LEGENDARY LOCALS OF ALAMOGORDO NEW MEXICO

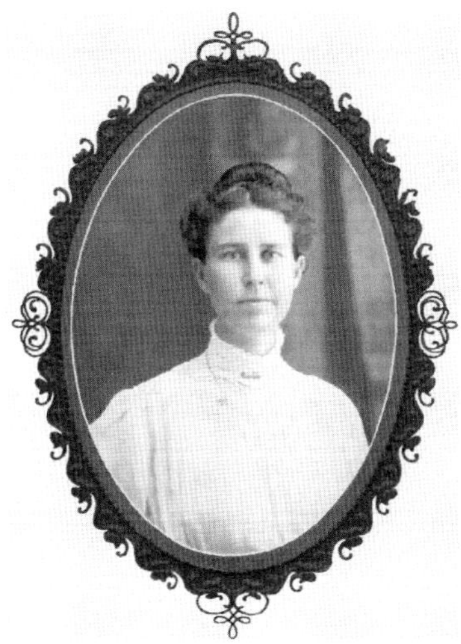

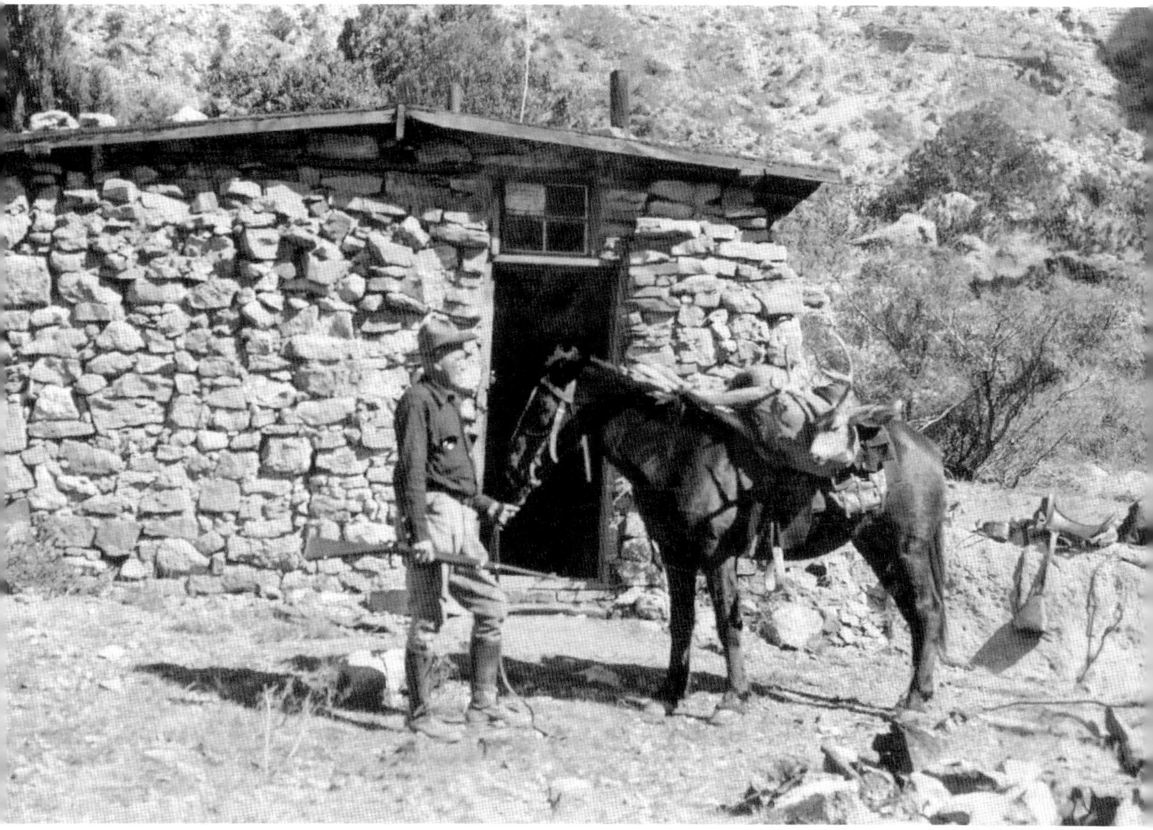

Frenchy's Cabin
Francois-Jean Rochas was a Frenchman who homesteaded in Dog Canyon. He lived in this hand-built rock cabin, farmed, and ran livestock. "Frenchy" died in 1894 from a gunshot wound to the chest. Whether he committed suicide or was murdered is often debated. Some theorize that he built the mysterious spiral staircase in the Loretta Chapel in Santa Fe. Archeologists Pete Eidenbach and Mark Wimberly, of Human Systems Research, excavated the cabin in the late 1970s. (Courtesy the Tularosa Basin Historical Society.)

Page 1: Mary Josephine Dudley
Mary Josephine Dudley, seen here around 1907, was the high-principled, beloved schoolmarm of Dudley School. The stucco building where she taught still stands at Maryland Avenue and Sixth Street. (Courtesy the Tularosa Basin Historical Society.)

LEGENDARY LOCALS

OF

ALAMOGORDO

NEW MEXICO

MICHAEL RAY SHINABERY

LEGENDARY LOCALS

ISBN 978-1-4671-0211-7

Legendary Locals is an imprint of Arcadia Publishing
Charleston, South Carolina

Printed in the United States of America

Library of Congress Control Number: 2015930746

For all general information, please contact Arcadia Publishing:
Telephone 843-853-2070
Fax 843-853-0044
E-mail sales@arcadiapublishing.com
For customer service and orders:
Toll-Free 1-888-313-2665

Visit us on the Internet at www.arcadiapublishing.com

Dedication
This book is for my son, Christopher.

On the Front Cover: Clockwise from top left:
Ed Dittmer, veteran and space chimpanzee trainer (Courtesy Michael Shinabery; see page 53), Bob Flotte, radio broadcaster (Courtesy Ed Thomas; see page 29), Frank Mackewich, stunt rider and police officer (Courtesy Frank Mackewich; see page 26), Joe Kittinger, Air Force test pilot and Vietnam POW (Courtesy New Mexico Museum of Space History; see page 51), Harold Davis, member of the 125th Signal Corps and participant in Joint Task Force 8 (Courtesy Harold Davis; see page 42), Ed Thomas, as Santa Claus (Courtesy of, and used with the permission of, Ed Thomas; see page 98), Maude Rathgeber, music teacher and activist (Courtesy Rathgeber family; see page 92), Isaiah and Johnnie Scott, teachers, counselors, and writers (Courtesy Scott family; see page 93), Linnie and Dr. David Townsend, authors and teachers (Courtesy Dave Townsend; see pages 22, 23).

On the Back Cover: From left to right:
Wyatt Atkins (second from right) and his staff at Atkins's auto dealership (Courtesy Wyatt Atkins; see page 80), Don Thorp (right), music teacher (Courtesy Don Thorp; see page 31).

CONTENTS

ACKNOWLEDGMENTS

Telling stories is one of man's earliest undertakings. I am grateful to those connected to Alamogordo who were gracious enough to invite me into their lives and tell me their stories.

I was fortunate to have a valuable resource of already-written history from such historians and writers as Dr. David Townsend, Clif and Barbara McDonald, and Pete Eidenbach. Dr. Townsend was also encouraging throughout my research.

Linnie Townsend edited the Things Remembered series for the Alamogordo and Otero County centennials. These two volumes were invaluable. She brought together a variety of writers who told their families' histories, as well as tales of the characters who played out life in Alamogordo since the town's founding.

I learned much from Randy Burroughs's Alamogordo's Own series, published in the *Alamogordo Daily News*. Obituaries from the newspaper were also informative.

Michael Shyne pointed me to those whose input and suggestions revealed tales waiting to be told. Thank you, Michael, for your enthusiasm and the conversations.

My thanks, too, go to the photographers whose images are included, first and foremost Ellis Neel, and Ed Thomas.

Don Larsen painstakingly compiled images from the Tularosa Basin Historical Society's archives. At the Alamogordo Chamber of Commerce, Tammy Brookbank and Candace Craine spent a busy morning scanning photographs.

Maude Rathgeber is a gem. She invited me to sit at her table and sift through family photographs taken more than a century ago. Her early family was integral to Alamogordo, and Maude's stories were entertaining and informative.

Many others, recently and over the years, have enlightened me, among them Wyatt Atkins, Ron Johnson, Wayne Mattson, George House, Harold Davis, Carl Clarke, Lloyd Berryhill, Junior and Betty Stoots, Carl and Jean Vallance, and Patti Brady.

My appreciation goes to Darrell Pehr, who called one day and said, "How would you like to . . . ?"

Finally, my heartfelt thanks go to Judy, because you, too, made a difference.

INTRODUCTION

There is a saying about New Mexico: In the Land of Enchantment, the mountains touch the sky. At times, the brilliant but unrelenting sun makes the craggy rocks black against an azure heaven. In the winter, the high-altitude snows make the eyes ache from the splendor. Between these mountain ranges are mile after mile of plains and high desert. And it is here that one finds Alamogordo, where a prehistoric sea once flowed, conquistadors marched across the landscape, and Native Americans sought sustenance.

Alamogordo is a crossroads of sorts. Physically, three highways enter and exit: US 70 and 54, and US 82 through Cloudcroft. More important, however, are the people who traverse these byways.

The saddled horse, covered and dray wagons, and the railroad brought early residents. That they came from around the country in the town's formative years is evident in the variety of architectural styles in the town. Wherever the newcomers hailed from, they injected a bit of home into the residences they built. Victorian and Tudor structures stood side by side with shotgun houses of the South, homes with walls made from local rock, and, of course, buildings erected in the traditional Southwest style.

As Alamogordo matured, so did the community's culture, coming a long way from 1884, when a teenaged cowboy, Oliver Lee, drove cattle from Texas because acreage in the Land of Enchantment was free and stretched beyond the farthest landscape. The custom and culture of the West is a coveted heritage not to be lost.

Alamogordo is a place where contributions in business, education, and the arts are considered worthwhile, appreciated, and remembered. Many people came with the military, choosing to stay after they were discharged or when they retired. Not surprisingly, what they learned in serving their country makes them valuable and strengthens the community.

Some who first called Alamogordo and Otero County their home went out into the world to make their name and fortune. Among them are nuclear physicist Edward Condon and Pulitzer Prize–winning cartoonist Bill Mauldin.

Others make Alamogordo their home for a time and then move on. Future Alabama governor George Wallace was a sergeant when he trained with bomber crews at Alamogordo Army Air Field. In the 1950s, a fighter pilot wanted off desk duty and back into the cockpit. When the Air Force declined, he answered a rather nondescriptive advertisement in a publication. A decade later, Gene Kranz was NASA's flight director.

Tales such as these were gathered while talking to the men and women who have made a difference. Hearing their stories was like finding a long-lost treasure. Their history is a piece of the community. If lost, the story will never be complete.

Many of the people found in these pages were not town founders and do not belong to a family that goes back generations. But, through their talents, they have made valuable contributions.

When my family and I moved here in 1993, I was fortunate. Bob Flotte soon hired me at KPSA AM. As a newscaster, I told stories. Later, *Alamogordo Daily News* editors Don McKinney, Richard Coltharp, and Darrell Pehr gave me the thumbs-up to go out and gather history. Today, I get to keep doing just that, hosting a morning talk show on KRSY AM, thanks to managers Phil Runnels, who saw the value in local radio, and Les Henke, who continues the tradition.

Now, who better to tell a community's history than its residents?

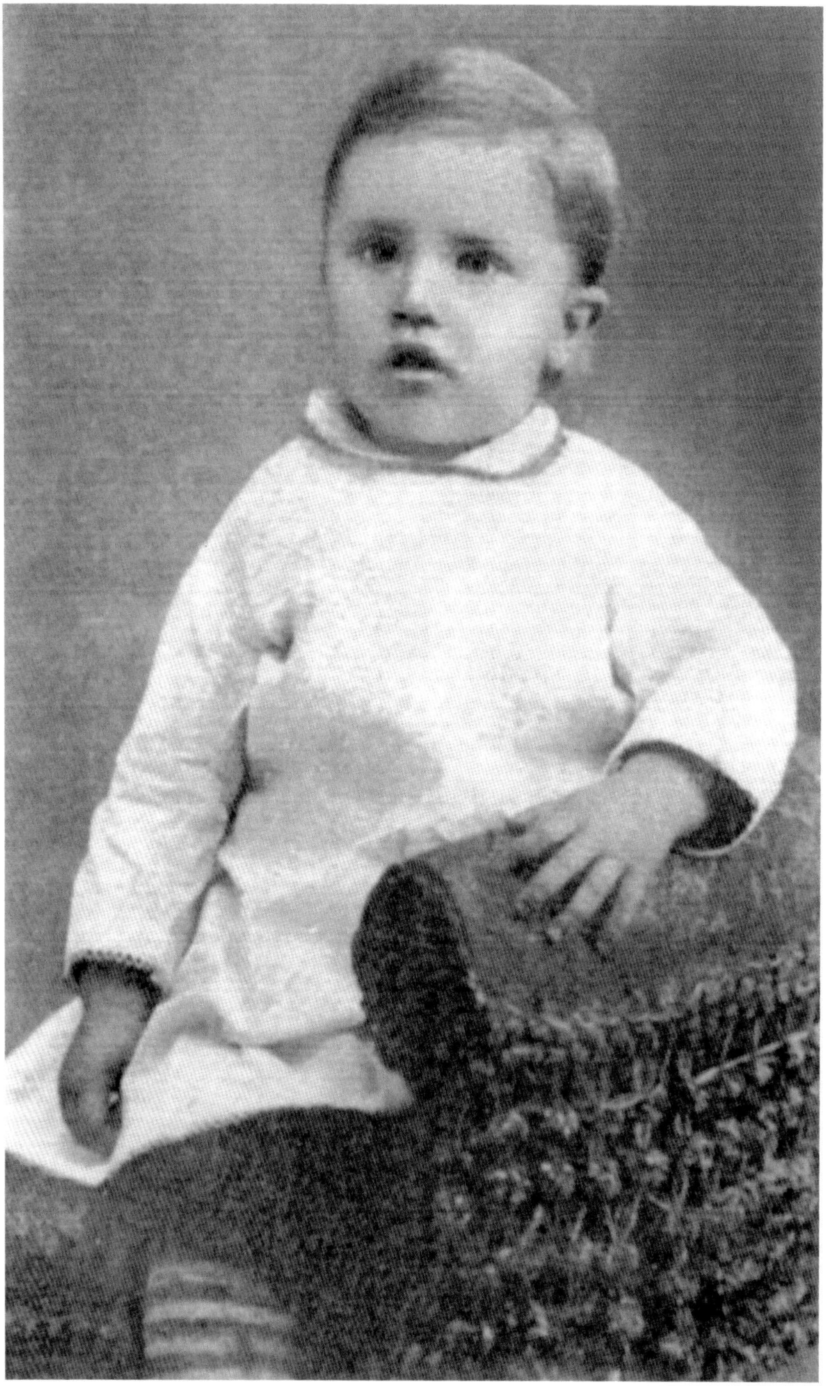

Lacy Simms as a Child

This may be the only known photograph of Lacy Simms with hands, as, two years later, the boy lost both arms below the elbows in an accident at a Texas cotton gin. (Courtesy the Tularosa Basin Historical Society.)

CHAPTER ONE

The Early Years

The railroad brought civilization to a desert that was once a prehistoric sea. In 1898, the El Paso & Northeastern line arrived. Brothers Charles Bishop Eddy and John Arthur Eddy pushed the line and created the Alamogordo Improvement Company. John Eddy bestowed the town's name. He described inspiration for the name in a letter on Alamogordo's 25th anniversary: "It devolved on me to name the stations on the railroad and in doing so, I sought to apply those of local characteristics or landmarks. It would have been natural therefore, to use the word Alamo, but it was objectionable because of its being so common and so many Alamos. In my cowboy days, one of my favorite camping places between Las Vegas and Seven Rivers, was on a little stream running into the east side of the Pecos, called Alamo Gordo. I had learned its meaning to be, a big or Rotund cottonwood, and upon seeing such a tree or the relic of such a tree, at the mouth of the Alamo Canyon, the name came back impressively to me."

John Eddy also convinced his brother and their lawyer, William Ashton Hawkins, to route water via ditches from the Sacramento Mountains to sustain thousands of trees he wanted to plant. He described his reasoning in his 1923 letter, saying: "I often wonder if the people of Alamogordo realize the great efforts put forth to provide the place with shade trees and particularly those of the park. It was early Spring when we were preparing the townsite, and of course, in its crude state, was forlorn enough. The prospect of a long hot summer, without a vestige of green was depressing. It was impossible to prepare the streets and set trees along them that season, but by great effort we might plant the park so as to have some trees growing." The company then went about building a park adjacent to the railroad stop so travelers could rest.

John Eddy also claimed credit for declaring temperance upon Alamogordo, except in an Alamogordo Improvement Company store on one block. He explained: "To have been constitutional, provision for its purchase for medicinal purposes, was essential. From experience in other towns, I had learned that this converted drug stores into salons, the druggists reaped its profit and the town its deficits. I think it demonstrated much to be the only rational temperance regulation."

The brothers bought the Shay railroad engines from the Lima Locomotive & Machine Company, in Lima, Ohio, to forge upward from Alamogordo's 4,300-foot altitude to some 8,600 feet into the Sacramento Mountains and what is today Cloudcroft. Along the way, they harvested trees, and two Alamogordo sawmills produced a quarter-million board feet a day.

To this new community, then, came the men and women who were the early educators and men of God, who advanced the livestock industry, and who created the White Sands National Monument. The seeds they sowed still produce today.

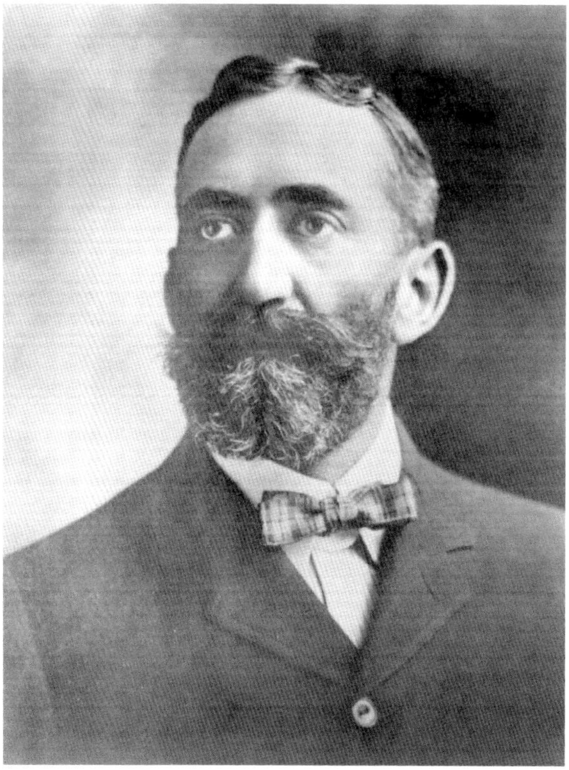

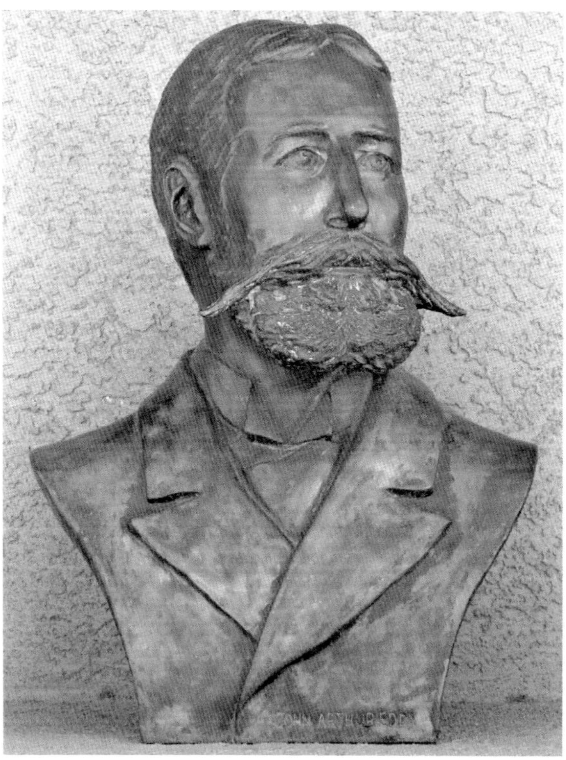

The Eddy Brothers

Charles Bishop Eddy (above) and his brother John Arthur Eddy (below) cofounded Alamogordo in 1898, along with their lawyer, William Ashton Hawkins. In 1897, the three purchased a defunct rail line out of El Paso, which financier Jay Gould was developing before his death. The Eddys laid track northward and created the Alamogordo Improvement Company. John named the town for the area's cottonwoods.

The brothers were still acquiring title to 940 acres from the federal government when they sold their first lot. The Eddys chose not to re-create what they considered the nightmare of Eastern towns, where unions led violent strikes. They sold reasonably priced lots; a turnkey house cost as little as $2,000. The first hotel went up in 1898 and had electric lighting. The next year, 150 buildings defined the skyline.

In 1900, John sold his interest to his brother for $100,000. Then, five years later, Charles sold the railway, land, water rights, and coal deposits for several million dollars. Both died in New York City in 1931. (Above, courtesy the Tularosa Basin Historical Society; below, courtesy Don Larsen.)

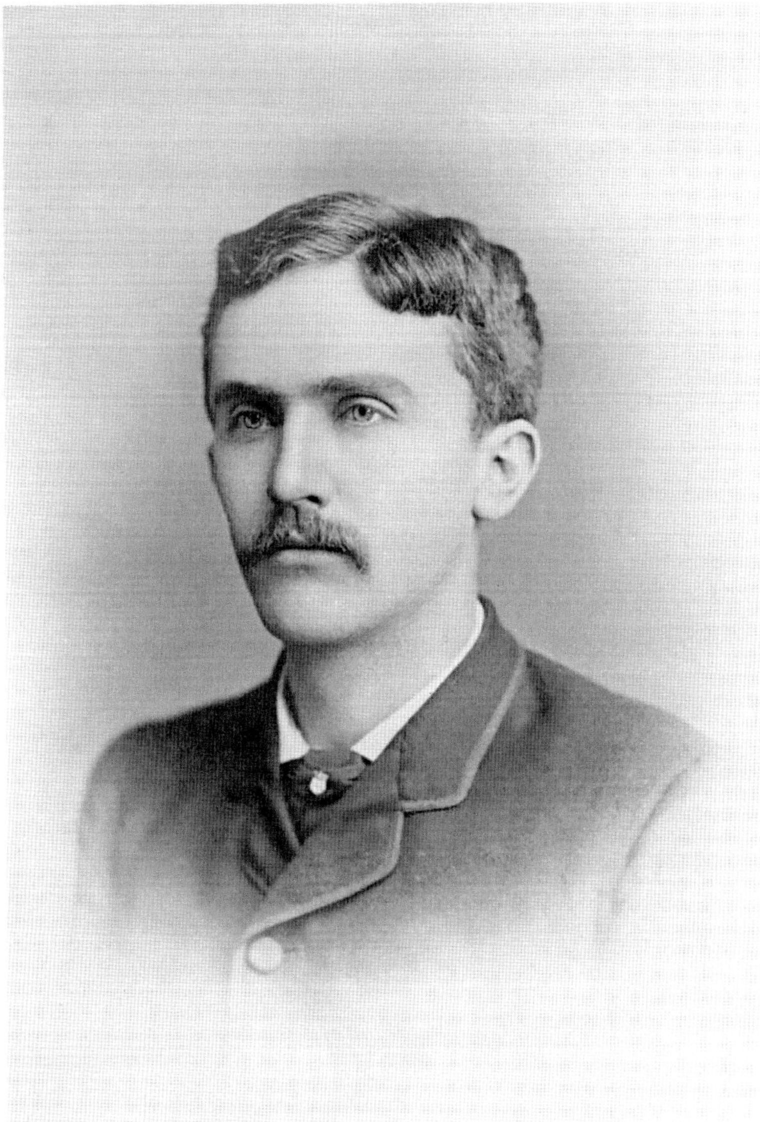

William Ashton Hawkins

Hawkins was a Tennessee native who, as a young adult, served with the New Mexico volunteers fighting against Geronimo and the Apaches. In 1903, he was part of the New Mexico Territorial Legislature. As attorney to the brothers Charles and John Eddy, Hawkins cofounded Alamogordo. The Eddys had built the community of Eddy (today known as Carlsbad) a decade earlier, but it had experienced social problems. Hawkins had suggestions as to avoid repeating those mistakes in Alamogordo. He proposed winding streets to cut down on the public's penchant for racing horses. Because the demon rum got out of hand in Eddy, Hawkins encouraged declaring Alamogordo a dry town. Except, that is, for one central location to control liquor. Hawkins believed such decisions would deny profits to the riffraff that gambled and the unscrupulous ladies displaying their wicked temptations.

Hawkins died in 1939 from injuries after falling from a horse. For his military service, he was buried in the Santa Fe National Cemetery. He is shown here as a young man in Nashville in 1883. (Courtesy the Tularosa Basin Historical Society.)

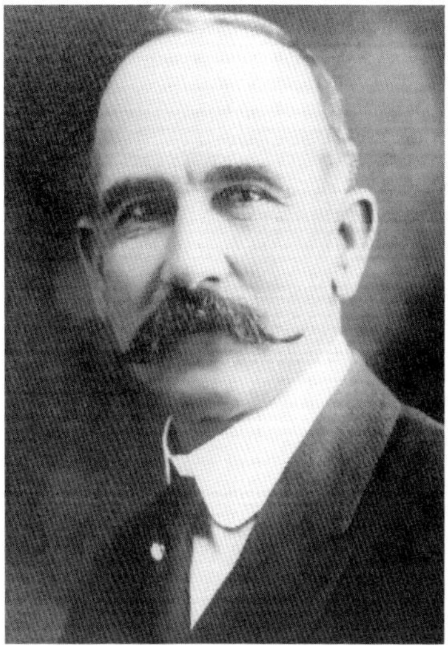

Oliver Lee

Lee was just 19 years old in 1884 when he convinced his doubtful half-brother, Perry Altman, to move their cattle from Buffalo Gap, Texas, to New Mexico. Their Circle Cross Ranch grew to a million acres. When beef prices plummeted in 1929 and the ranch went bankrupt, Lee bred horses for the cavalry. From 1918 to 1930, he served terms as a state senator and representative. Lee died in 1941 and is buried in Alamogordo. A son, Don Lee, purchased property adjacent to the Circle Cross and formed the Hat Ranch. Charlie Lee, Don's son and a state senator as well, ran cattle there with his son, Bebo Lee. (Courtesy the Tularosa Basin Historical Society.)

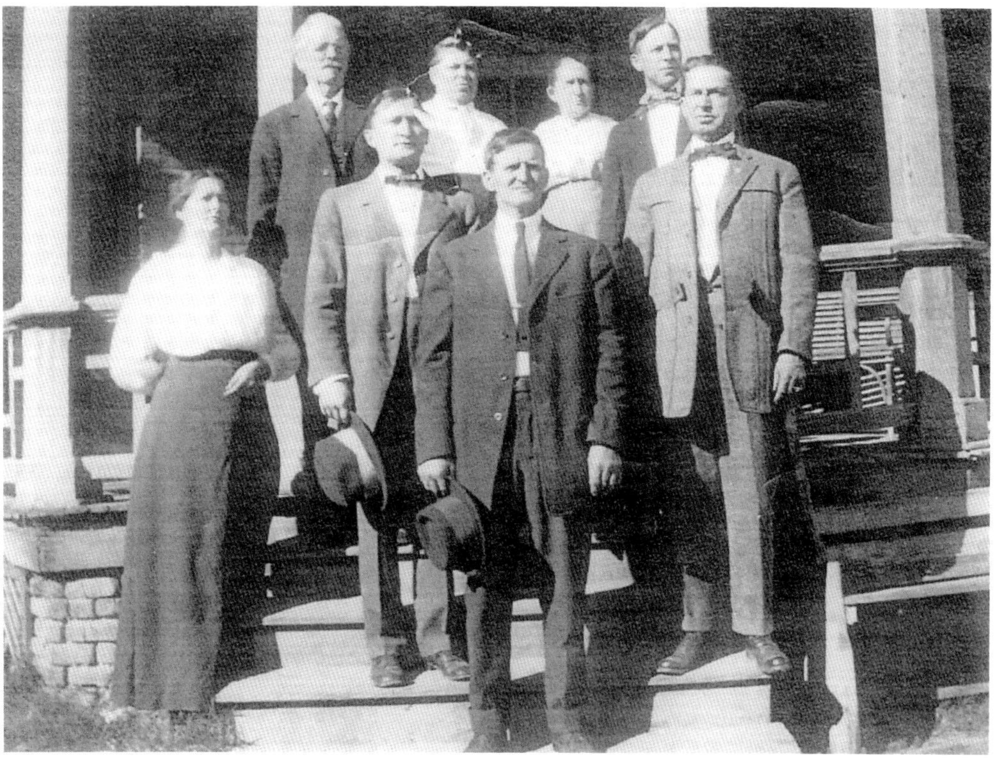

George B. Oliver

While with the 19th Mississippi Infantry during the Civil War, Oliver was recuperating from illness when he got homesick. He trudged off and convinced his wife and boys that prosperity awaited them in the West. The family made their home in Cooper, Texas, before resettling in Roswell. When Oliver set out for Alamogordo, he swore to his wife he would not shave or get a haircut until he had $500 in the bank. He earned the money, sent for his family, and grew prosperous as a retailer. Oliver is seen here at upper left. The others are, clockwise, Jess Oliver, Eliza Rowan Oliver, Williard or Clifford Oliver, Edward Lee Oliver, Frank "Flute" Oliver, Tobie Oliver, and Mary Verda Bedford. (Courtesy the Rathgeber family.)

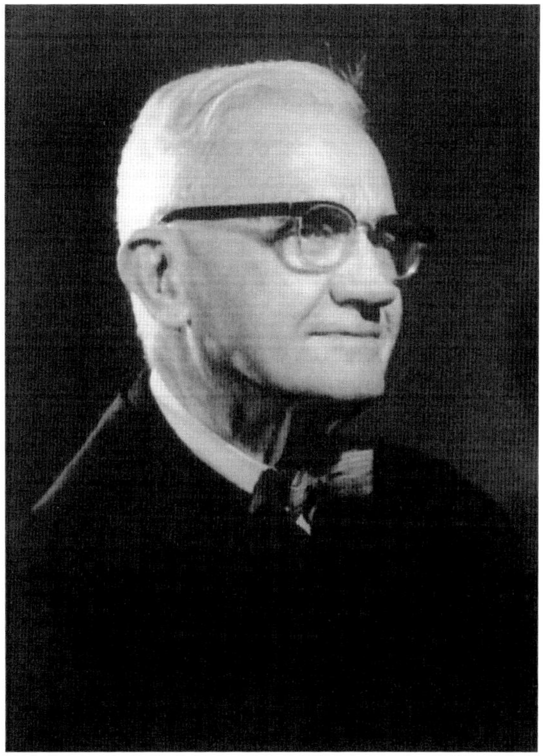

Lacy Simms
Simms was five years old when a cotton gin in Texas sheared off both arms below the elbows. His father told him not to expect any coddling. When Simms arrived in Alamogordo in 1905, he had artificial arms, but he soon tired of the prosthetics and buried them. Simms founded the town's first day care; was a minister at First Presbyterian Church as well as at Spanish-speaking congregations nationwide; and was a Civil Air Patrol chaplain. He also taught school, was a county superintendent, and even became a pianist and painter. (Courtesy the Tularosa Basin Historical Society.)

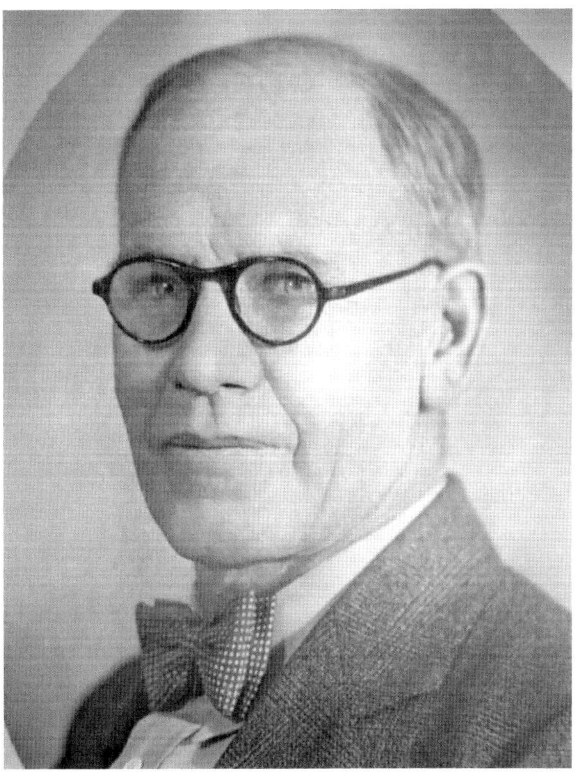

Tom Charles
Known as the father of White Sands National Monument, Charles was editor of the *Alamogordo News* and owner of the Tom Charles Insurance Agency. He urged the congressional delegation to preserve the geologic wonder, and in January 1933, Pres. Herbert Hoover signed a proclamation creating the monument. Charles was the first superintendent; until Congress appropriated funds, he earned $1 a year and paid for his own gas and office supplies. He died in 1943 and is buried in Monte Vista Cemetery. (Courtesy the Alamogordo Chamber of Commerce.)

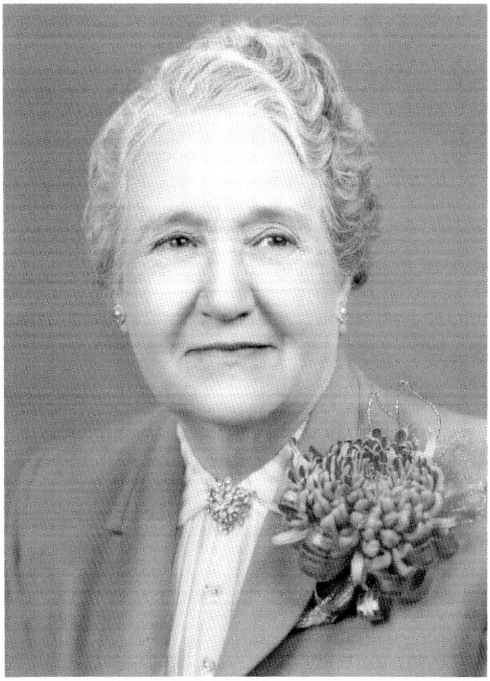

Bula Charles

Bula, Tom Charles's wife, was socially active as a USO hostess, president of the New Mexico Federation of Women's Clubs, and the first woman on the Alamogordo Chamber of Commerce Board of Directors. After her husband's death, she managed the family insurance agency. Not only was she frequently mentioned in the newspaper, but she won many awards for her newspaper and magazine articles. She also published history books. Bula Charles died in 1974. (Courtesy the Tularosa Basin Historical Society.)

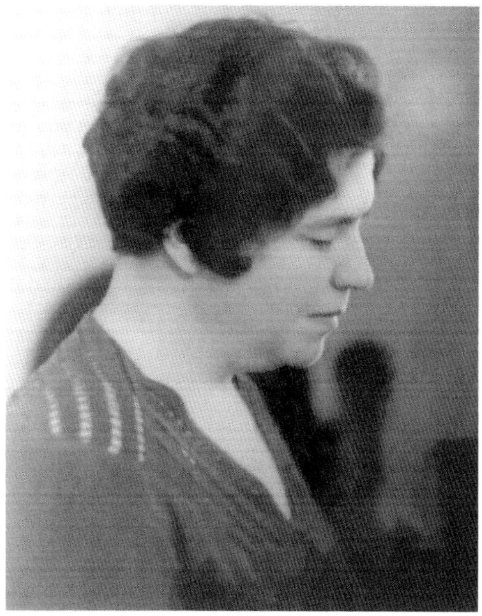

Elizabeth Garrett

Sheriff Pat Garrett's daughter lost her eyesight not long after she was born. After getting her education at the Texas School for the Blind, Garrett came to Alamogordo and taught music at the New Mexico School for the Blind and Visually Impaired. She served on the board of regents and wrote "O Fair New Mexico," which the New Mexico Legislature adopted as the state song in 1917. Garrett eventually moved to Roswell, taught piano, and died in 1947. (Courtesy the Barbara McDonald Collection.)

CHAPTER TWO

The Law

Alamogordo has a long history of colorful people dedicating their careers to the law. High-profile cases have been tried in the Otero County Courthouse, at the corner of Tenth Street and New York Avenue. New Mexico's 12th Judicial District covers both Otero and Lincoln Counties. Diana Martwick serves as the first female district attorney, elected after Scot Key's service (1996–2007). Key is the only DA, to date, to serve three terms. Prior to Key, Bert Atkins was the first district attorney ever reelected. After district judge Frank Wilson retired from the bench, he entered the pastorate.

In 2006, Court TV came to town when the district tried Cody Posey. At the age of 14, he was accused of killing his father, stepmother, and stepsister. Attorney Gary Mitchell defended Posey. Mitchell, a Ruidoso attorney, is no stranger to controversial defendants within the courthouse.

The community mourned when it lost a former officer in the 9-11 terrorist attacks, and residents rallied after an Otero County sheriff's deputy lost his life in December 2004. Billy Anders and Bob Hedman rushed to a call of "argument with shots fired" in the Sacramento Mountains. When the deputies arrived at an isolated cabin, they found blood on the ground by the front door. When confronted, a suspect retreated, locking himself inside with a little girl. Hedman snuck to the rear, where the gunman ambushed the deputy. Anders, hearing the shot, ran to Hedman, but he was not certain Hedman was dead. The gunman quickly moved into a dark position outside the front door, using the three-year-old girl as a shield. The girl was the daughter of a woman whom the deputies suspected the assailant of killing. Anders was ambushed as the suspect ran toward him. When the suspect fired, a .357 Magnum round passed through the left sleeve of Anders's uniform jacket. Returning fire high and left in order to avoid the child, Anders wounded the gunman, perhaps fatally, rushed the girl to safety, and then returned to Hedman. But his partner was dead on the back porch. Anders returned to the front and, finding the suspect moving, fired another shot, ending the rampage. An independent analysis showed the suspect's blood on a jack handle near his body, the object possibly intended as a weapon. The man's murdered pregnant girlfriend was found in a cabin closet. Cloudcroft-area citizens, shocked when Anders was charged for the man's death, raised $65,000 for his legal expenses. Anders was locked in a Santa Fe maximum-security prison cell for 10 months. When he was released, he returned to Cloudcroft.

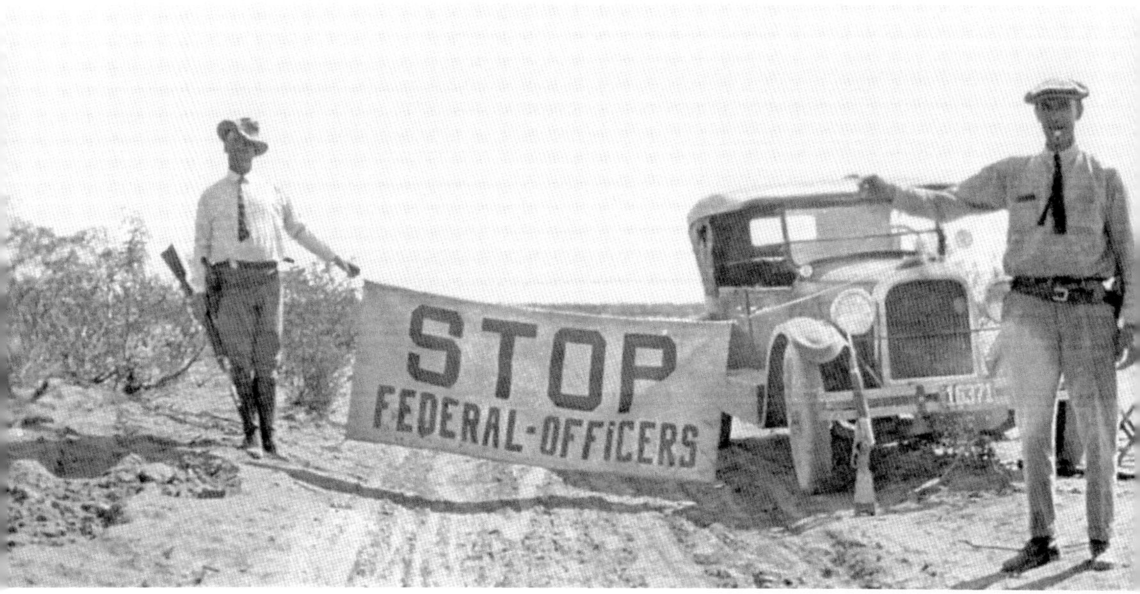

Sheriff Howard Beacham

Elected in 1920, Beacham (right) vigorously enforced Prohibition. As a result, he was not reelected until 1935. In the interim, he was a federal investigator for the Department of Justice, Bureau of Prohibition. Beacham set up roadblocks, such as the one seen here with Agent Edward Crossett. He once stopped a driver smuggling alcohol inside a stack of lumber. In August 1928, Beacham shot at an airplane attempting to take off with five cases of whiskey. Beacham made a lamp from the plane's damaged cylinder, which is on display at the Tularosa Basin Historical Society. Also shown at the society is his "jinxed" carbine, which caused the deaths of three persons who borrowed it. (Courtesy the Tularosa Basin Historical Society.)

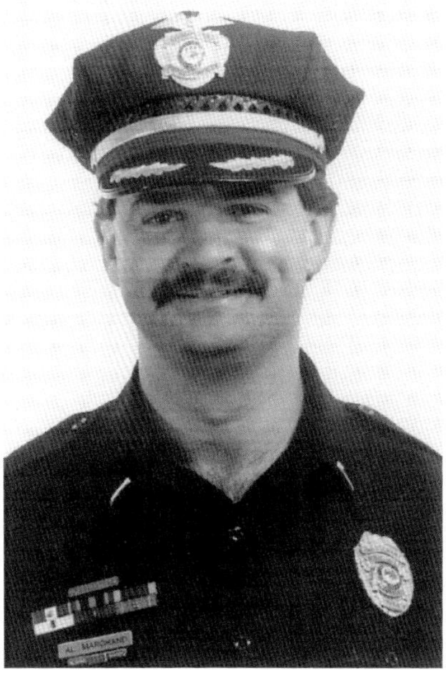

Al Marchand

When Marchand retired after 21 years as a police officer, he announced that he wanted to pilot commercial airplanes. To get his foot in the industry's door, Marchand hired on as an attendant with United Airlines. On September 11, 2001, he was aboard Flight 175 when Al-Qaeda terrorists crashed the plane into the South Tower of New York's World Trade Center. (Courtesy the Alamogordo Police Department.)

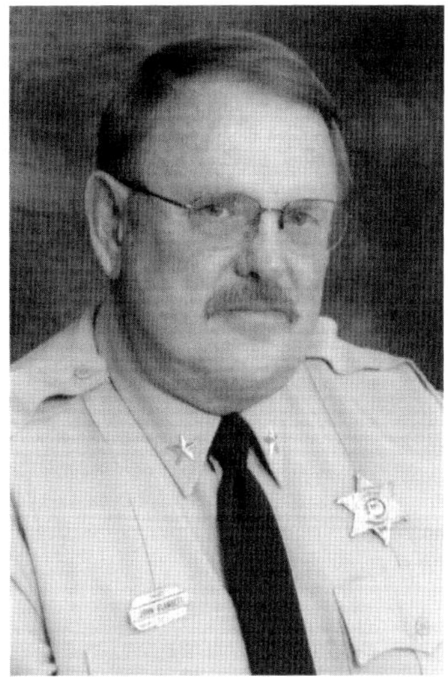

Sheriff John Blansett

Blansett was at a gym when he heard the radio call that deputies were struggling to quell a raucous bar fight. Blansett, a bear of a man, rushed to the scene with his gun tucked into his sweatpants and waded into the fray. He had come to Alamogordo in 1984, after 11 years with the Sacramento County, California, sheriff's department, where he received the Silver Star for gallantry. In Alamogordo, he spent a year and a half with the Department of Public Safety before joining Otero County. Then, three years later, Blansett was elected to his first of two terms as sheriff. He returned to patrol until 2002, when he was elected to two more terms. He is the longest-serving sheriff, with a total of 12 years. (Courtesy John Blansett.)

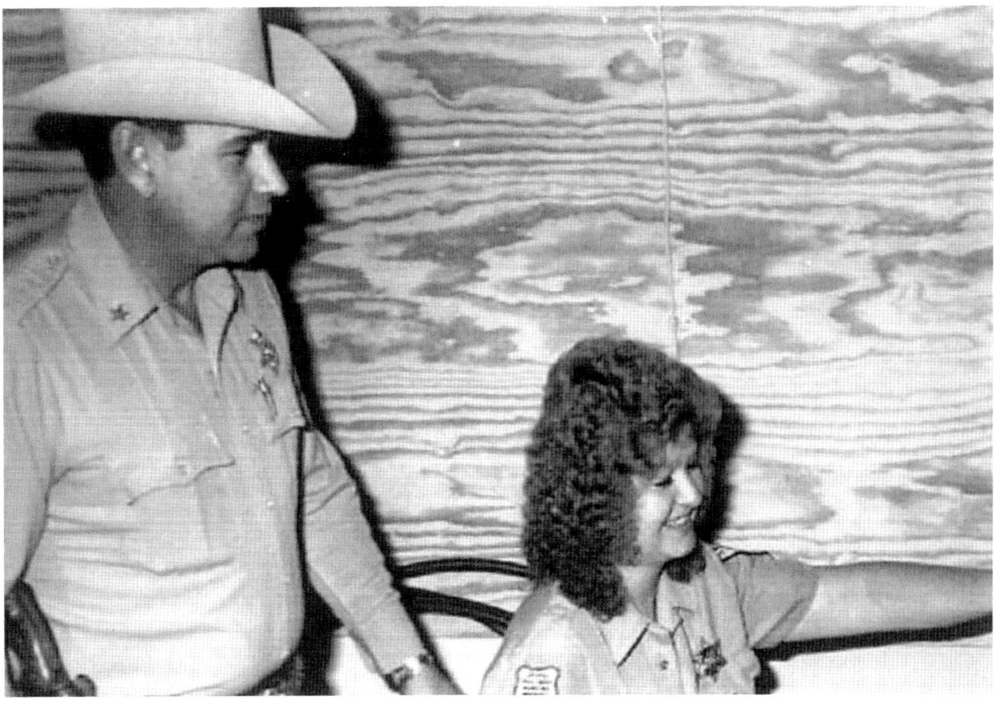

Sheriff John Lee

When the 1993 Brady Bill required sheriffs to foot the bill for background checks, Lee (seen here with dispatcher Jean Braziel) called the legislation "slavery"—if he could not afford to do the checks, he would go to jail. Lee sued and lost, but he focused attention on the mandate's unfairness, and the Supreme Court struck down that provision. Lee was 18 when he asked the sitting sheriff for a job; he was told to come back when he was 25. He joined the Marines and subsequently served in other law-enforcement agencies until the Alamogordo Department of Public Safety hired him. In 1989, he became Sheriff John Blansett's chief deputy, and in 1992, he was elected to his first of three terms, making him the longest consecutively seated sheriff in Otero County. John Lee campaigned for Megan's Law, which requires sex offenders to register. (Courtesy Lee family.)

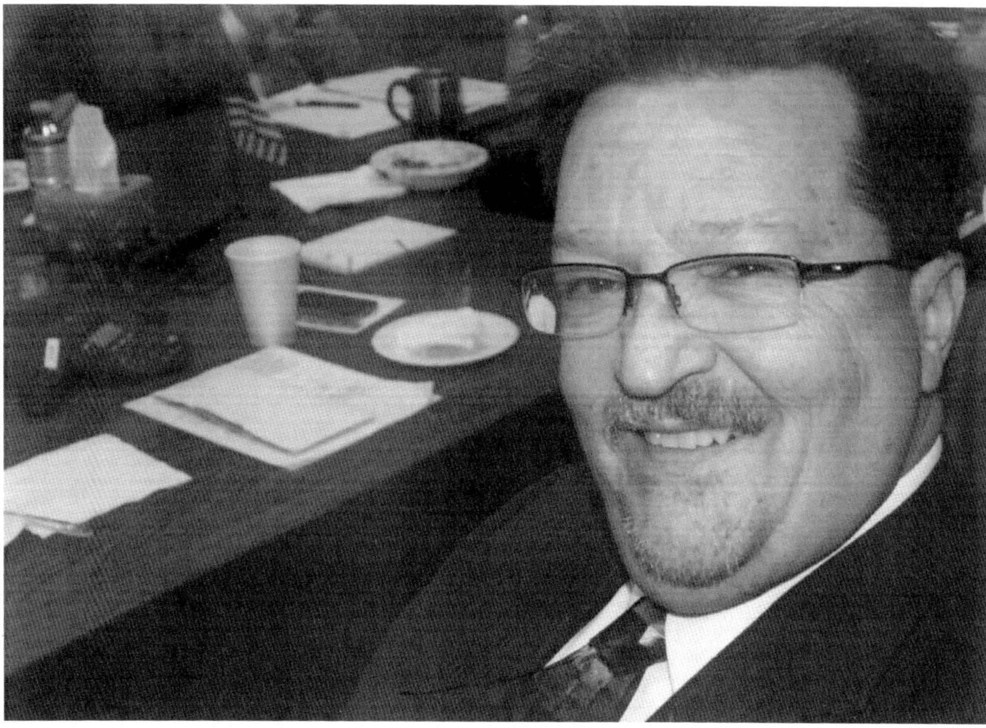

Bert Atkins

Atkins was the first district attorney ever reelected in the 12th Judicial District. First elected in 1988, Atkins campaigned on creating a major crime unit to consolidate all law-enforcement and prosecutorial agencies. He had not been in office long when a female Allsup's employee was abducted and murdered. The new crime team spent months gathering forensic and DNA evidence, and Atkins got a conviction. He also secured conspiracy and evidence-tampering indictments against family members of the murderer, who were suspected of helping to conceal the crime. (Courtesy Bert Atkins.)

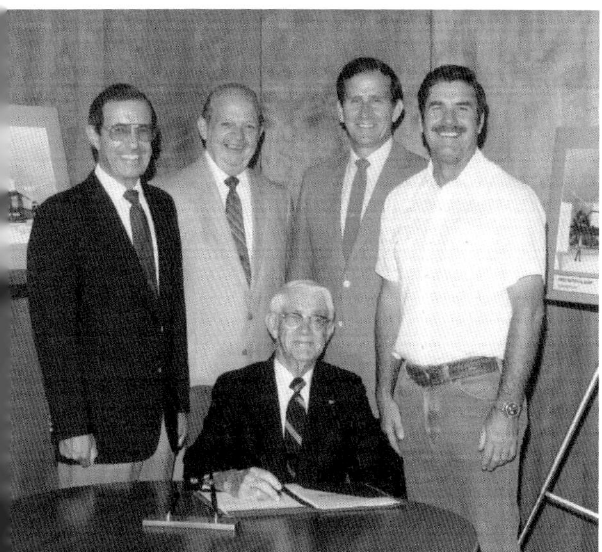

George Fettinger

Fettinger began his legal career in Alamogordo in 1958 and became an expert in Native American law. He argued two landmark cases before the Supreme Court. A state representative for 20 years, Fettinger chaired the House Judiciary Committee. He was an advocate of junior colleges, and the George E. Fettinger Student Services Center at New Mexico State University–Alamogordo is named in his honor. Fettinger, who served on the First National Bank Board, is seen here at left in 1986, planning the bank's annex. The others are, from left to right, Wyatt Atkins, George Abbott (seated), Kenneth Hutt of Pioneer Abstract & Title, and Jeff Gentry of Gentry Construction. (Courtesy Wyatt Atkins.)

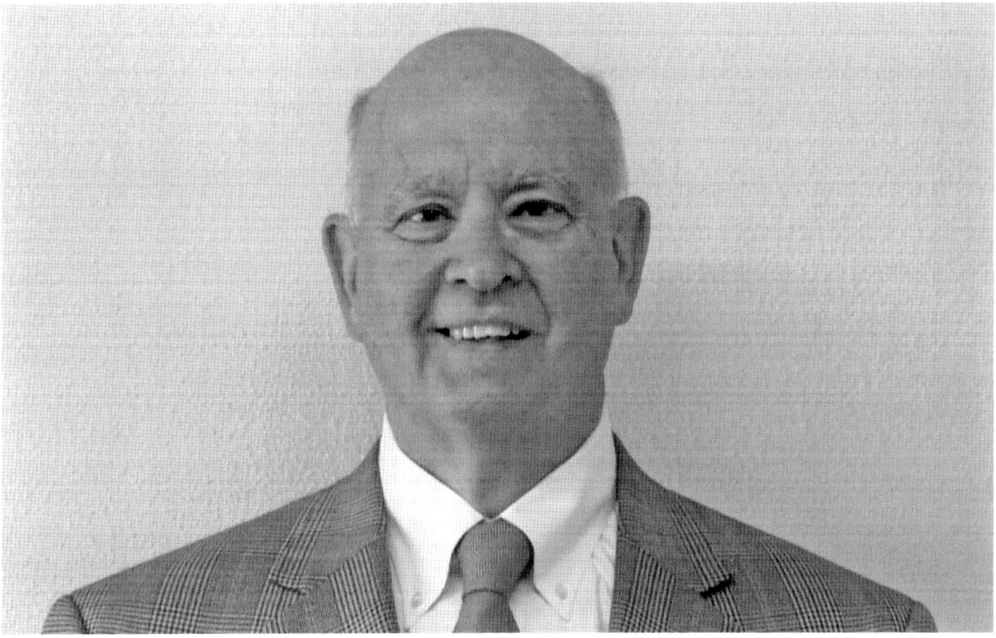

Randy Burroughs
Alcohol distribution and consumption was prohibited for 100 years in Alamogordo's original townsite, until Burroughs, of the law firm Burroughs & Rhodes, argued to have that overturned. "The Safeway Case" in early 1990 opened up liquor sales in businesses. Burroughs's early law career was with George Fettinger. Burroughs wrote briefs on two Indian cases presented to the US Supreme Court. *Mescalero v. Jones* defined the limits to which New Mexico could tax sovereign Indian resources. Burroughs was named Outstanding Young Man in America three separate times by the nonprofit Outstanding Young Man in America organization. (Courtesy Randy Burroughs.)

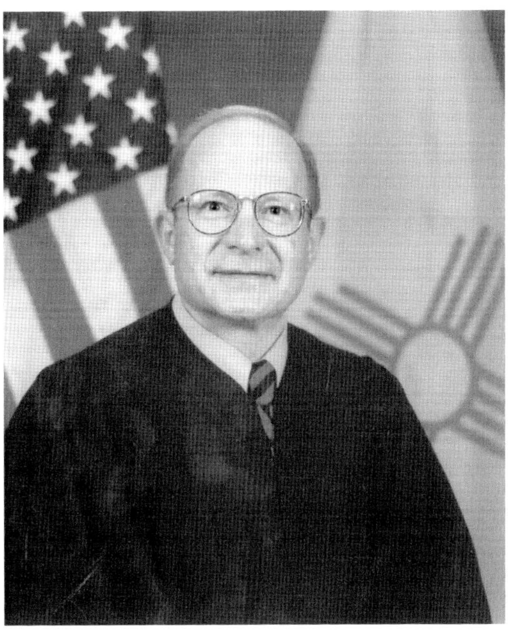

Judge Richard Stokely
In 1998, Stokely was elected a magistrate. His court was located on Alamogordo's north side, and the detention center was on the south. Stokely and Judge Ted McCutcheon, also newly elected, drove to the jail, eliminating dangerous prisoner transport and saving thousands of dollars. Several years later, their courts were among the first in the state to receive video arraignment technology. When the dollar amount for civil actions increased to $10,000, the two judges arranged to train volunteer mediators. Stokely and McCutcheon's courts were honored for Best Customer Service, as voted by clients using the court. (Courtesy Richard Stokely.)

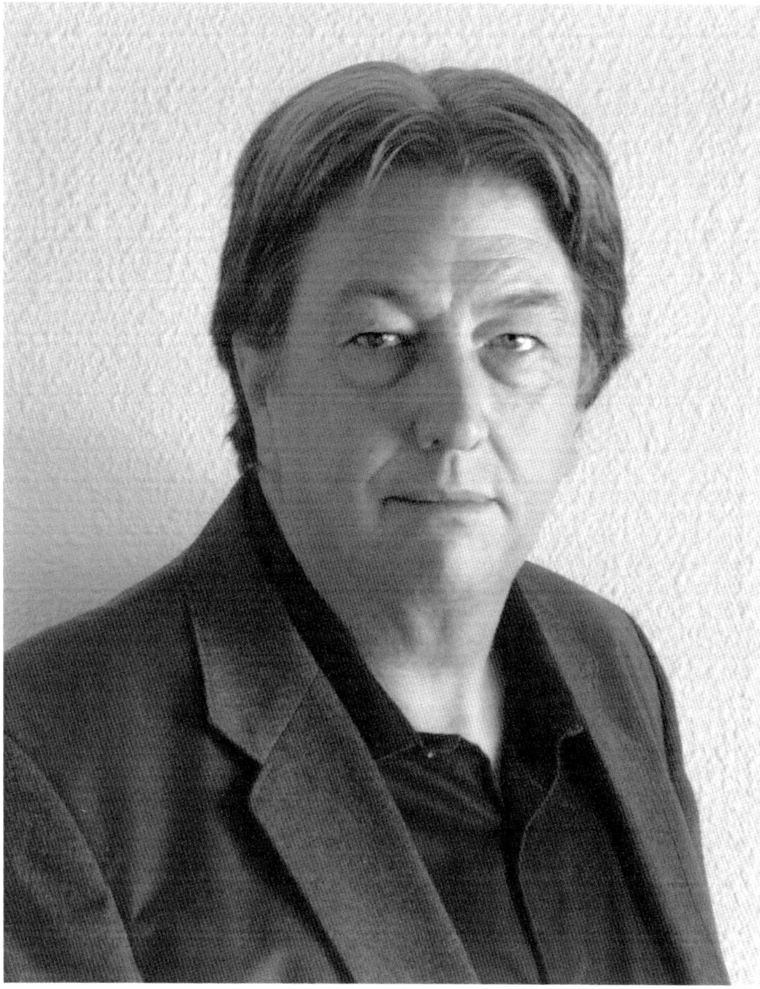

Judge James Waylon Counts

Counts has presided over several high-profile cases, including murder defendants Lenny Holly and Cody Posey. In 2004, Counts sentenced Holly, an Alamogordo High School basketball star who played for the New Mexico Slam and semipro ball in Europe and Mexico, to life in prison. The New Mexico Supreme Court upheld Counts's ruling.

Posey was 14 in 2004 when he shot his father, stepmother, and stepsister on newsman Sam Donaldson's Lincoln County ranch. Court TV broadcast the 2006 trial, which lasted several weeks. Prosecutor Sandra Grisham, under District Attorney Scot Key, convinced a jury that the teenager was guilty. However, his defender, Gary Mitchell, argued for treatment over prison. Counts concurred, placing Posey with the Children, Youth and Families Department until he turned 21.

Counts came to Alamogordo after graduating from the University of New Mexico School of Law and practicing in Albuquerque. He worked in the city attorney's office before being appointed a district judge for eight months in 1994. Counts then practiced privately for two and a half years. In 1997, he began prosecuting drug offenses for the DA. Counts was reappointed to the district bench in 1999. The New Mexico Supreme Court named him a water judge to adjudicate water rights. He was chief judge from 2007 to 2010 and has served on the Judicial Education and Training Advisory Committee and the Statewide Courthouse Security Committee. In 2006, he received the Outstanding Judicial Service Award from the state bar. (Courtesy Irene Mirabal-Counts.)

CHAPTER THREE

Arts, Entertainment, and the Media

Once in a great while, someone rehashes an old local adage that simply is not true: "There's nothing to do in Alamogordo." In fact, the opposite is the case. The community has musical theater, as well as band and choir concerts rife with local talent. The Flickinger Center for Performing Arts brings world-class entertainers to the stage, ranging from musicians and magicians to acrobats and actors. It is not unusual for artists to spend time working with the area's young talent, as jazz trumpeter Maynard Ferguson did in 1999. Authors and astronauts have come to town. Actor, singer, and songwriter Ronny Cox, who was born in Cloudcroft, has returned to perform his unique music.

There are holiday festivals in Alameda Park, which is also home to the oldest zoo in the Southwestern United States. Hot-air balloons lift off from White Sands National Monument during the annual White Sands Balloon Invitational. Astronomy clubs hold star parties. The New Mexico Museum of Space History features monthly Launch Pad lectures, runs the annual Rocketeer Academy summer camps, and, on Founder's Day, invites visitors to tour the museum and build and launch a model rocket, all for free. A walk through the Tularosa Basin Historical Society museum is a trip back in time. Downtown, one can see a family-friendly film in the revitalized Historic Sands Theater. Several parades a year trail down Tenth Street. There is rodeo and the annual Otero County Fair. Rotary Little League attracts hopeful future sluggers who, in the summer, can savor sitting in the stands with a hot dog and watch the White Sands PupFish play semipro baseball. Whatever the sport, whatever the season, the schools' athletes are on the courts and on the fields.

Distinguishing art, entertainment, and events in the media is not easy, as, more often than not, these areas intertwine. Artists know that nature never fails to inspire, with desert landscapes and towering vistas of the Sacramento Mountains. Those who appreciate such beauty have long admired what Ernie Lee Miller has captured on canvas over the decades. Pat Beatty's paintings of the white sands are legendary. A Depression-era Peter Hurd mural is preserved on the old federal building, at the corner of New York Avenue and Eleventh Street.

Writers weave their tales in the imagination. Michael McGarrity has set plots of his bestselling novels in the region, much as Eugene Manlove Rhodes did long ago. For historians such as Dr. David Townsend, Pete Eidenbach, Linnie Townsend, and Clif and Barbara McDonald, ensuring that history is not forgotten is the printed word's goal.

Radio stations up and down the AM and FM dials offer news, talk, Top 40, oldies, country, and sports, all to entertain and inform.

Without a doubt, there is always something to do in Alamogordo. On any day and in any week, an activity or event is on the calendar.

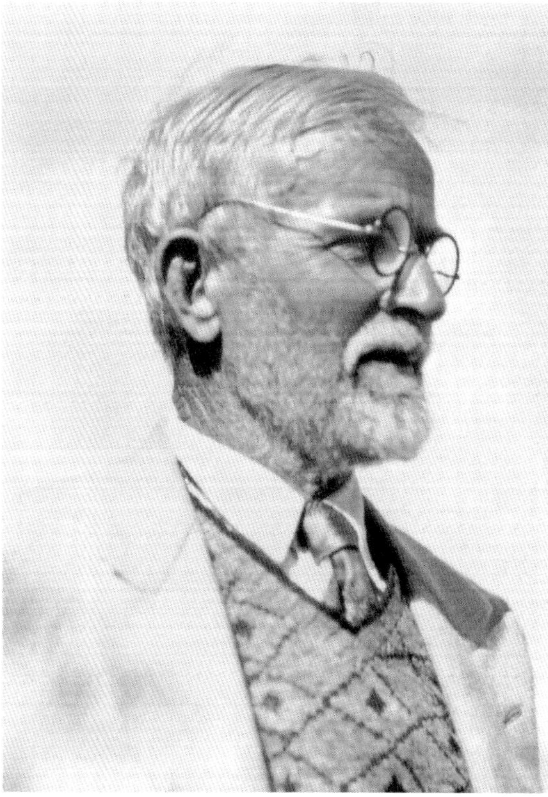

Eugene Manlove Rhodes

Rhodes was a cowboy, miner, and rancher who wove those he met and befriended, including Oliver Lee, into characters in his Western stories and poetry. Ironically, much of his writing was done after he "exiled" himself to New York. Novels such as his 1927 masterpiece *Paso Por Aqui* endear him to Alamogordo readers. Born in Nebraska in 1869, Rhodes moved with his family to New Mexico in 1881. His stories were serialized in popular magazines. In 1896, two of the defendants suspected of killing Col. Albert Fountain and his eight-year-old son, Henry, hid out on Rhodes's ranch in the San Andreas Mountains. That is where Rhodes was buried after he died in California in 1934. (Courtesy Barbara McDonald Collection.)

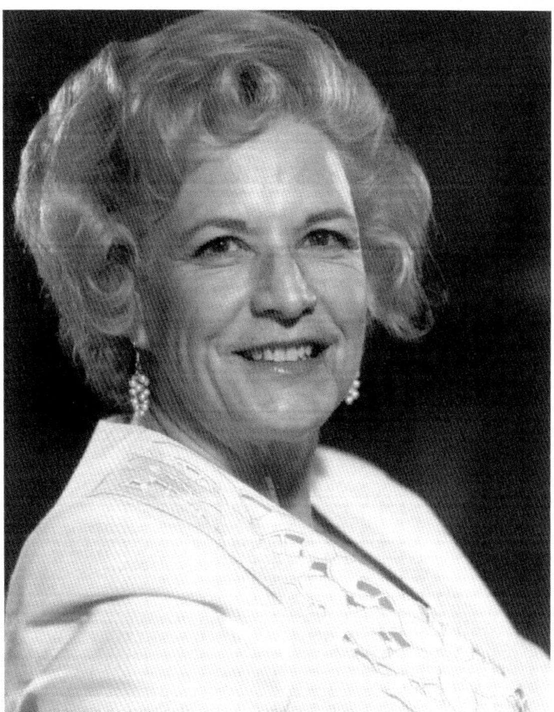

Linnie Townsend

Townsend was Alamogordo's "poet literate." The beloved English professor at New Mexico State University–Alamogordo edited several books on area history, including the Things Remembered series for the Alamogordo and Otero County centennials. Gov. Bruce King appointed her to the New Mexico School for the Blind and Visually Impaired Board of Regents. Townsend battled Parkinson's for six years. At her 2014 service, her friends recited her favorite poetry. (Courtesy David Townsend.)

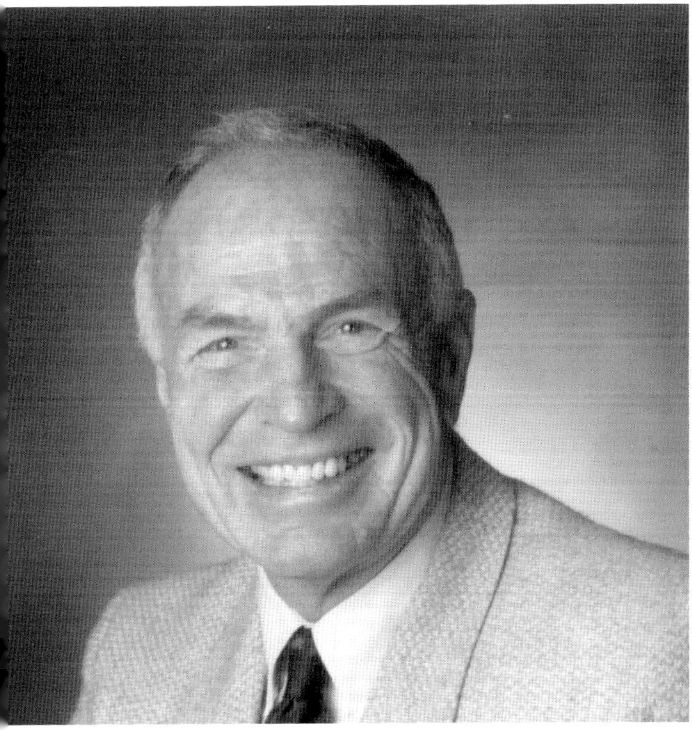

Dr. David Townsend
Alamogordo's history lives, thanks to Townsend, who authored such books as *Centennial: Where the Old West Meets the New Frontier* (with Clif McDonald) and *Lacy at Ninety*. The library at New Mexico State University–Alamogordo, where he taught history for more than three decades, is named for him. Townsend was also the campus director from 1978 to 1982, served as a state representative, and, in 1969, served on New Mexico's Constitutional Convention. In 1998, the New Mexico Endowment for the Humanities bestowed upon him the honor of Special Friend to the Humanities. (Courtesy David Townsend.)

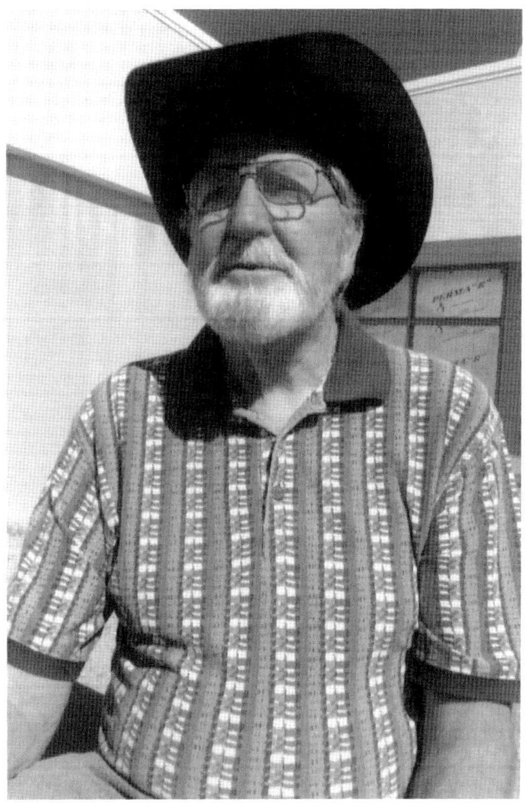

Sid Benson
A cowboy poet, Benson blends humorous stories with Western custom and culture. He was 20, in 1958, when he began writing poetry. Words came naturally, as his ancestors were pioneer newspaper people in the West. Benson became hooked on the cowboy genre after hearing Waddie Mitchell, the "Buckaroo Poet," perform at a Michael Martin Murphy concert. (Courtesy Michael Shinabery.)

Ernie Lee Miller

There was no money for art lessons while growing up during the Depression, but Miller drew anyway with her crayons and pencils. The family came to Alamogordo after their Tularosa bakery burned down, and local artists took her under their wings. She watched Peter Hurd paint his mural on Alamogordo's old post office. Eventually, as a young adult, Miller attended art classes in Albuquerque. While her New Mexico–themed paintings are sold in many galleries, local residents see her bronze sculptures every day in Founder's Park, which commemorates the region's early and notable residents. (Courtesy Don Larsen.)

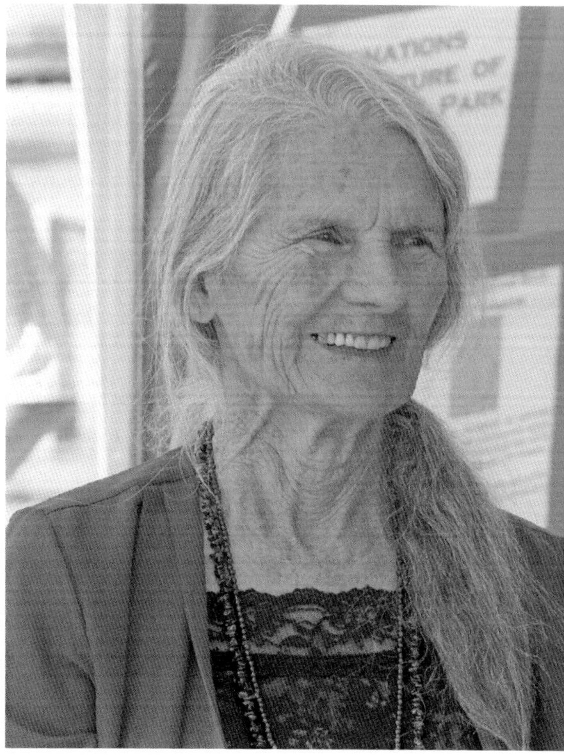

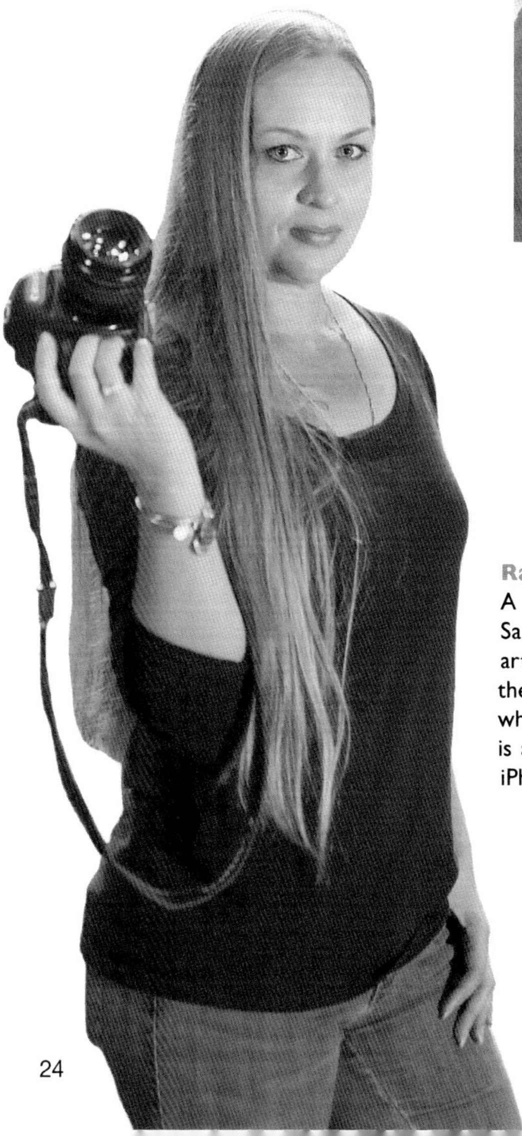

Rachel Telles

A photographer, Telles spent 2011 capturing White Sands National Monument. The result was the fine-art book *White Sands—A Photographic Journey*. Her theme was "reside," or what she said nature does while man is not watching. Her second book, *Vignettes*, is a compilation of average objects snapped with her iPhone. (Courtesy Rachel Telles.)

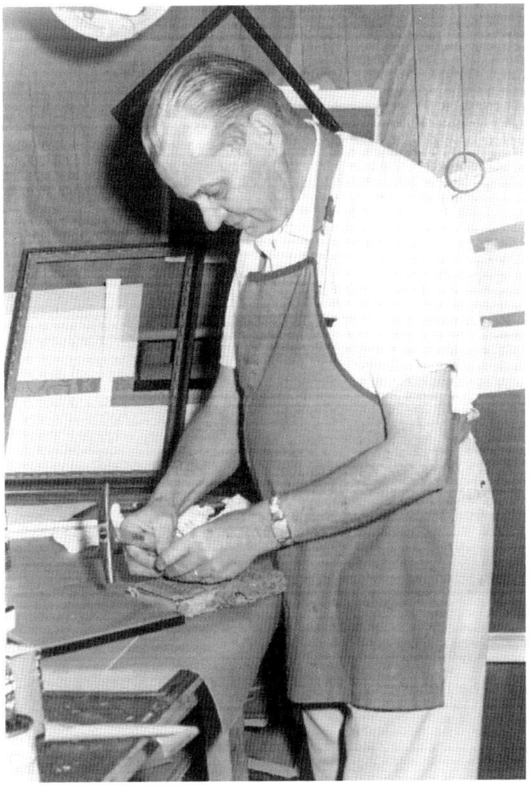

Carl Ness
Traveling while in the Merchant Marines gave Ness an appreciation for nature's never-ending features. His favorite, though, was the Southwest, and Ness's landscape paintings gave beauty to nature melding with man's detritus. Peter Hurd and his wife, Henriette Wyeth-Hurd, were friends. At Holloman Air Force Base, Ness was DynCorp's lead draftsman, and his artwork was on the thank-you cards the base gave to every departing airman. Ness died in 2003. (Courtesy Linda Ness-Gulley.)

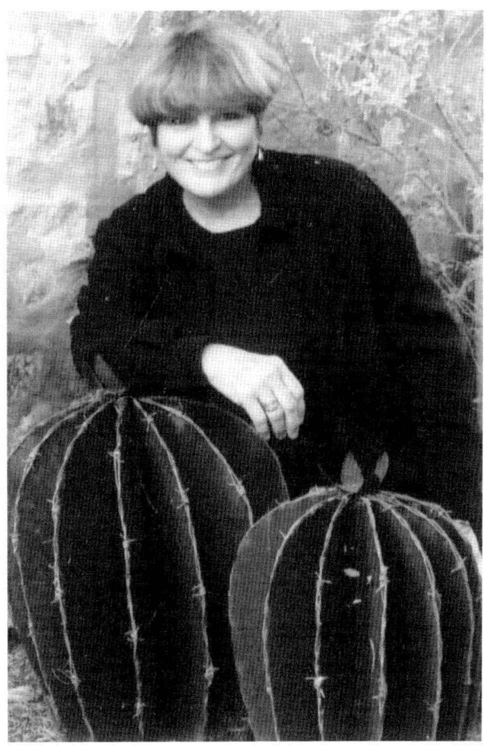

Penny Simpson
Since 1977, Simpson has painted her watercolors and acrylics in New Mexico, and many of her works have won state and national awards. She opened Penny Artworks in Alamogordo in 1985 and moved to Las Cruces nearly 25 years later. Her work depicts very realistic fruit, flowers, and still lifes, with dramatic lighting. Simpson's work hangs in galleries in Las Cruces, Mesilla, and Albuquerque, where she exhibits at the annual Weem's International ArtFest. (Courtesy Penny Simpson.)

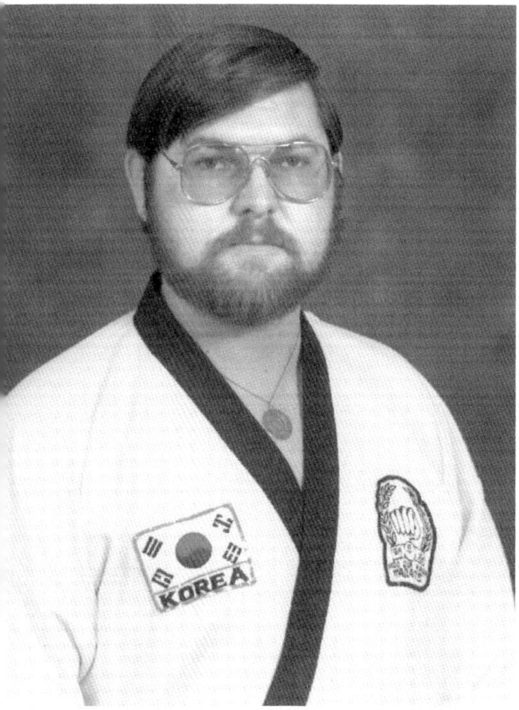

Johnny Rardin

Rardin first studied martial arts at age 11 and earned his black belt in 1975. He later became a teacher; one of his students, Linda White, became his wife. The couple taught martial arts for 24 years, taking students to tournaments in New Mexico, Texas, and Arizona. In 1996, Rardin was chosen for the US Martial Arts Team. He came in fourth in the world in sparring at the World Cup Games in Australia. Rardin retired from the sport in 2000, when he started teaching grandchildren of his former students. He is now assistant manager of First National Bank's North Branch. (Courtesy Johnny Rardin.)

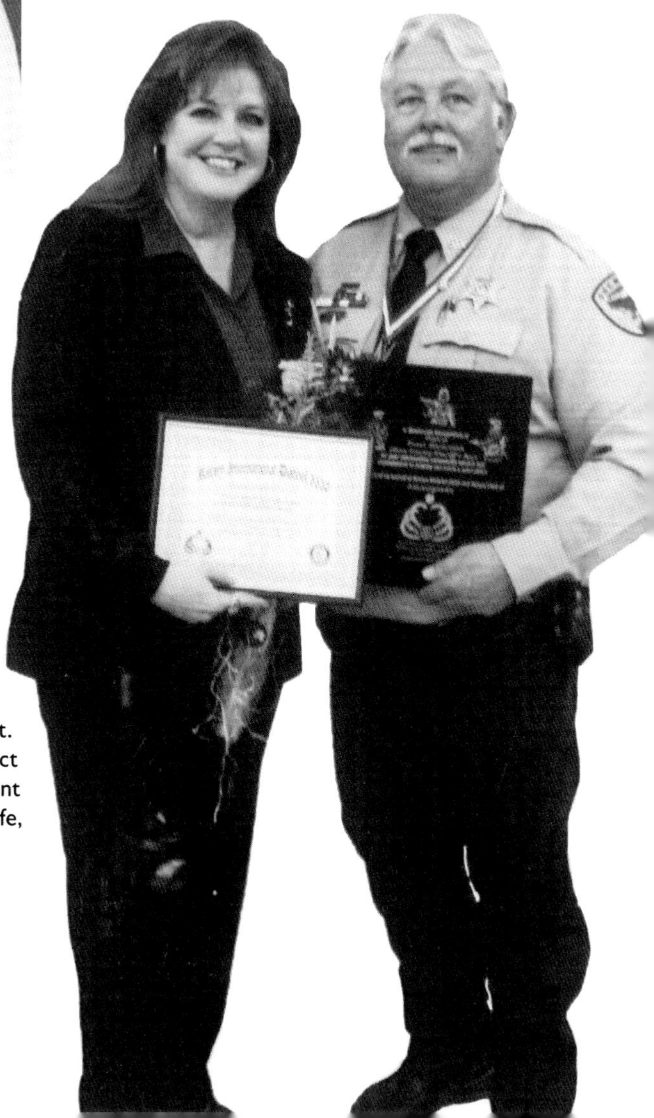

Frank Mackewich

Before he became a highly decorated police officer, Mackewich was a professional stunt rider known as "Fearless Frank." He performed throughout the United States and Canada, driving up two-foot-wide ramps to leap over increasingly longer lines of vehicles. On his last professional jump, Mackewich hit the last two cars and slid unconscious across the asphalt. In 2012, in Albuquerque, Rotary District 5520 honored him for his law-enforcement service. He is seen here with his wife, Lorraine. (Courtesy Michael Shinabery.)

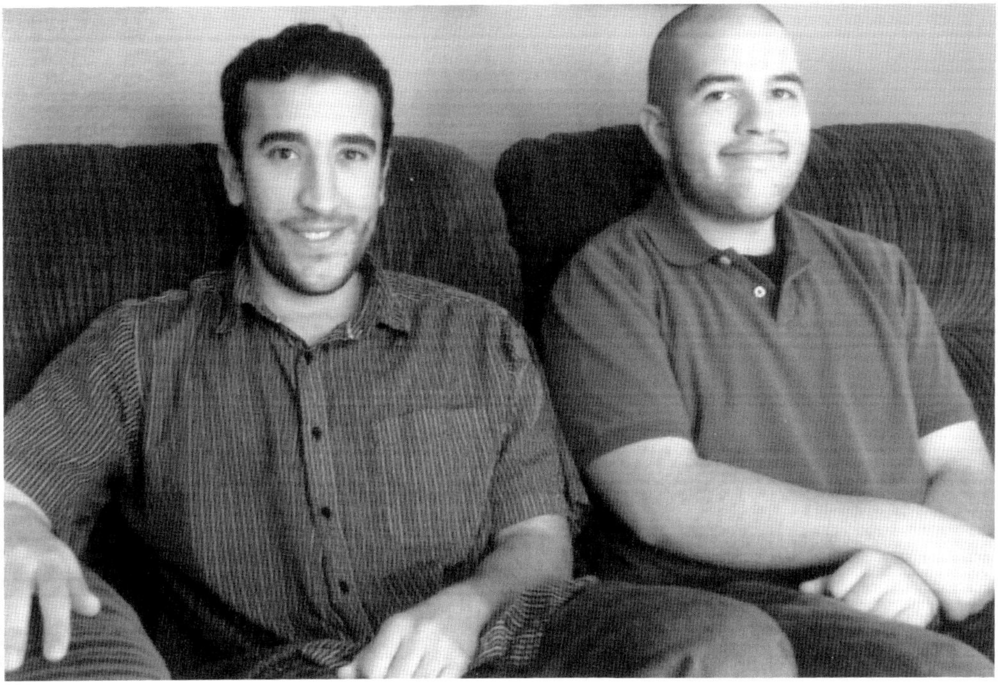

House Brothers
Not long after Josh House (left) graduated from New Mexico State University, his dad saw an advertisement for actors for the television show *Manhattan*. Josh and his brother Ben (right) were called two weeks after applying, and they have worked steadily in television and film. With his Middle Eastern looks, Josh has played everything from Italians to Israelis to terrorists. Ben is also a playwright. (Courtesy Michael Shinabery.)

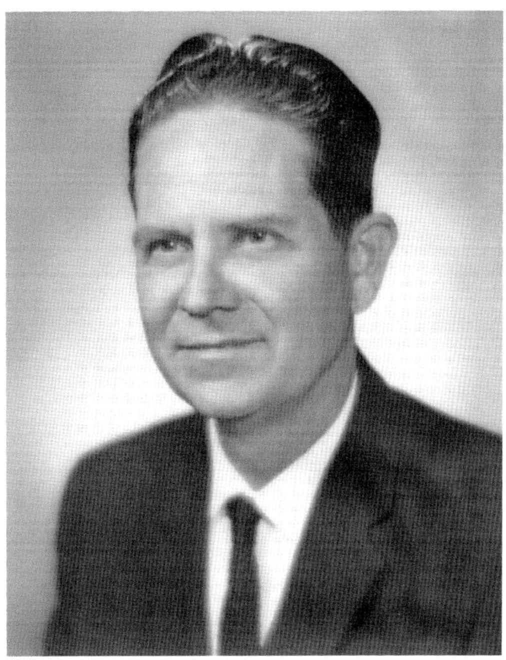

Wayne Phelps
Phelps bought Alamogordo's first radio station, KALG, just three months after it went on the air on June 28, 1950. Holloman Air Force Base deputy commander James Joy spoke at the ceremony, along with state senator Murray Morgan, state representative Herb Bays, and county agent Walter Wade. In August 1951, Phelps recorded the dirt-turning ceremony for the new high school for later broadcast. In August 1954, he was aboard the inaugural Continental Airlines flight to Denver. Phelps sold KALG to Bob Flotte in 1977. Today, the station is KRSY, but it resides in the same building, still at 1230 AM, and it has the same telephone number. (Courtesy the Tularosa Basin Historical Society.)

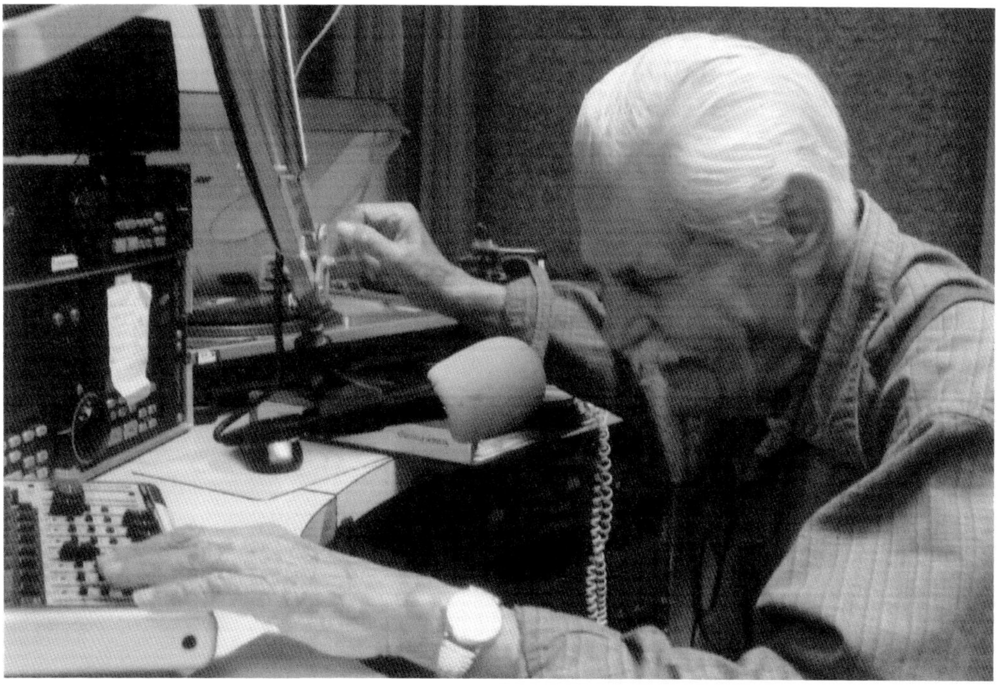

Ron Johnson

Johnson plays big-band music on KRSY's *Sweet and Hot and All That Jazz*. He came to Alamogordo in 1951 after playing woodwinds for many celebrated artists: Reggie Childs; Louis Prima, at New York's Hotel Commodore; Ina Ray Hutton's all-male band; Lou Walters's (Barbara Walters's father) Latin Quarter; Ray Anthony; and on the road with Charlie Spivak. Johnson's day job for 33 years was at Land-Air DynCorp. Except for a three-year absence from the station (then KALG) in the mid-1950s, Johnson has continually hosted programs, including *Music of Yesterday and Today, Styled the KALG Way*. He has also appeared as "Dr. Feelgood, the Medicine Man for the Blues." (Courtesy Michael Shinabery.)

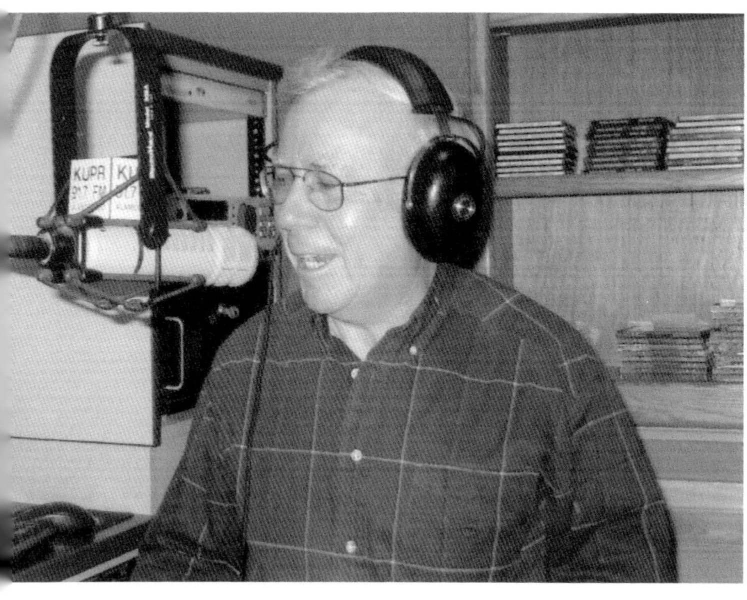

Ken Wilson

Wilson worked in broadcasting before coming to Alamogordo as an award-winning State Farm agent. Radio, though, never quite left his blood, and for many years, he pulled from his vast collection of music to host oldies shows. He is seen here as "Captain Ken" on KUPR FM. At his pre-funeral viewing, instead of soft music, his family played recordings of his shows. (Courtesy Michael Shinabery.)

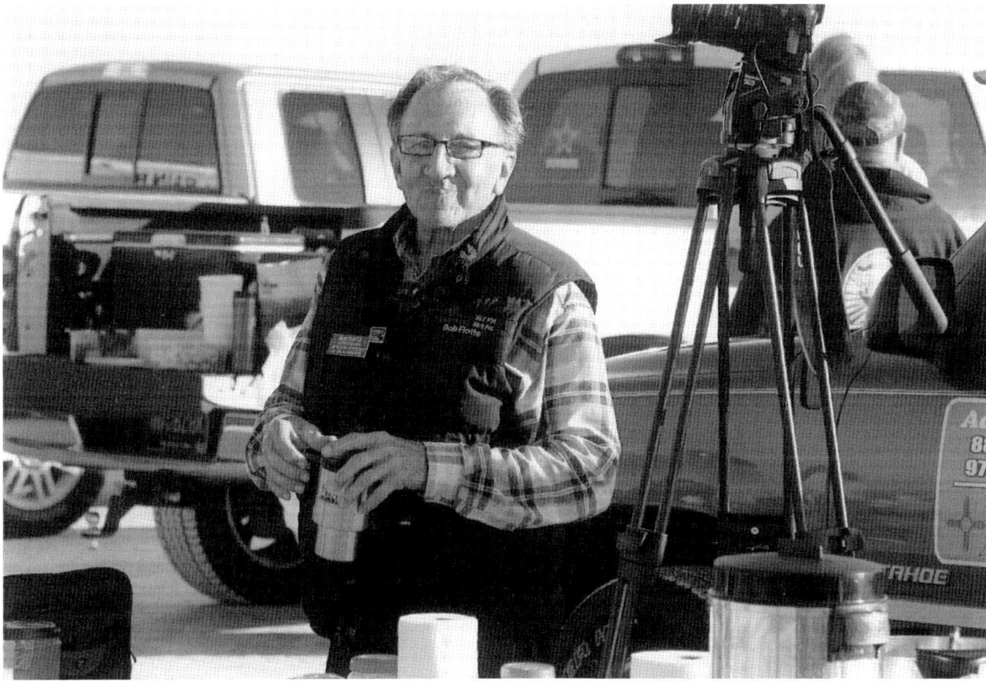

Bob Flotte

In 1977, Flotte arrived in Alamogordo as KALG's new owner. He changed the call letters to KPSA, an inspired reference to the phrase *que pasa*, Spanish for "what's happening?" Flotte's most memorable reporting was in 1982, when the space shuttle *Columbia* landed at White Sands Missile Range. When the train carrying recovery equipment came through town, Flotte rushed to the US 54/70 overpass. Listeners responded, descending en masse, so shocking the train's engineer that he braked to a stop. After the shuttle landed on March 30, NASA recognized Flotte's accurate reporting when it directed astronauts Jack Lousma and C. Gordon Fullerton to him for their first interview. (Courtesy Ed Thomas.)

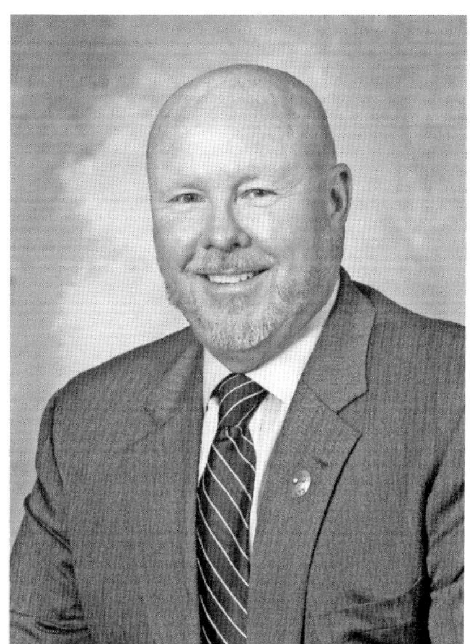

Bill Burt

Burt, a disc jockey in Illinois, Florida, Texas, and California, worked with a pre-syndicated Rush Limbaugh and was a rock 'n' roll drummer before he and his wife, Donnie, bought 94KEY in 1988. Today, Burt Broadcasting owns four successful radio stations. A Christian and a conservative, Burt has donated untold hours to youth, including as the voice of Alamogordo High School Tiger basketball and football, and as master of ceremonies for the Sertoma Scholarship Pageant. A state senator, his many honors include Citizen of the Year from the Alamogordo Chamber of Commerce; the Chamber Ambassador's "Top Gun;" and the New Mexico Broadcasters Association's Broadcaster of the Year and medium-market Owner of the Radio Station of the Year. A tireless supporter of Holloman Air Force Base, Burt has been a Wingman since 2006. (Courtesy Alamogordo Chamber of Commerce.)

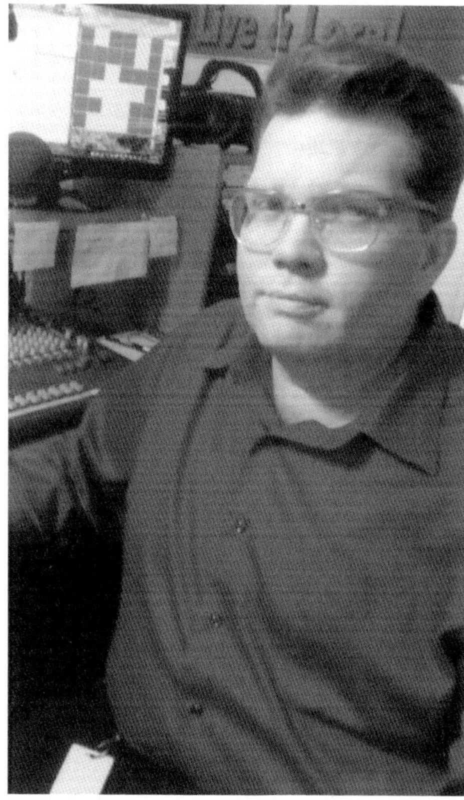

Jason Curtman

Curtman is passionate about bringing back the nickel soda pop. Maybe not literally, but he certainly seeks a return to the ambience of a simpler time. Curtman takes his campaign to the airwaves every week, broadcasting from Alamogordo to more than 20 radio stations across America. With rebroadcasts, the show, which mixes music and comedy from 1935 to 1979, airs 110 times weekly. Born in St. Louis, Curtman was seven when his pastor dad dragged the family to Yankee territory. When he reached his early 20s, Curtman hightailed it out of Michigan and back to Missouri. There, he worked in security and private investigations and subsequently wore the uniforms of a county sheriff's deputy and municipal police officer. Curtman moved to Alamogordo to work as a recruiter for a Fortune 500 company. He is a singer who sounds a lot like Elvis Presley, and he has released CDs that contain not just covers of music popular during the nickel-soda era but original compositions as well. (Courtesy Michael Shinabery.)

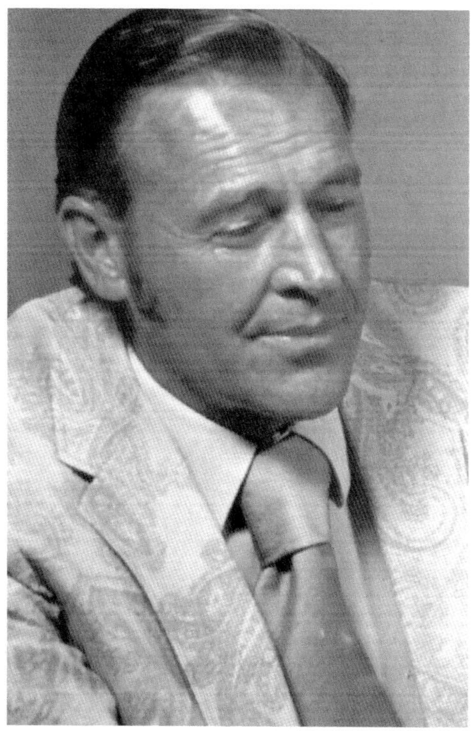

Calvin Boles

Before he died in 2004, Swedish and German filmmakers produced documentaries on Boles and his Yucca Records label. Boles released 237 vinyl singles, as well as albums, all recorded in his garage and at KALG AM. His artists included Bobby Fuller, and Bob Taylor and the Counts (with members Jim Reese and Willie Nelson). For a time, Boles owned a publishing company in Nashville, where a daughter married Faron Young's son, Robin. (Permission to use from Ron Johnson, from the album *We Lit the Candle of Love, and Blew It.*)

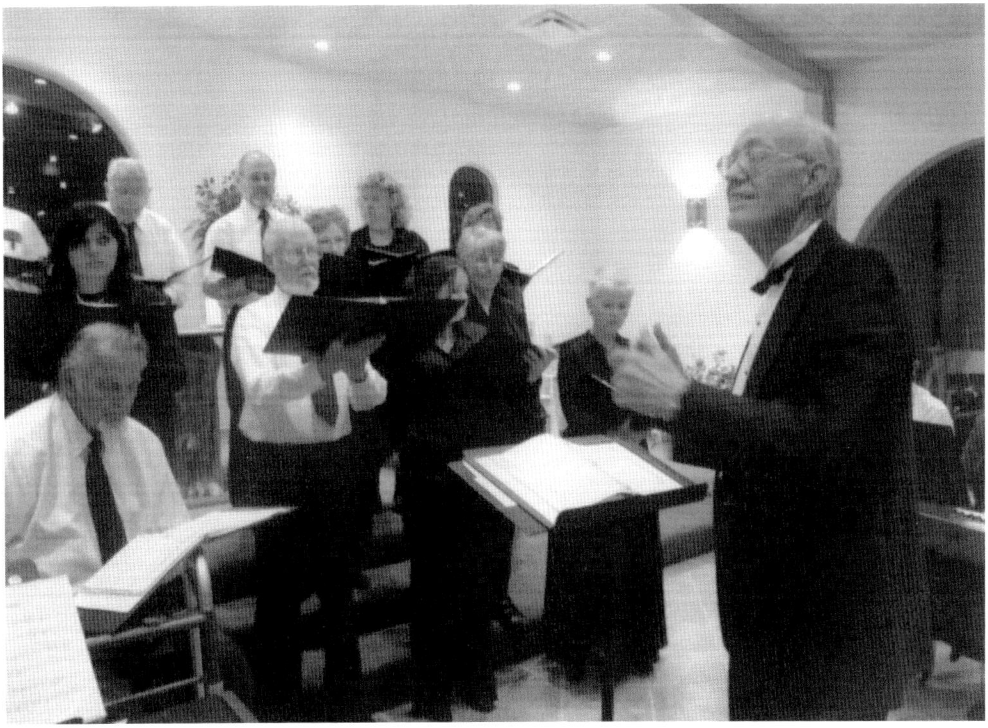

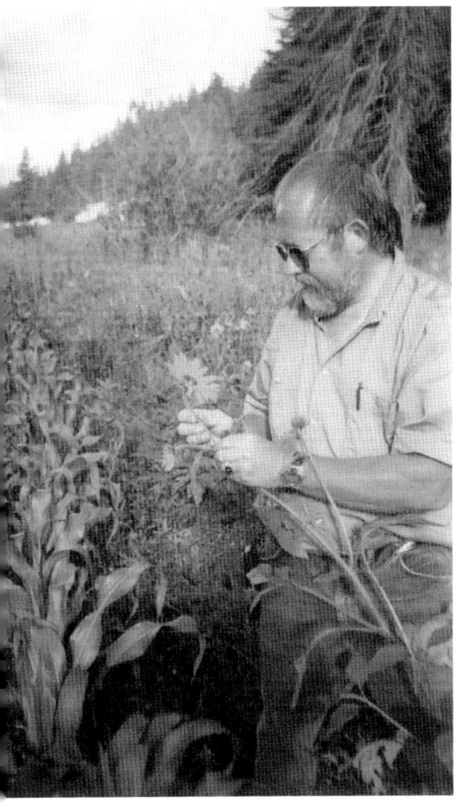

Don Thorp

Thousands of area students lifted their voices in harmony over the quarter-century that Thorp taught music in Alamogordo. After settling in Alamogordo in 1966, Thorp inspired students at Alamogordo High School and directed community choirs and church worship. He also adjudicated vocal festivals and choral contests to encourage youth to make music a lifelong avocation. (Courtesy Don Thorpe.)

Bill McClain

McClain learned piano while listening to his mom worship God on her piano. Never formally trained, McClain began writing and recording his own music, released several albums, and played in area restaurants. He and his wife, Lynda, were invited to perform on God's Learning Channel, in Midland-Odessa, Texas, and they then went to Brazil on a concert tour. His calming music has been used in Alzheimer's wards and senior facilities. Diagnosed with cancer in 2009, McClain continued his ministry until his 2011 death. By then, he had performed in front of millions of people. (Courtesy Lynda McClain.)

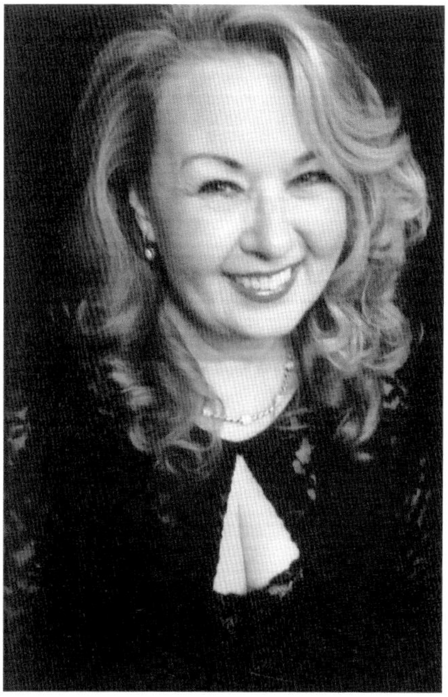

Donnie Burt

Burt was four when she stepped out at church and sang a solo. She has not stopped. At eight, she traveled throughout Southern California with church musicians, and at 16, she was a paid singer on a weekly radio church service. While a young woman, she toured Sweden, Denmark, and Norway as a soloist. She has performed in musical theater, has sung on television and radio jingles, is a featured singer with the Flickinger Center for Performing Arts' House Band, and was talent coach for Miss Alamogordo/Miss Otero County. Her sons, both Alamogordo High School graduates, work in Los Angeles. Jarrod Burt is a television and film editor on such projects as *Keeping Up with the Kardashians*, *In the Company of Strangers*, *Grey Skies*, and *The Challenge*. Aaron Burt, a successful actor, graduated from Hollywood's American Academy of Dramatic Arts. He has had roles in the films *Then Again*, *Seekers*, and *What We Can't Have*. (Courtesy Donnie Burt.)

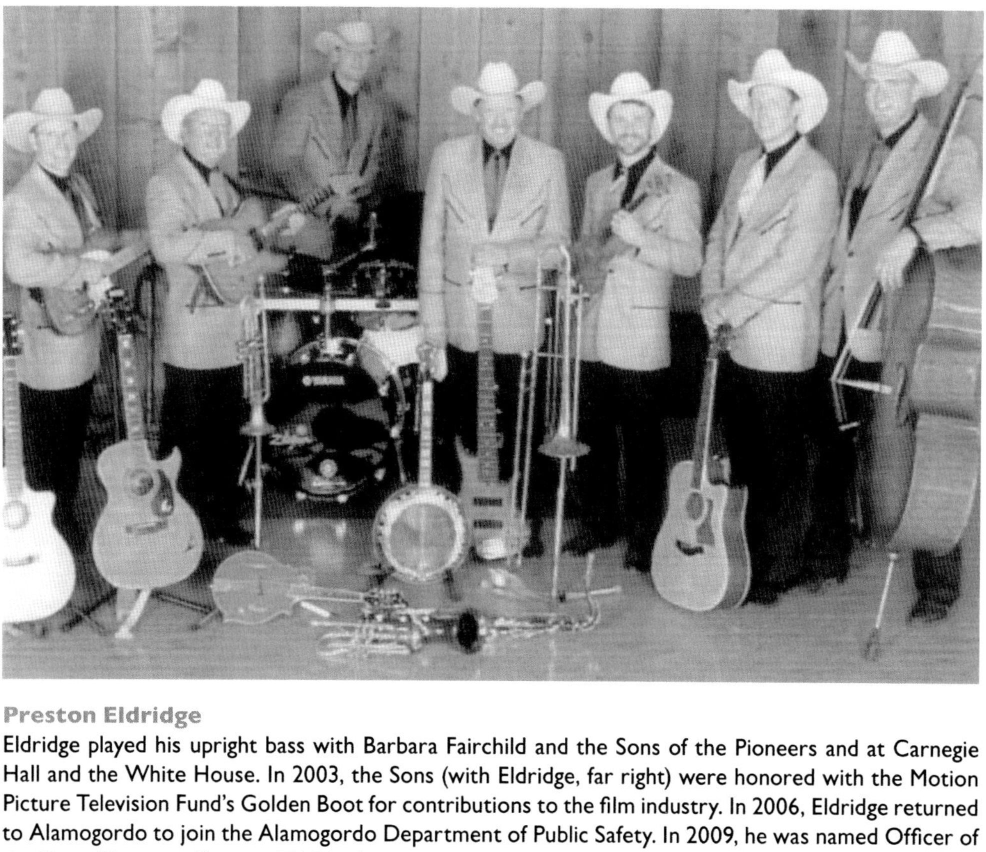

Preston Eldridge

Eldridge played his upright bass with Barbara Fairchild and the Sons of the Pioneers and at Carnegie Hall and the White House. In 2003, the Sons (with Eldridge, far right) were honored with the Motion Picture Television Fund's Golden Boot for contributions to the film industry. In 2006, Eldridge returned to Alamogordo to join the Alamogordo Department of Public Safety. In 2009, he was named Officer of the Year. (Courtesy Preston Eldridge.)

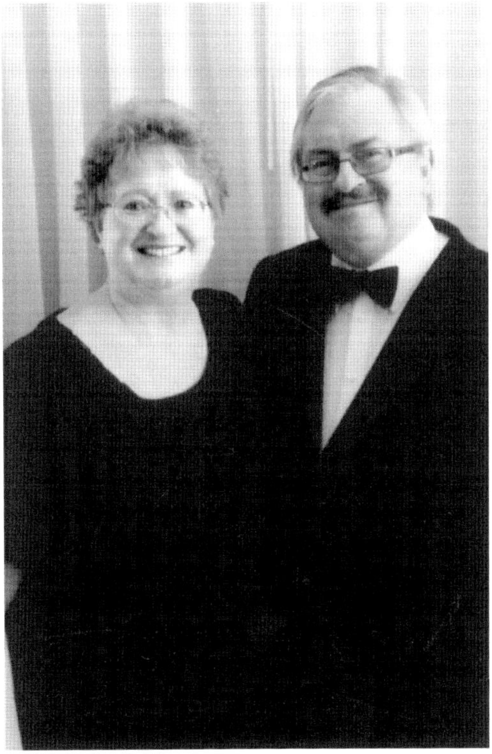

Cheryl and Paul Hughen
Cheryl left a secure job at White Sands Missile Range in 2005 to pursue her dream: opening Classifiddles Studio to teach violin. An accomplished musician, she plays in the Southwest and Roswell Symphonies. Paul, who teaches beginning bass, also plays in the Southwest Symphony, as does their daughter, Melody. The couple has scores of private students, and Cheryl is an assistant teacher at Imago Dei Academy. (Courtesy the Hughens.)

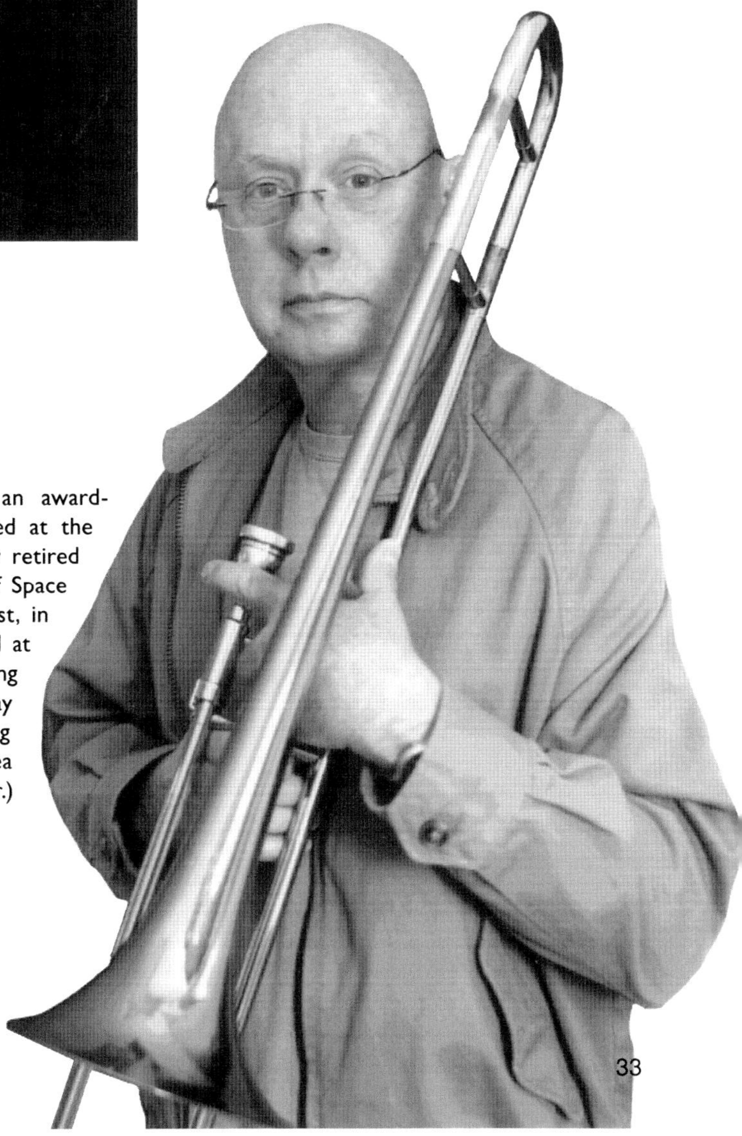

Ron Keller
A US Navy veteran, Keller is an award-winning photographer who worked at the *Alamogordo Daily News* and is now retired from the New Mexico Museum of Space History. A talented jazz trombonist, in 2013, he founded the House Band at the Flickinger Center for Performing Arts. The local musicians play several concerts annually, including at Christmas to raise funds for area organizations. (Courtesy Ron Keller.)

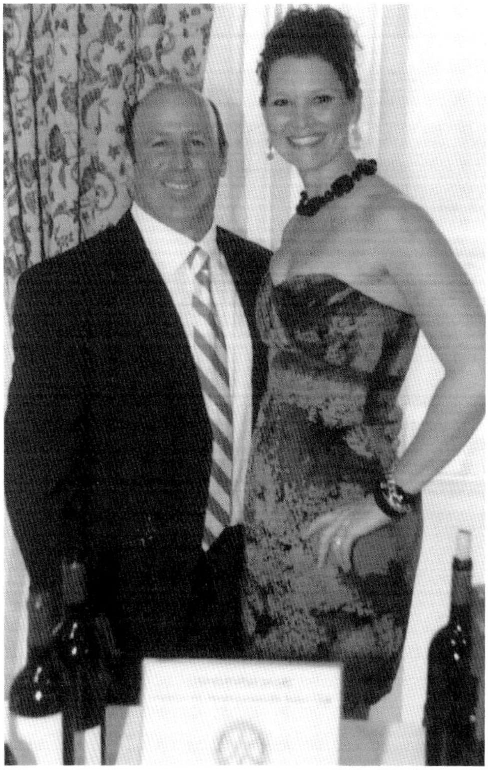

Amanda Foster

Foster was a popular morning-show host on KRSY FM and a talented singer who wanted to expand her musical abilities. She headed to Tennessee to write with country singer and former Otero County resident Colt Prather. Foster became vice president of development for the Hendersonville (Tennessee) Area Chamber of Commerce and is a fitness instructor. She is married to Hendersonville mayor Scott Foster. (Courtesy Amanda Foster.)

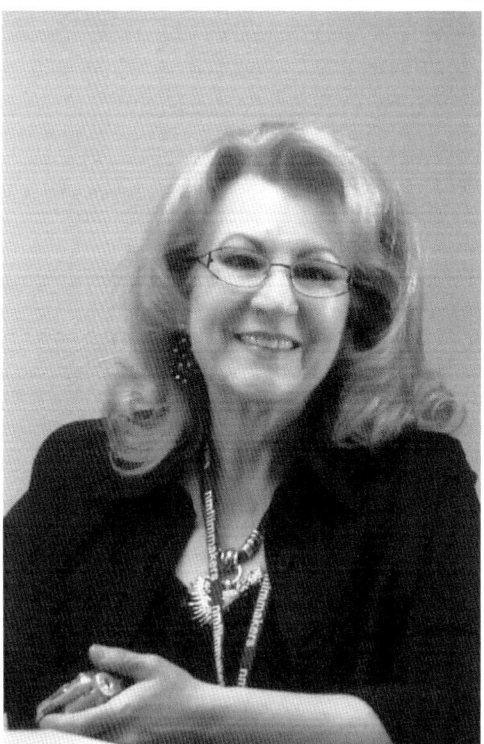

Jan Wafful

Wafful is the City of Alamogordo's film liaison. The list of movies she has helped bring in for location shooting includes the first two *Transformers* films, *The Men Who Stare at Goats*, and *The Book of Eli*. She works with documentary producers, too, including those for A&E, National Geographic, History Channel, NBC, the BBC, and Foolish Earthling Productions. (Courtesy Jan Wafful.)

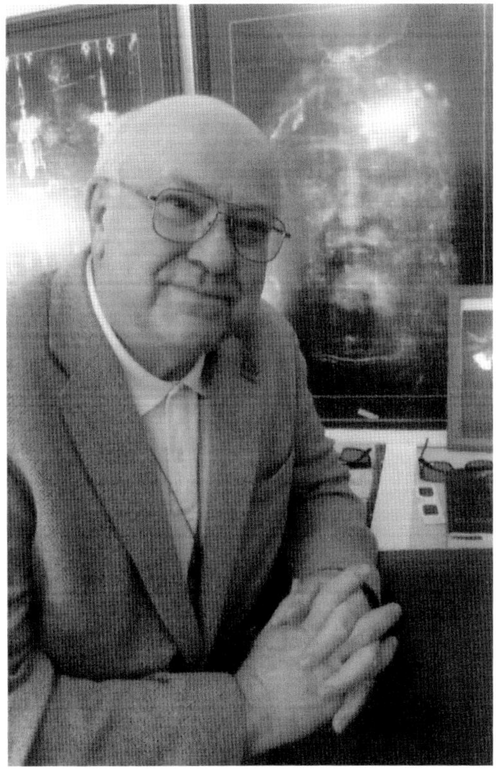

Deacon Pete Schumacher
In the mid-1970s, Schumacher was product engineer for the VP8 Image Analyzer, which he calibrated on a picture of the Shroud of Turin. He was startled to see a 3-D image emerge, his first step toward establishing that the face is that of Jesus Christ. Schumacher, a Catholic deacon, now operates the Shroud Exhibit and Museum in downtown Alamogordo. (Courtesy Michael Shinabery.)

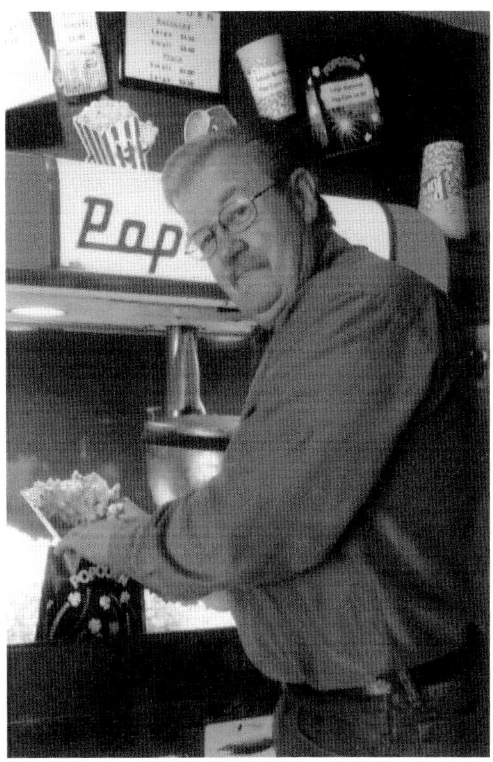

Bill Oechsner
In 1982, Oechsner was standing in the KVBA Christian Television studio, housed in the old Sands Theater, while his wife sang the theme of a Saturday-night program. Oechsner asked what he could do to help. Program host Bob Broome was also the engineer and so had to continually leave the stage to address problems. So, after a month of Saturdays listening to Oechsner's inquiries, Broome told Oechsner he was the new host. Oechsner became station manager eight years later. In December 2013, volunteer Dan McKee proposed reopening the Sands to show family films. Renovation was undertaken by 40 Holloman Air Force Base volunteers through the Big Give, including reinstalling the original seven-foot-tall Voice of the Theater speaker, the 1950s Manley Aristocrat popcorn machine, and the original 25-foot silver screen. (Courtesy Michael Shinabery.)

Margaret Flickinger

Flickinger came to Alamogordo with her husband and set about bettering the community. In 1998, she donated funds to purchase the old Sierra Theatre, which now bears her name: The Flickinger Center for Performing Arts. She threw herself into the renovation until she died unexpectedly the next year. Her legacy lives on in the facility that brings world-class artists and musicians to Alamogordo. (Courtesy Flickinger Center for Performing Arts.)

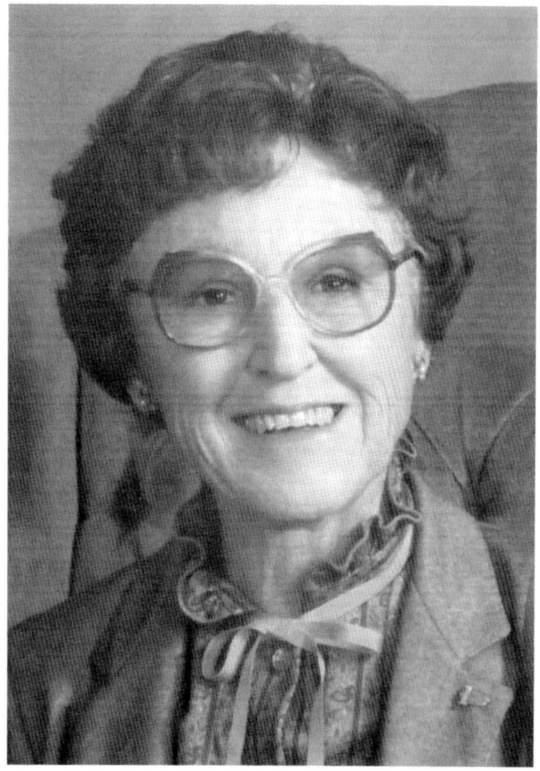

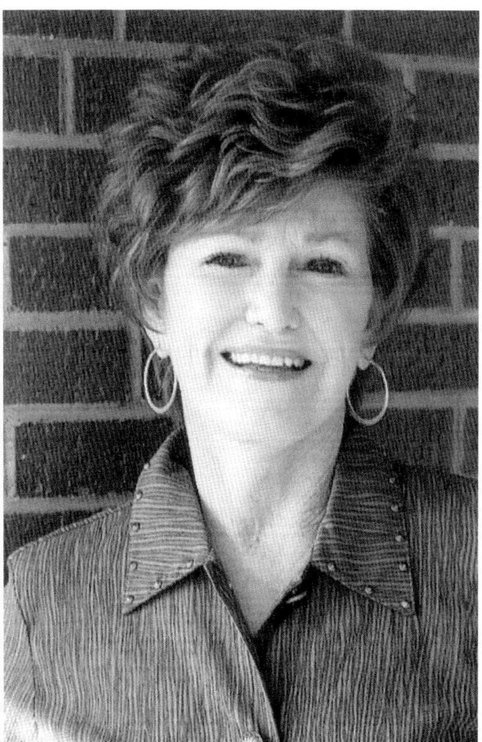

Teresa Ham

When Ham joined the board of the new Flickinger Center for Performing Arts in 1988, she scraped gum off the seats and mopped up soda spills at what was the old Sierra Theater. Margaret Flickinger had provided the purchase funds, and when she died, Ham chaired the Million Dollar Capital Campaign to complete the conversion. She raises funds to bring schoolchildren to performances and initiated the Annual Support Campaign to maintain the Flickinger as Alamogordo's cultural center. (Courtesy Teresa Ham.)

CHAPTER FOUR

The Military and Space

In Alamogordo, space was never the final frontier, but it was the force that changed the frontier of a Western small town. The transformation began with an act of war more than 3,000 miles away. In the early 1940s, the British were coming . . . to Alamogordo. The British Overseas Training program was slated to prepare flight crews in New Mexico's skies. Until, that is, the Japanese attacked Pearl Harbor. With war inevitable, England stayed home. However, America now needed a base, and in 1942, the Alamogordo Army Air Field began training bomber crews. Unfortunately, the rushed pace to prepare for war resulted in many crashes. A high number of young pilots and crew members perished before ever deploying overseas.

At the same time, the US government established White Sands Proving Ground. To do so, it confiscated property, both deeded and leased. The Army roared up to front doors and ordered families to move. The ranchers sacrificed land, as well as water and mineral rights—for most of them, patriotism was more important than materialism. They believed that, when America won the war, home on the range would once again be home sweet home. That was true for many, but only for a time. Eventually, the government claimed the property for good. The festering wounds of confiscation never healed. In 1994, US senator Pete Domenici sponsored legislation to pay Americans fair value for their losses. However, a well-known regional axiom came into play: Lawmakers in the East simply do not understand rural life in the West. Domenici's bill, the last attempt at justice, failed.

After World II, the Army air field became Holloman Air Force Base. White Sands Proving Ground, farther away, became the White Sands Missile Range (WSMR). Both were vital to the space race. German engineers arrived in the area to help the Army develop America's rocket and missile programs. Balloons launched from the Tularosa Basin, carrying the first men to the edge of space. Dr. John Stapp rode rocket sleds to learn about force trauma on the human body, slamming to a stop at 43 times the force of gravity. On Stapp's air-powered Daisy Track, Capt. Eli Beeding endured a brief moment of 83 g's, and he survived. In order to prove that living and working in the hazardous environment of space was possible, two chimpanzees trained at Holloman. *Mercury* 7 astronaut Gus Grissom once visited. Pres. John Kennedy landed at Holloman before visiting White Sands. In the early 1960s, New Mexico pitched WSMR as the ideal launching location; after all, years of flight-testing and data proved that the remote region was ideal.

Today, Holloman alone puts more than $1 million a day into the area's economy. The base, coupled with WSMR and McGregor Range, make up the largest contiguous landmass in the Department of Defense inventory. Military and space history are preserved at the New Mexico Museum of Space History, the International Space Hall of Fame, the American Armed Forces Museum, and at a memorial, spearheaded by Armando Quinones, honoring residents who served in the 82nd Airborne.

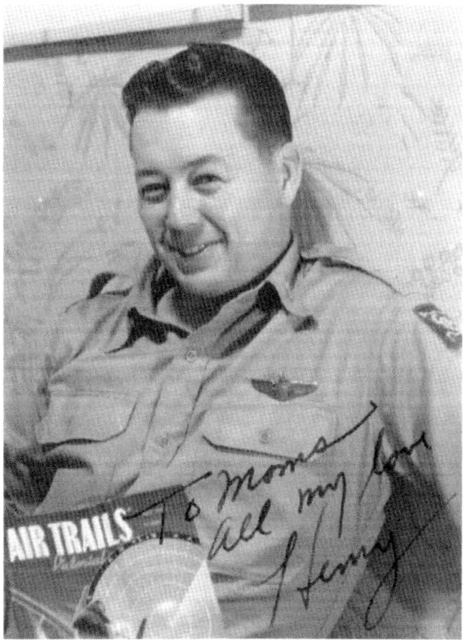

Col. Henry Godman

Godman flew B-17s in World War II and, for a time, was Gen. Douglas MacArthur's pilot. Godman once descended too fast into Melbourne, Australia, and gave MacArthur a nosebleed. However, the general came to trust his judgment after Godman informed an enraged MacArthur that his plane was unfit to fly, and Godman's suspicions proved true. He once participated in a rodeo in Spain to raise funds for orphans' homes and children's hospitals. Godman chronicled his experiences, including his lifelong journey to find faith in God, in his autobiography *Supreme Commander.* (Courtesy Godman family.)

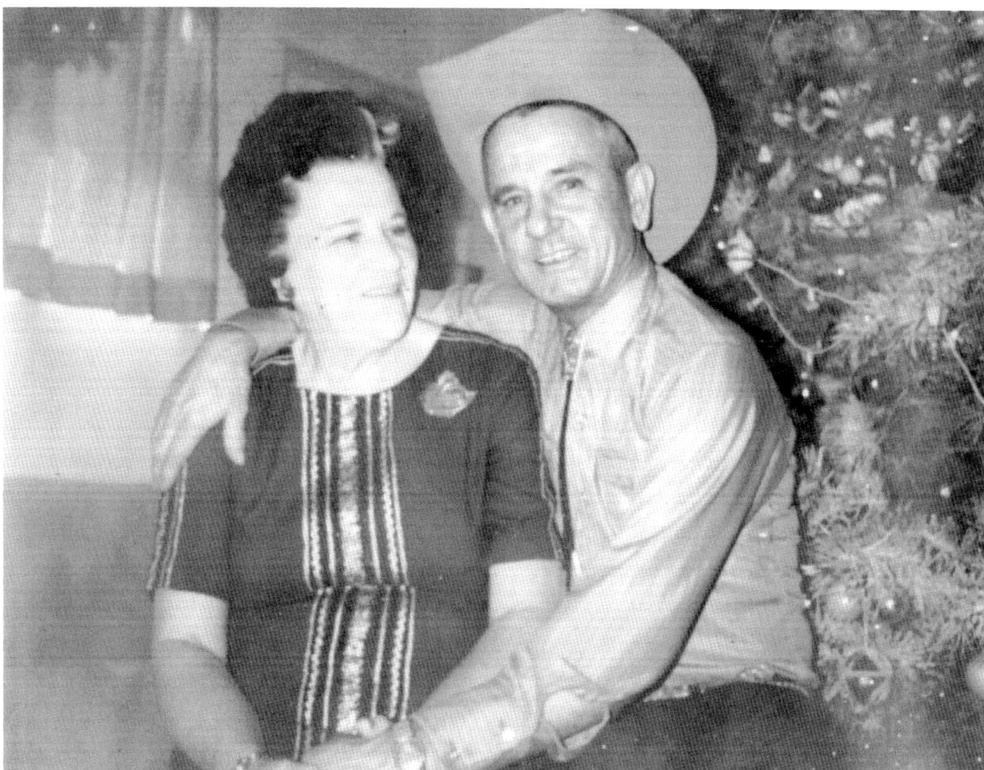

The Burrises

Laura and "Snooks" Burris lived in their ranch house for two years before the US government seized the property to create White Sands Proving Ground. The stress caused a quick divorce. In February 1942, Laura, pregnant with her daughter Patti, rode horseback through a raging snowstorm to move livestock per the Army's orders. Her only help came from neighboring cowboys. She went on to serve 14 years on the state school board. (Courtesy Patti Brady.)

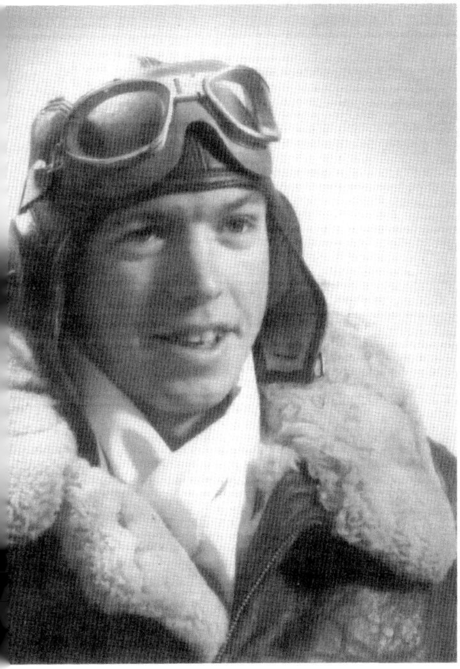

Jack Rathgeber

Rathgeber was a 23-year-old naval aviator when the United States dropped the atomic bombs on Hiroshima and Nagasaki. One morning aboard ship, Rathgeber learned he was one of eight pilots chosen to fly over Japan and search out opposition. They carried bombs, rockets, and machine guns with which to fight back. The Corsair F4U-4 fighter-bombers catapulted off the USS *Intrepid*, but never encountered the enemy. After hours of flying, they approached their final target, the emperor's palace. Rathgeber told his family that his parting shot was dropping his filled urine bag atop the palace.

After serving in Korea, Rathgeber married Maude Oliver. She informed him that she was not about to be a Navy wife, so he retired and spent 30 years at White Sands Missile Range, participating in classified research and development at Ryan Aeronautical Company (later Teledyne Ryan). His responsibilities included flight engineer, base manager, and flying remotely piloted vehicles. He died in 2011. (Courtesy Rathgeber family.)

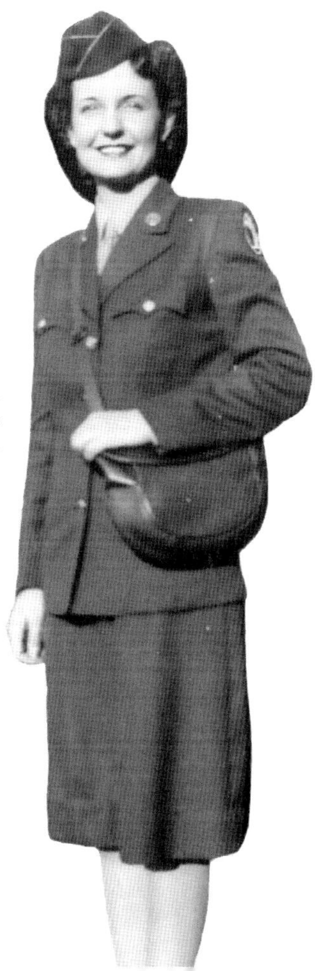

Frankie Edwards Saulnier

When Edwards learned her brother was shot down over Germany during World War II, she joined the Women's Army Corps. He had been flying with the Royal Air Force because he was too young for America's Army Air Corps. Working at the Pentagon, Frankie Edwards learned of his whereabouts. After marrying Edward Saulnier, she moved to Alamogordo and worked at Holloman Air Force Base as the commander's secretary until she and her husband built the KOA. (Courtesy Marcia Stirman.)

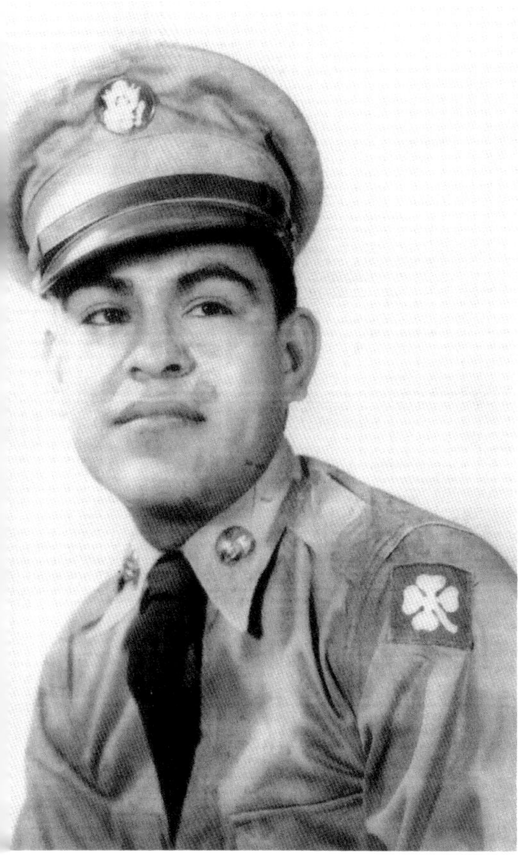

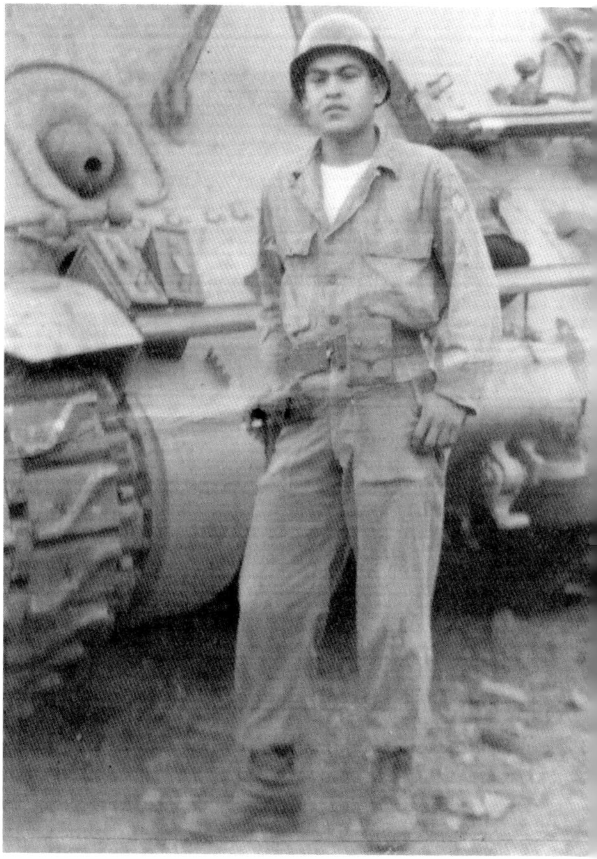

Willie Estrada
An Alamogordo native, Estrada was 23 when he gave his life for his fellow soldiers in September 1952. North Koreans had the 245th Tank Battalion hemmed in, even keeping medics from reaching the wounded. The 15-hour battle culminated when the enemy swarmed American tanks. Estrada signaled to his fellow soldiers that he would cover their retreat. The Koreans tossed grenades into Estrada's tank, and he quickly threw them back. Estrada was slashing enemy soldiers with his dagger when the Koreans slammed his hatch shut, trapping him inside. One soldier scribbled on the tank, "Brave fighter." About that time, a counterassault arrived from another American battalion. Estrada lived long enough to open his eyes to medics. The South Korean government posthumously bestowed that nation's highest military award on Estrada and named a training camp for him. Fort Knox, Kentucky, has an Estrada Avenue, and, more than 45 years later, the Alamogordo City Commission renamed the civic center the Sgt. Willie Estrada Memorial Civic Center. The battle tale was even told in a comic book. Estrada was posthumously awarded the Distinguished Service Cross, but his family has not given up on having the Congressional Medal of Honor bestowed as well. (Both courtesy Estrada family.)

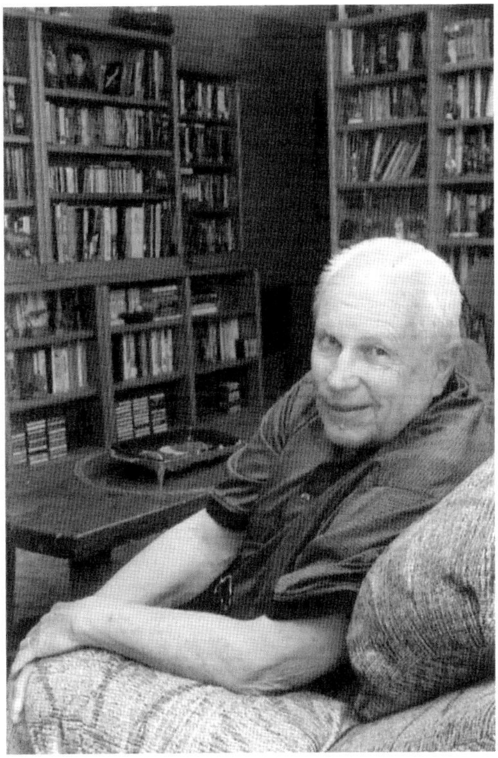

Wayne Mattson

Mattson spent nearly 20 years as a volunteer archivist at the New Mexico Museum of Space History. He cataloged thousands of books and transcribed nearly 70 years of military-related articles from Alamogordo newspapers. A graduate of the Naval Academy at Annapolis, Mattson transferred to the Air Force. Under commander Paul Tibbits, who had flown the atomic bomb to Hiroshima, Mattson flew B-47s for Strategic Air Command. During Vietnam, he piloted covert combat missions in a O-2A. In 1969, Mattson arrived at Holloman Air Force Base as chief of operations of the 6585th Test Group's Target Drone Division. He cowrote *We Develop Missiles, Not Air!* for the Department of Defense, Air Combat Command, Legacy Program. Just two days before his February 2012 death, the museum presented Mattson with the annual Community Service Award for his efforts to educate the public on space history. (Courtesy Ron Keller.)

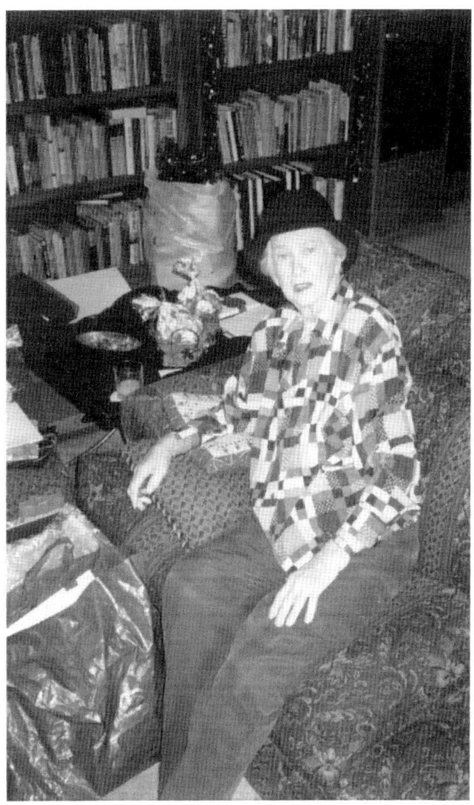

Sue Burroughs

Burroughs and her family came to Alamogordo in 1958, and she soon became secretary at Holloman Air Force Base for a German scientist during Operation Paperclip. Subsequently, Burroughs spent 12 years as secretary for a succession of base commanders. She is best known for her paintings of "local colors," more than 700 Southwest scenes from the 1950s through 2008 that still hang in homes and offices. She died in 2010. (Courtesy Randy Burroughs.)

Frank Gentile

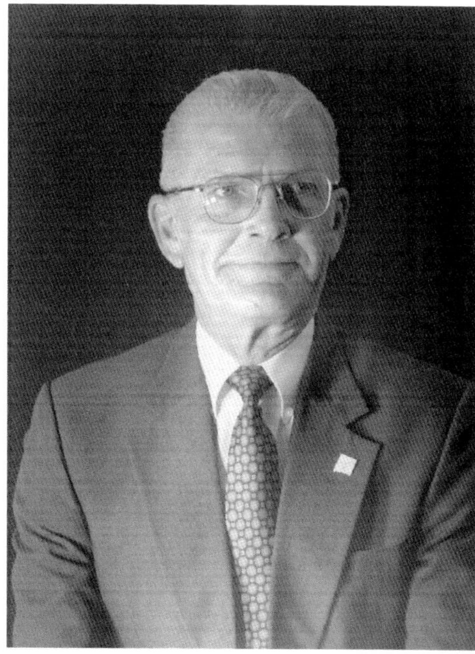

As an airborne battlefield controller, Chief Master Sergeant Gentile flew 239 combat missions, earning, among many honors, the Distinguished Flying Cross. At Holloman Air Force Base, Gentile was the first senior enlisted advisor. He became vice president at Western Bank, executive director of the Alamogordo Chamber of Commerce and Otero County Economic Development Council, and a city commissioner. Gentile founded the Retired E-9 Group, whose members held the highest enlisted rank in any military branch. (Courtesy Alamogordo Chamber of Commerce.)

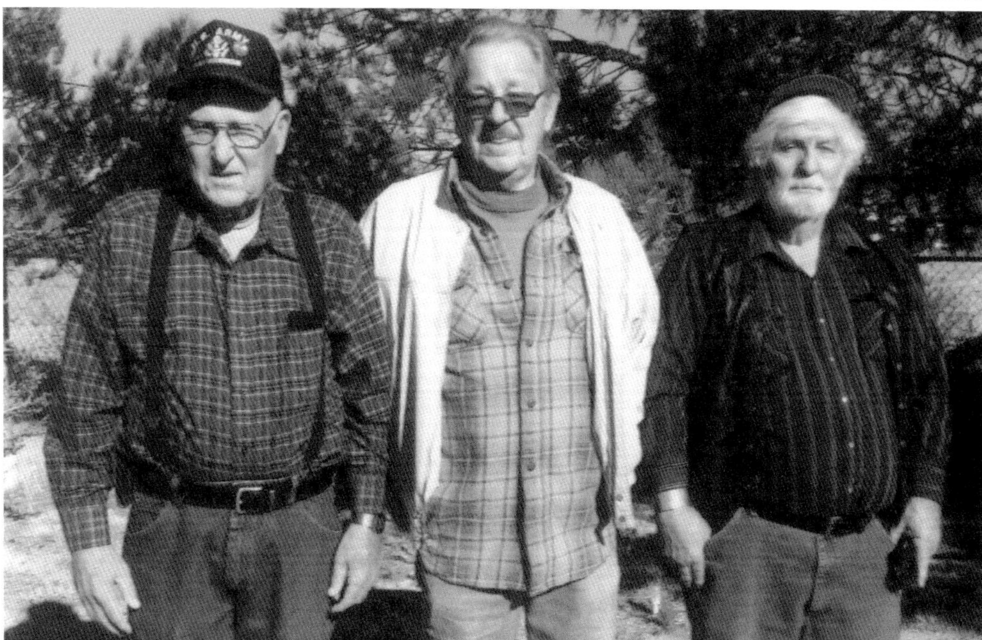

Nuclear Veterans

Harold Davis (left), Carl Clarke (center), and Lloyd Berryhill witnessed early-1960s nuclear testing in the Pacific Islands, known as Operation Dominic, part of Joint Task Force 8. Davis, an Army radio operator with the 125th Signal Corps, watched a warhead melt atop a Thor missile. Clarke, part of the Air Force 6th Weather Squadron, was on Palmyra Island. Berryhill, a Navy veteran, served on Christmas Island. Clarke died just two weeks after this photograph was taken in January 2015. (Courtesy Michael Shinabery.)

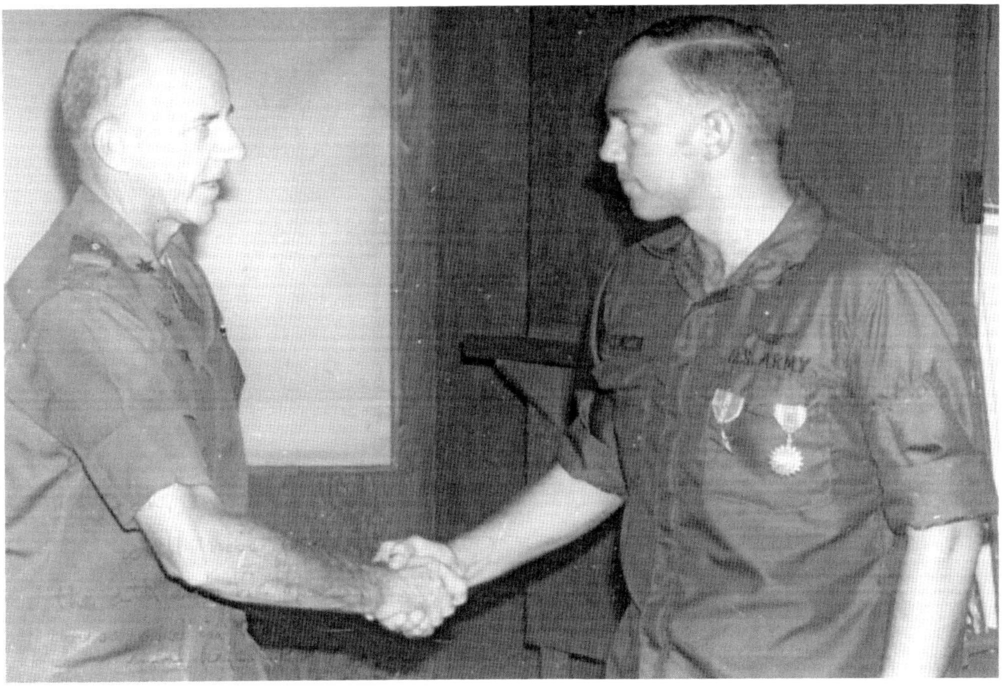

Jack Smith

The Huey helicopter in which Smith (right) flew combat missions in Vietnam, and with which he evacuated wounded, is now displayed at the Tulsa Air and Space Museum. Smith logged 1,600 hours for the 1st Air Cavalry Division and then for the 20th Engineer Brigade. Before leaving Vietnam, Brig. Gen. K.B. Cooper (left) recognized Smith for his service. Smith now honors his fellow veterans as a member of VFW Post 11999's Color Guard. An enrolled IRS agent, he prepares taxes and is also Cloudcroft's municipal judge. Smith has participated in Amazon Outreach, making multiple trips to Brazil to build church and school buildings for locals. (Courtesy Jack Smith.)

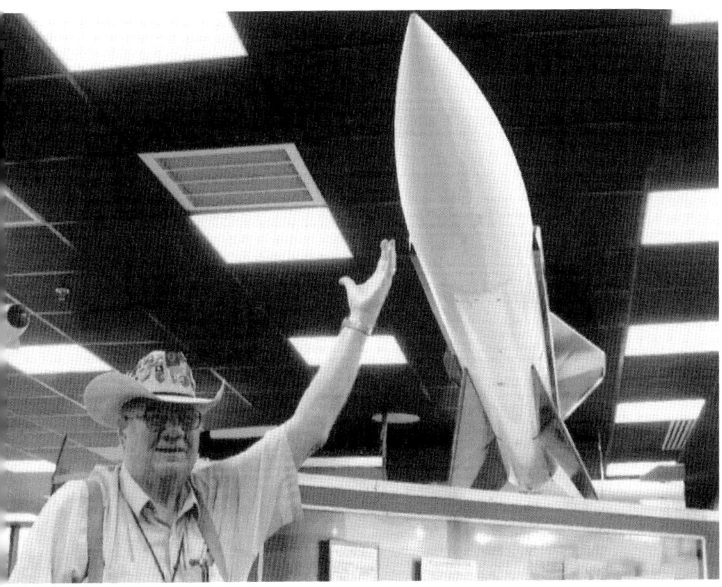

Paul Vigneault

In 1958, "Viggy" Vigneault became the first HAWK missile instructor at Fort Bliss, El Paso, Texas. He traveled the world in this capacity until retiring from the Army in 1976. For the next 11 years, Vigneault worked for HAWK's manufacturer, Raytheon. At the New Mexico Museum of Space History, he enlightened visitors about the missile's legacy, shown here under the HAWK. (Courtesy Ron Keller.)

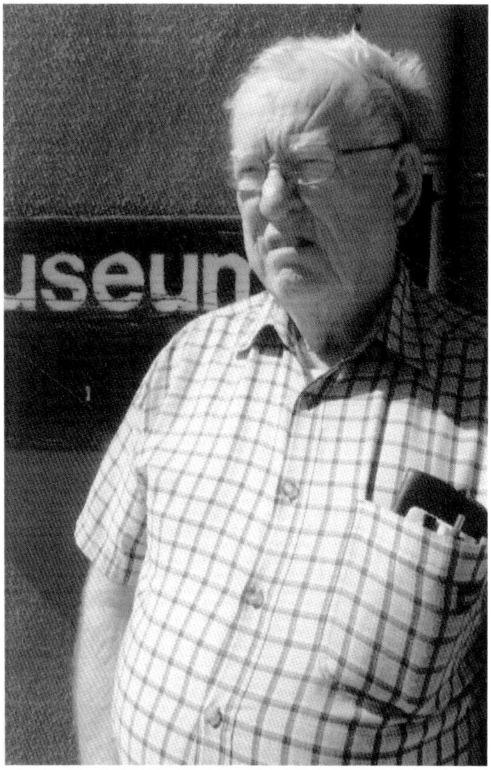

Don Larsen

Senior Master Sergeant Larsen worked on test and development for Gemini and Apollo, among other programs, at Edwards Air Force Base, California. An Air Force Vietnam veteran, Larsen was a weapons expert at Langley Air Force Base, Virginia. After retiring, he worked in quality assurance for the F-117A Nighthawk at Holloman Air Force Base. He also set up the base and 49th Fighter Wing historical displays in the lobby of Holloman's command building. His active-duty, civil, and volunteer service totaled nearly 45 years with the Air Force, which honored him in 1998 with a Certificate of Volunteer Excellence. Larsen now volunteers at the Tularosa Basin Historical Society. (Courtesy Michael Shinabery.)

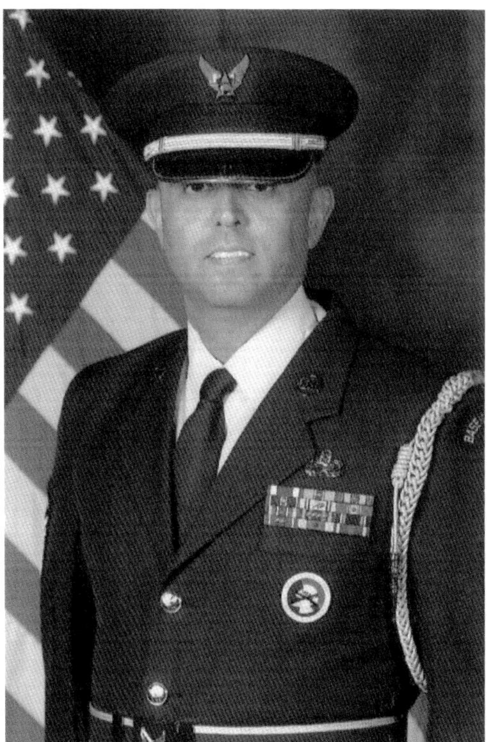

Paul "Chez" Sanchez

Arriving at Holloman Air Force Base in 2005, M.Sgt. Paul Sanchez rapidly took over the Steel Talons Honor Guard, helping perform USAF ceremonies for area service members and veterans who had passed on. Retiring in 2009, he now serves with the Patriot Guard Riders as a ride captain, still assisting with military funerals. "Chez" simply says that he will "Stand for them, until they stand for him." (Courtesy Paul Sanchez.)

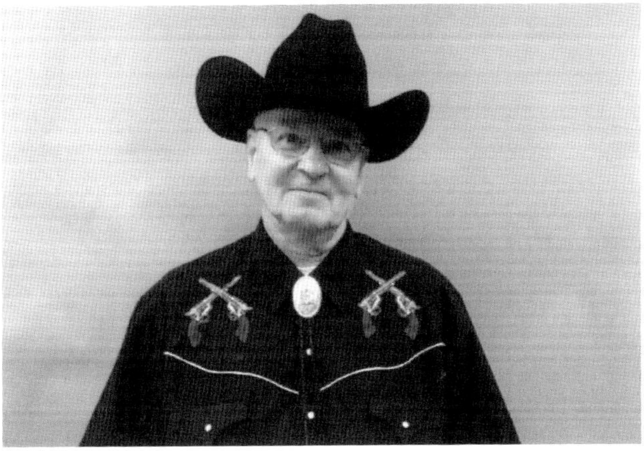

Jim Ernst

Ernst is an assistant state captain with the Patriot Guards, who ensure that veterans and active-duty military, as well as police and first responders, get full honors at their funerals. As a member of the Lincoln–Otero County Veterans Advisory Council, Ernst, who served in the Air Force for 20 years, provides input to state and federal lawmakers on veterans' issues. (Courtesy Jim Ernst.)

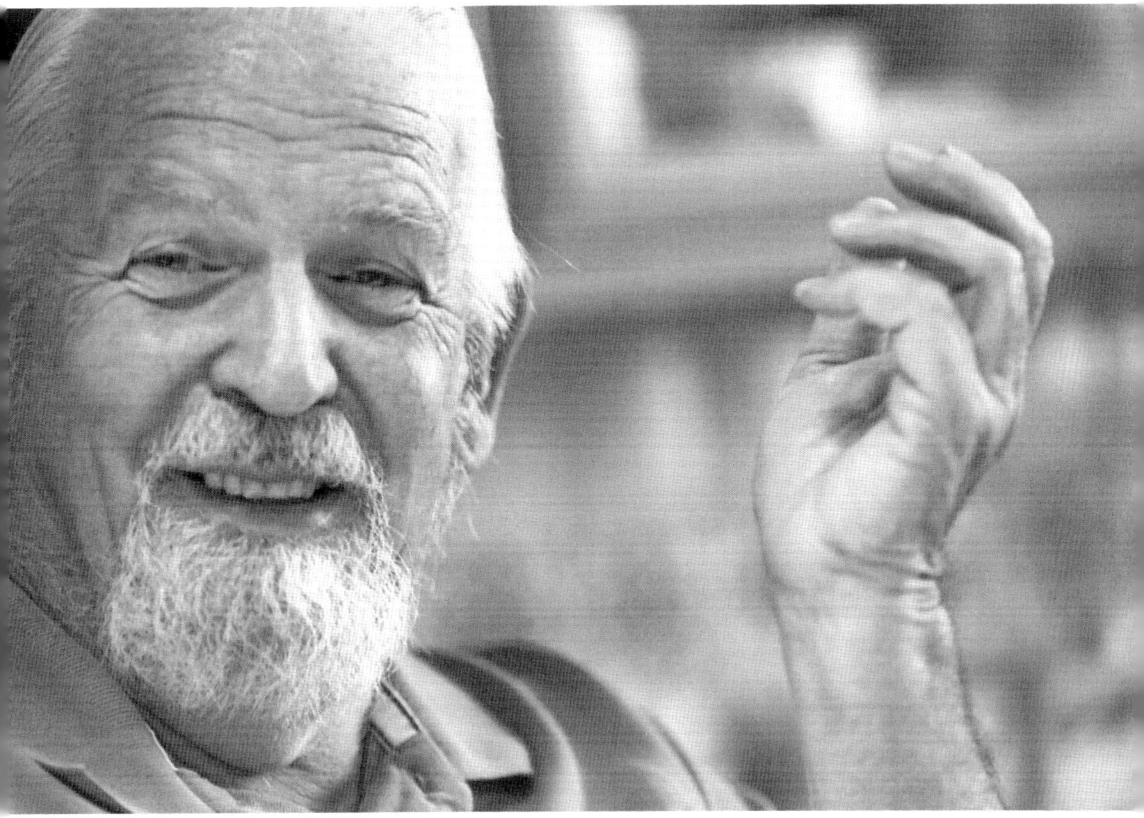

Sgt. Lyn Buchanan

When he was assigned to the Army's Remote Viewing team, Buchanan's official records were sealed. He entered the covert world. At Fort Meade, Maryland, he not only trained to view classified targets, he also eventually trained others. His work ranged from looking for hostages in the Middle East to gathering foreign weapons technology. He became the unit's database manager and a trainer, as well as a computer systems analyst at the Defense Intelligence Agency. In Alamogordo, after the CIA declassified remote viewing, Buchanan began training civilians and recruiting volunteers from among them to aid law enforcement in finding missing children. He chronicled his experiences in his book *The Seventh Sense*. (Photograph by John Zeuli; used with the permission of Lyn Buchanan.)

Maggie Fazenbaker

Fazenbaker (right, with Alex and Eric Chase) was just 11 in October 2004 when she started Operation Soldier Smiles. The year before, her father was deployed to Operations Iraqi Freedom and Enduring Freedom. His childhood church in Pennsylvania sent a care package to his duty station, but by then, he had returned home. Maggie saw the package arrive in Alamogordo and wanted to repay the kindness. A year later, Col. Rich Treadway, the 49th Fighter Wing vice commander at Holloman Air Force Base, brought the Fazenbakers care packages that a Ruidoso church had gathered. But Holloman had no means to send them overseas. The Fazenbakers made telephone calls and found a willing ear at Fort Bliss, El Paso, Texas, and were asked if the family might take on a care-package project. Maggie proudly declared, "I will!" The goal was to comfort those serving in war zones. With the permission of her principal at Chaparral Middle School, she collected paperback novels, candy, and Chapstick from her classmates. She marched into businesses and set up collection boxes, and she asked for funds from service clubs. Hundreds responded. Care Package Parties (seen here) were held primarily at St. John's Episcopal Church, or, on special occasions, at First National Bank. In 10 years, Operation Soldier Smiles sent 15,338 packages. In February 2010, the Army asked the Fazenbakers if they could provide specialized packages to troops rendering aid in Haiti following a massive earthquake. Within three days, the family met the need. (Courtesy Fazenbaker family.)

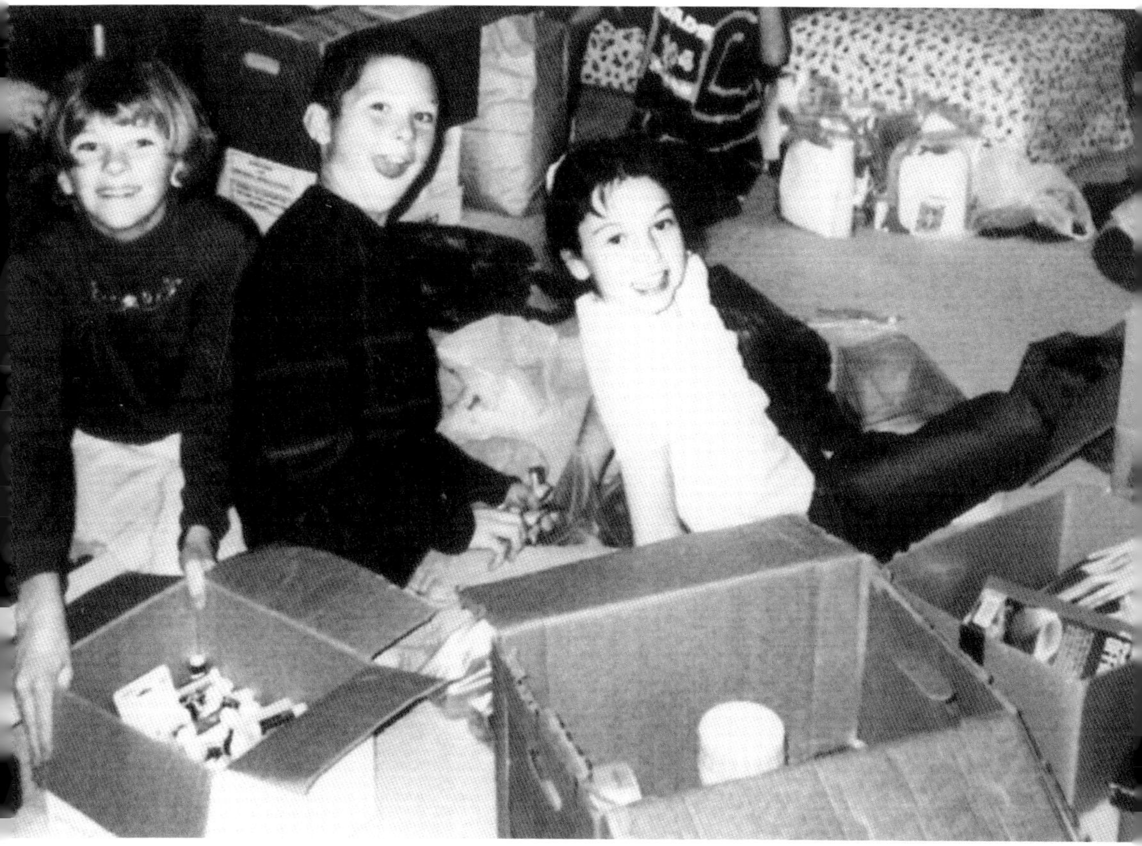

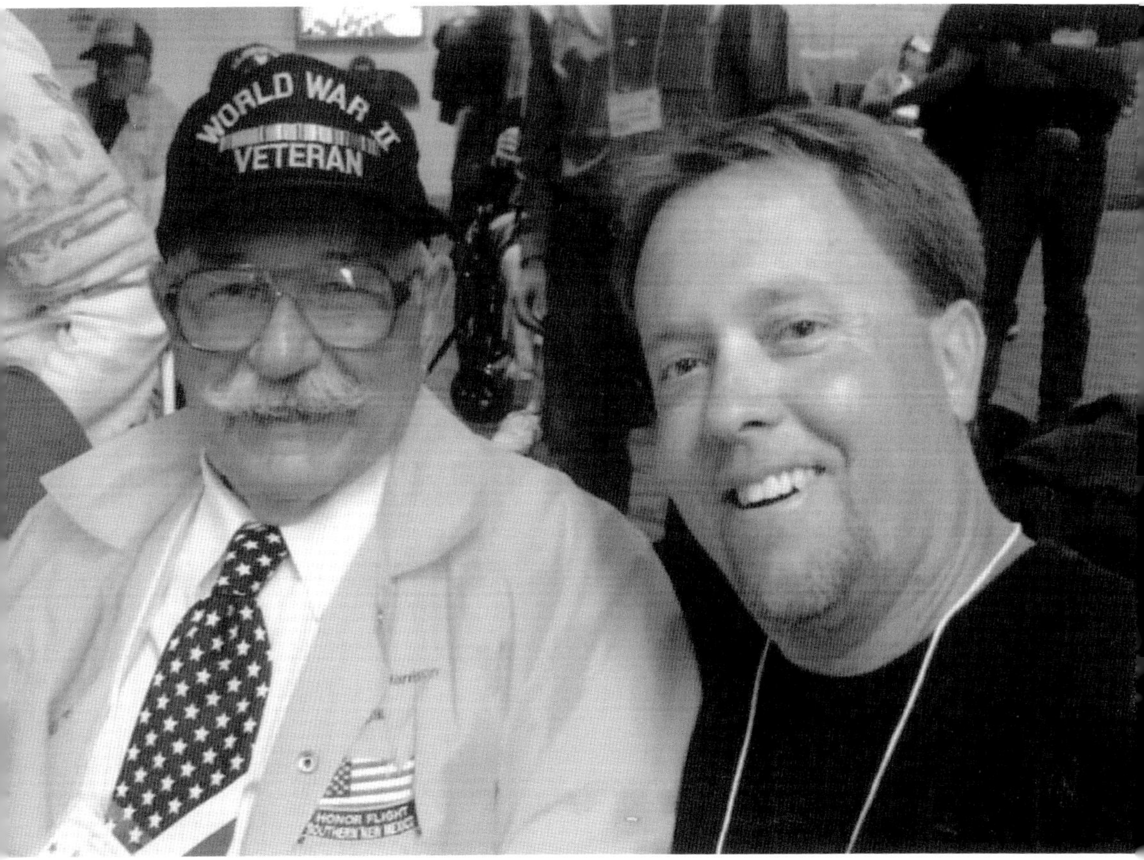

Dale Lindley

Lindley did not just want to teach middle school history, he wanted to participate in history. In 2011, he joined the Honor Flight of Southern New Mexico and El Paso, which escorts veterans to Washington, DC, to see the memorial for the war in which they fought. Lindley's first escort was Bill Harrison (shown here), and Lindley's job was to make sure the World War II vet enjoyed the trip of a lifetime. Lindley photographed the event and organized 300 pictures into an album. He was so moved that he joined the board of directors. Today, as operations coordinator, he ensures that the annual trips are trouble-free. That was a challenge in October 2013, when the federal government was shut down during that year's Honor Flight. Lindley, his fellow escorts, and their veterans did not let barriers stop them. After all, he points out, these were the soldiers from the Greatest Generation who had fought for freedom on foreign soil; to them, a wooden barricade was nothing.

A 1986 Alamogordo Senior High School graduate, Lindley is also ride captain for Southeastern New Mexico Patriot Guard Riders. In addition, he is a founding member of the Alamogordo Mustang Club. (Courtesy Dale Lindley.)

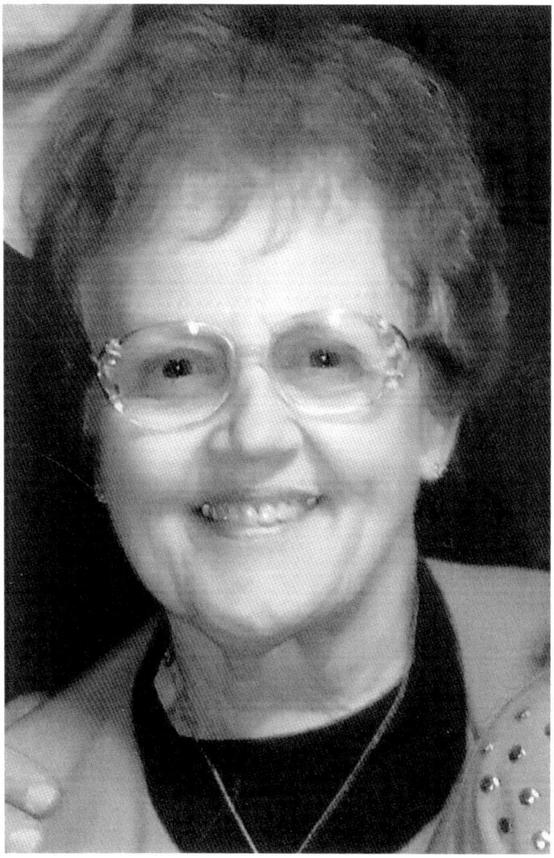

Marie Wuersching

For 14 years, Wuersching and other military-focused citizens sat in front of Alamogordo's grocery stores, selling raffle tickets to raise funds to build the Armed Forces Museum. What she collected, along with grant funding, bought the land and raised the building, which opened in 2011. In addition to the countless hours she and the other volunteers give to the museum, on military holidays, they place flags on veterans' graves. Wuersching began her venture into history when she started volunteering as secretary and curator at the Sacramento Mountains Historical Society, where one of her duties was transcribing hundreds of hours of "old-timer" interviews. (Courtesy Erich Wuersching.)

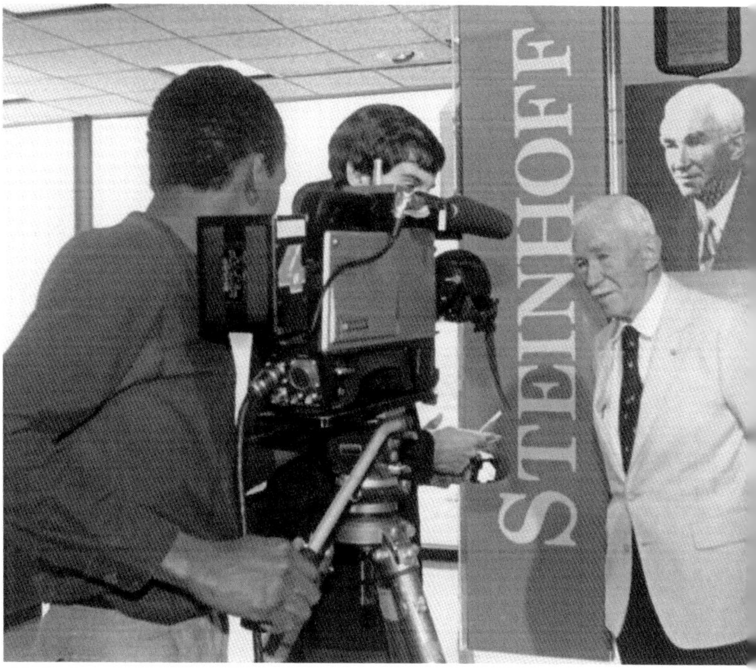

Dr. Ernst Steinhoff

Steinhoff, who developed the German V-2's guidance system, came to the United States at the end of World War II under Operation Paperclip. At White Sands Proving Ground, he helped advance the Army's rocket program. He then worked on various missile programs at Holloman Air Force Base. He is seen here in 1979, being interviewed at his induction into the International Space Hall of Fame. (Courtesy New Mexico Museum of Space History.)

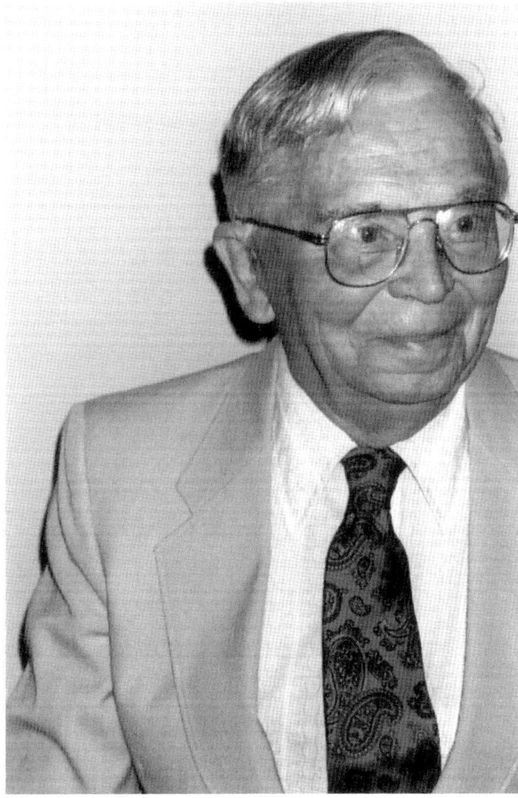

Dr. Martin Jaenke

Dr. Martin Jaenke escaped war-torn Europe in the Berlin Airlift. He fled ahead of his family because of his unpopular political beliefs. His wife, Eve, followed with the children after the Russians arrested her slipping through the Iron Curtain and roughed her up. Jaenke worked at Holloman Air Force Base on missile guidance and at the Test Track Central Inertial Guidance Test Facility. The Jaenkes became citizens in 1958. In 1969, the Daughters of the American Revolution presented Eve with the Americanism Medal. She was the first naturalized citizen to be so honored. (Courtesy New Mexico Museum of Space History.)

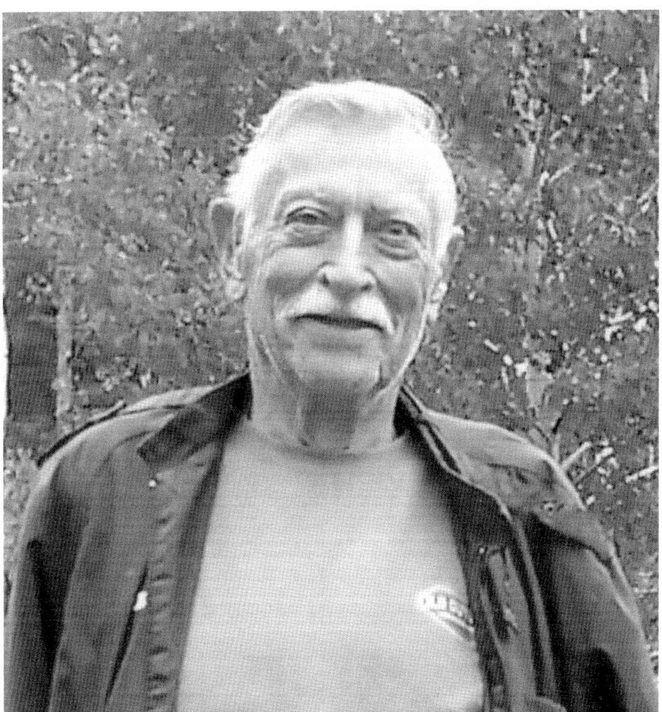

Robert Callaway

Callaway was a high school freshman when a German V-2 was launched from White Sands Proving Ground and smashed into the Sacramento Mountains. The next day, Callaway and three friends hitched a ride to the site in the bed of a red Ford Model B pickup. When cleanup was finished, guards let the boys salvage wiring panels, as well as tanks to convert into portable welding tanks. Callaway flew F-84s in the Air Force. He owned Callaway's Firestone, served two terms as a city commissioner, and has been a member of the Alamogordo Lions Club for more than half a century. (Courtesy Robert Callaway.)

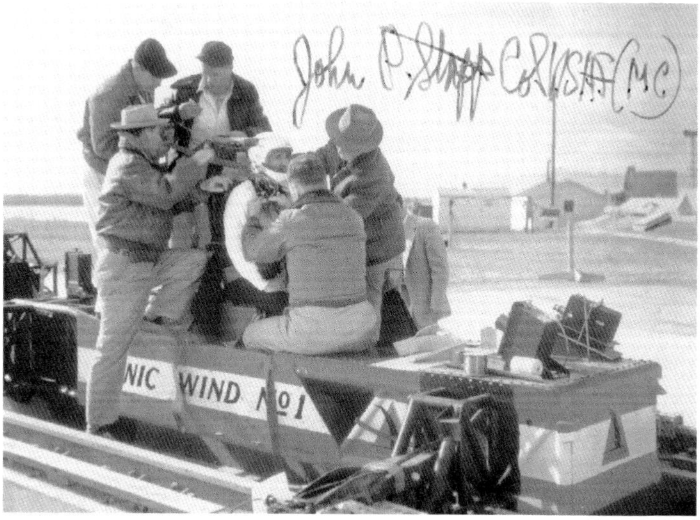

Dr. John Paul Stapp

Time magazine called Stapp "The Fastest Man on Earth." He rode 29 increasingly faster rocket-propelled sleds as part of a study into how blunt-force trauma affected the body. During stops as abrupt as 43 times the force of gravity, Stapp suffered black-and-blue eyes and broken bones, and he lost six fillings when they shot out of his mouth. Because he knew he would leave in an ambulance, Stapp always parked his Cadillac and an ambulance at the track's end.

Stapp began his study in 1947 at Muroc Army Airfield, California (now Edwards Air Force Base). His last ride was atop *Sonic Wind I* on December 10, 1954, at Holloman Air Force Base (above). The pusher rockets ignited; five seconds later, Stapp hit 632 miles per hour. A water-brake system slammed him to a stop in 1.4 seconds, resulting in temporary blindness from retinal hemorrhaging. He began campaigning for vehicle seat belts and again made international headlines when Alamogordo police ticketed him for driving 40 miles per hour in a 25-miles-per-hour zone. The justice of the peace dismissed the charge, recharged a Capt. Ray Darr, and paid the $12.50 fine himself. Famed racer Smokey Yunick (below, right) came to Alamogordo to have lunch with Stapp four years before he died at age 89. They discussed ways to make racing safer for drivers. (Above, courtesy Tularosa Basin Historical Society; below, courtesy New Mexico Museum of Space History.)

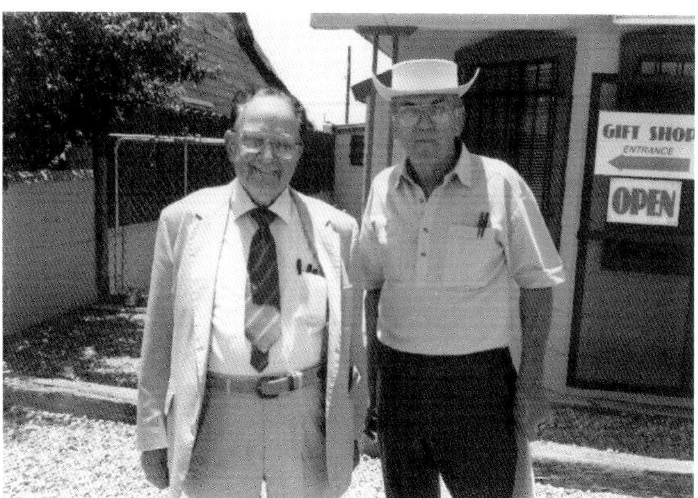

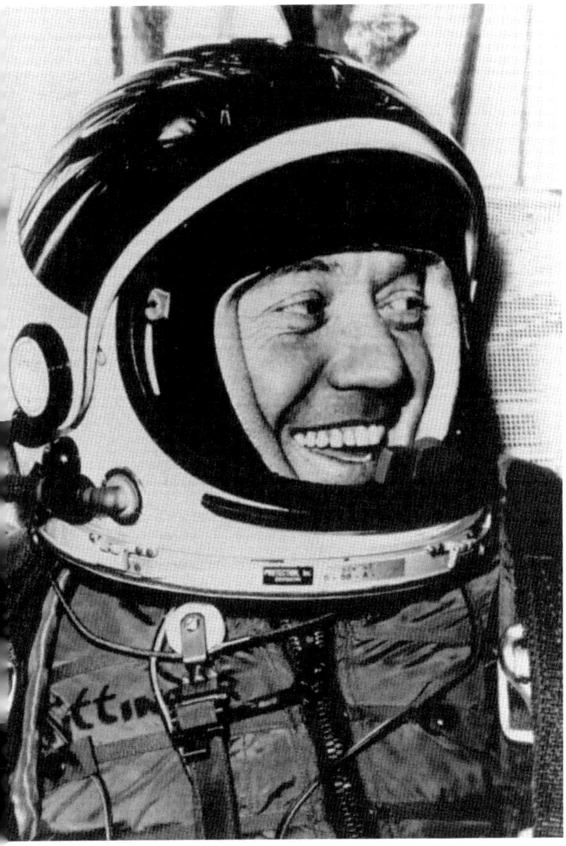

Capt. Joe Kittinger

Kittinger trained at Holloman Air Force Base to fly the first *Manhigh* balloon to discover what weightlessness might inflict on the body and mind. He reached 96,000 feet altitude in 1957. In 1959 and 1960, Kittinger made three jumps out of open gondolas during Project Excelsior to test suits and parachute systems. On the first jump, a 16-second delay leaving the gondola caused a parachute malfunction. Kittinger spun twice every second and lost consciousness. A second parachute deployed and saved his life. His second jump was trouble-free. During the third ascent, Kittinger's right glove failed to pressurize, rendering his hand useless. Refusing to inform the ground crew and abort the mission, Kittinger stepped out at 102,800 feet. He free-fell 13 miles in four minutes and 36 seconds before his parachute unfurled.

In Vietnam, Kittinger's F-4 Phantom was shot down, and he suffered for several months in the infamous Hanoi Hilton. Kittinger is seen below in an F-4 cockpit while revisiting Holloman in 2012. (Left, courtesy Tularosa Basin Historical Society; below, courtesy Michael Shinabery.)

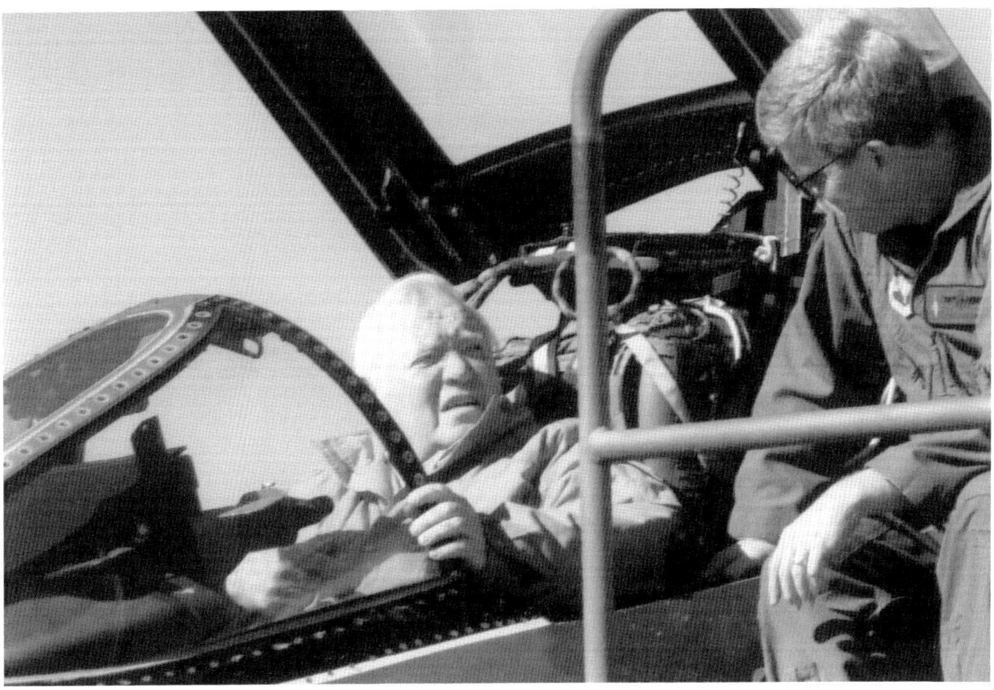

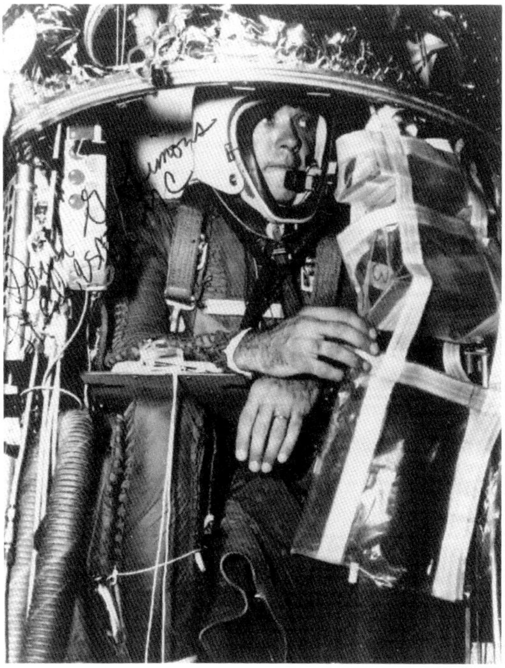

Dr. David Simons
Simons spent 32 hours in his *Manhigh II* craft in August 1957, floating at the edge of space to study how isolated humans might react in severe situations. He set a new balloon-flight record, and the Associated Press dubbed him "the Christopher Columbus of outer space." Simons became a clinical professor and coauthored books on overcoming pain. He died in 2010 at age 87. (Courtesy New Mexico Museum of Space History.)

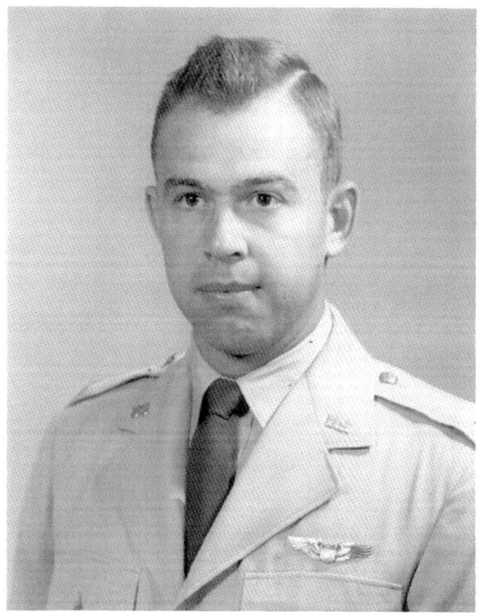

Lt. Clifton McClure
McClure was launched aboard *Manhigh III* in a gondola three feet in diameter and nine feet high, pulled aloft by a balloon. Floating at the edge of space, the capsule's heat caused McClure's body temperature to rise to 108.5 degrees Fahrenheit. The ground crew feared he would die, but McClure fully recovered after descending from 98,850 feet. (Courtesy New Mexico Museum of Space History.)

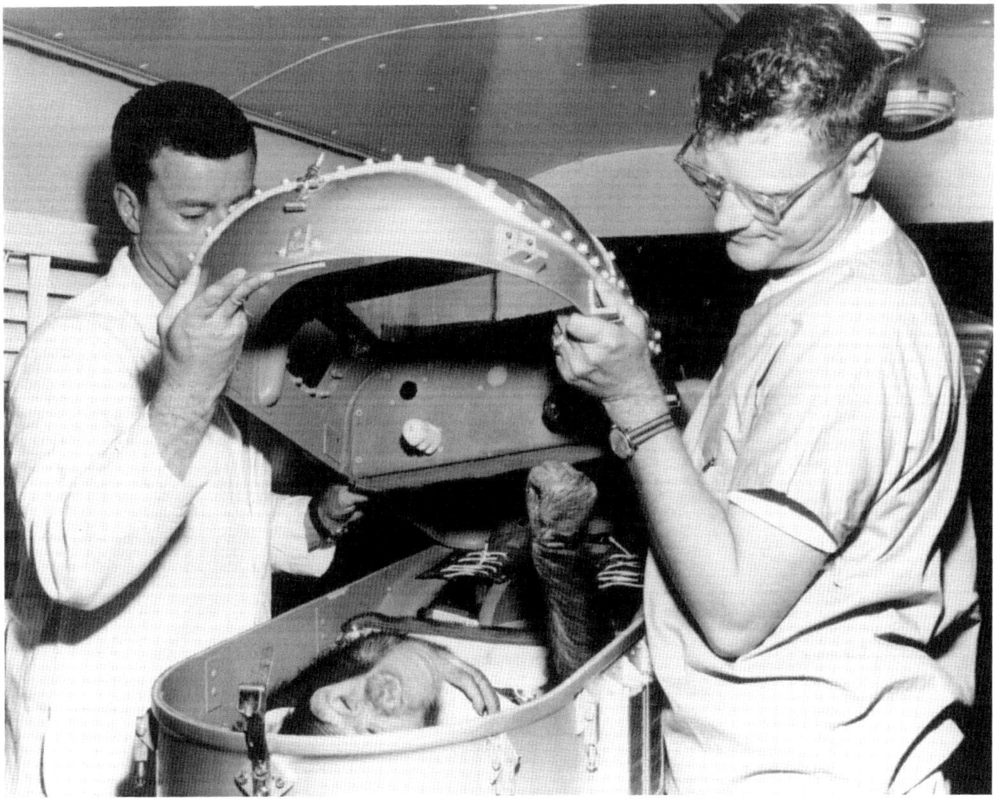

Ed Dittmer

Dittmer's military career began in World War II with the 1st Cavalry Division. He joined the Army Air Corps in 1946 and continued serving through Korea and Vietnam. When Holloman Air Force Base began training chimpanzees for space, Dittmer worked with HAM (an acronym for Holloman Aero Medical) and Enos. He is shown here with HAM at Cape Canaveral. From 1957 to 1960, Dittmer participated in *Manhigh* and Project Excelsior balloon flights. During training for *Excelsior III*, the balloon plummeted to Earth. Dittmer sped to the scene. Because he refused to stop for a pursuing officer, he was able to save the pilot, whose throat had been slit. (Courtesy the New Mexico Museum of Space History.)

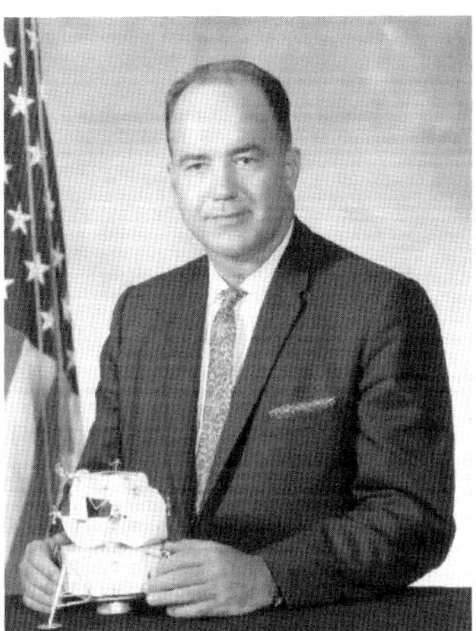

Paul Haney

Haney was NASA's first information officer, news division chief, and the voice of Mission Control. In 1958, Haney set up the protocols for media access. He unknowingly preserved much of NASA's daily history after he hired stenographers to transcribe press conferences and astronauts' communications. Haney, who had the trust of families such as the Kennedys, went on to work for England's broadcast networks and the *Economist* magazine. In 1965, he helped wrestle an armed hijacker to the floor while aboard a National Airlines flight. (Courtesy New Mexico Museum of Space History.)

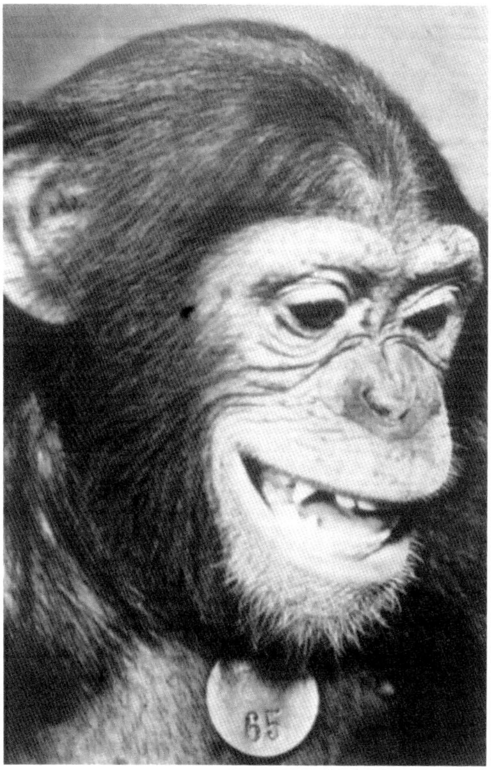

HAM

HAM, the first chimpanzee in space, proved that man could work in the hostile environment. An acronym for Holloman Aero Medical, where he was trained, HAM lifted off on January 31, 1961. Ed Dittmer helped train the chimp in psychomotor skills. HAM, who never flew again, is buried at the New Mexico Museum of Space History. (Courtesy New Mexico Museum of Space History.)

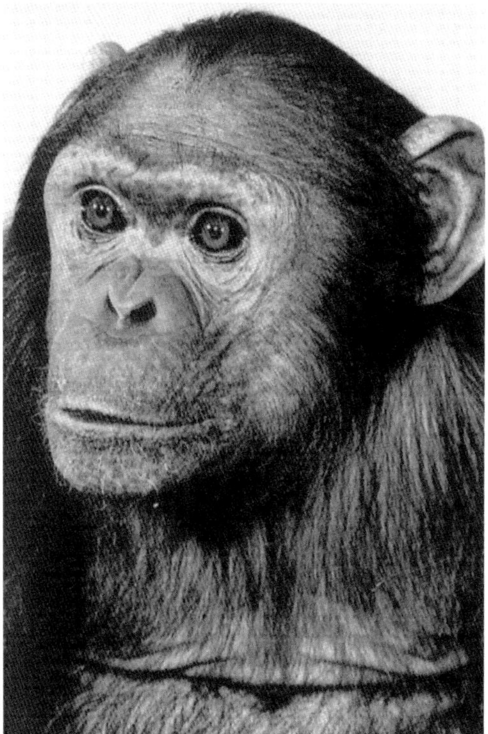

Enos

The chimpanzee Enos preceded astronaut John Glenn, completing two orbits of Earth on November 29, 1961. Enos completed trained tasks to prove one could work for extended periods in space. Ed Dittmer trained Enos at Holloman Air Force Base. The chimp died on November 4, 1962, from the African dysentery disease shigellosis. (Courtesy New Mexico Museum of Space History.)

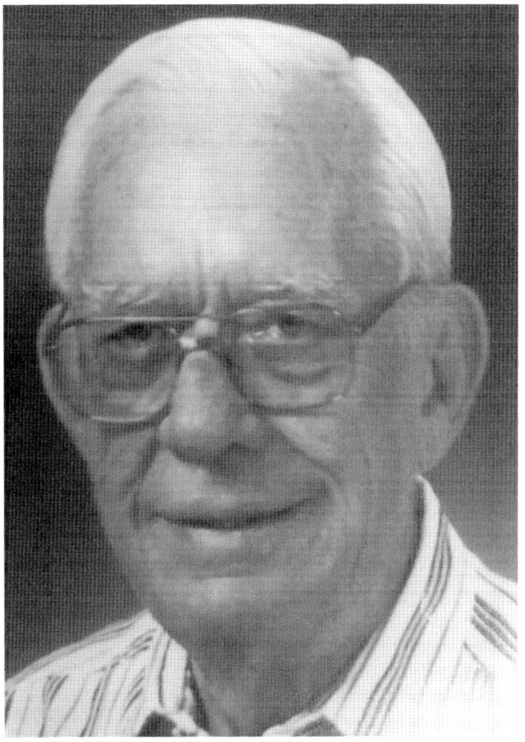

Dwight Ohlinger
In 1973, Ohlinger, a businessman and former mayor, realized that Alamogordo needed a facility to preserve the region's contributions to the space race. On October 5, 1976, the International Space Hall of Fame opened. The weekend commemorated several space milestones, including Robert Goddard's 94th birthday, the 19th anniversary of the Soviet Union's *Sputnik I* flight, and the anniversary of Germany's first successful launching of a V-2 from Peenemunde. (Courtesy New Mexico Museum of Space History.)

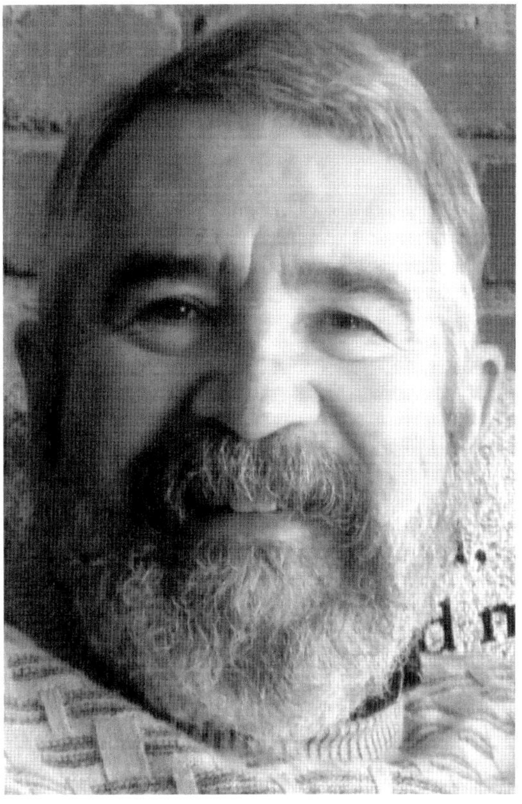

George House
House is the longest-serving curator of the New Mexico Museum of Space History. Over nearly 29 years, he acquired artifacts with ties to space history. He counts among the most important artifacts he helped secure the World War II weapon JB-2 Loon, reverse-engineered from the German "Buzz Bomb." During House's tenure, aerospace companies visited the museum to study engines on display, as they had not kept their technology. (Courtesy Michael Shinabery.)

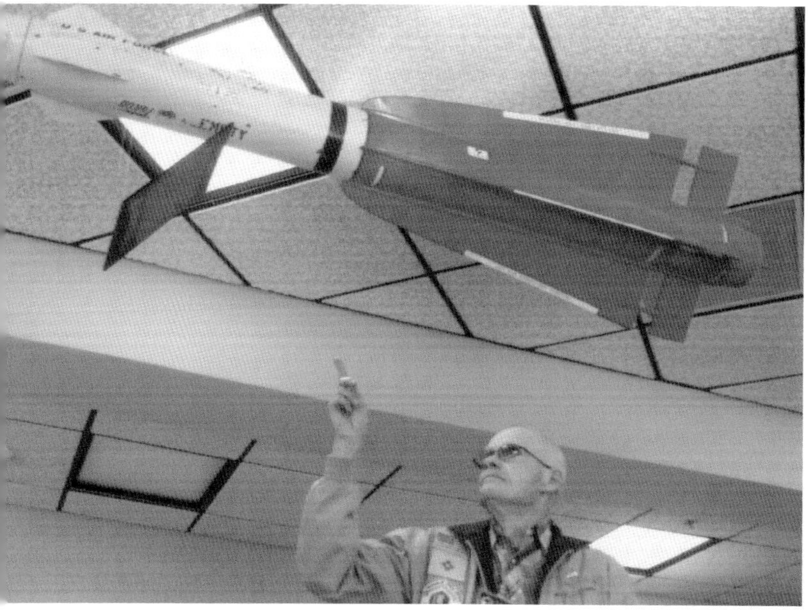

Mike Smith

Smith culled data from the film of classified tests at Holloman Air Force Base's Range Control and then White Sands Missile Range. Subsequently, he was the New Mexico Museum of Space History's registrar. Here, he points out the Falcon missile while giving a tour. Smith is also a published poet. He became a lifelong friend of Clyde Tombaugh after taking an astronomy class in 1963 with the discoverer of Pluto. (Courtesy Michael Shinabery.)

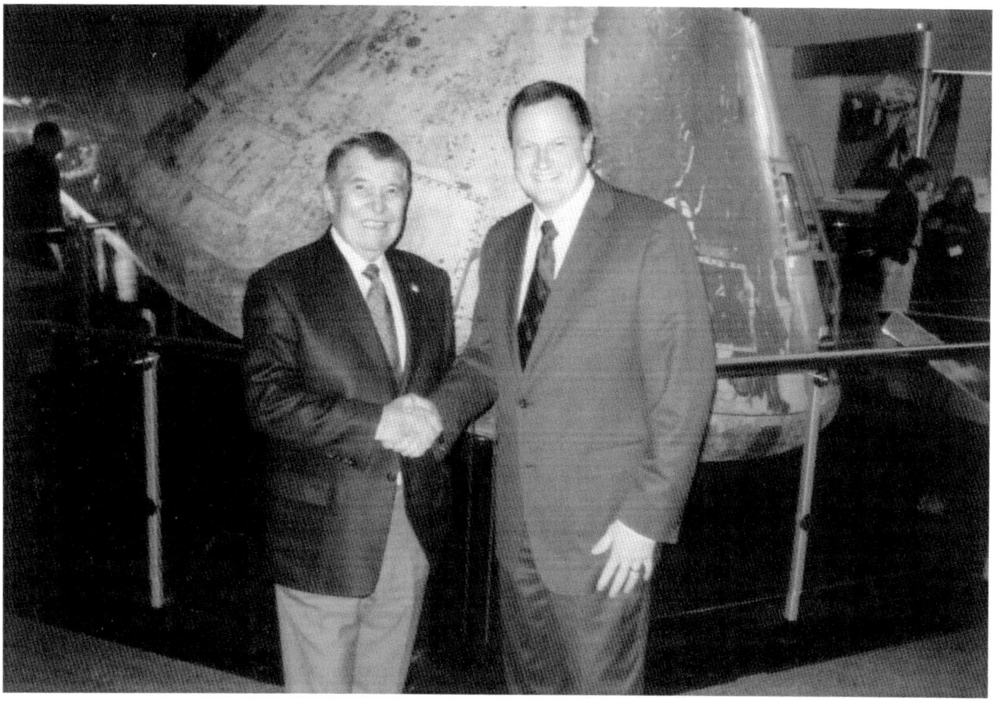

Chris Orwoll

Orwoll (right) became director of the New Mexico Museum of Space History in 2012. A 1986 graduate of the US Naval Academy, Orwoll served as a nuclear-submarine officer onboard the USS *Ohio* missile submarine, USS *Tucson* attack submarine, and USS *Dolphin*, the Navy's last diesel submarine. Orwoll served as president and CEO of the Kansas Cosmosphere and Space Center. His military background and his association with numerous space explorers and pioneers, such as Wally Schirra (left), has resulted in many new ideas and exhibits at the museum. (Courtesy Chris Orwoll.)

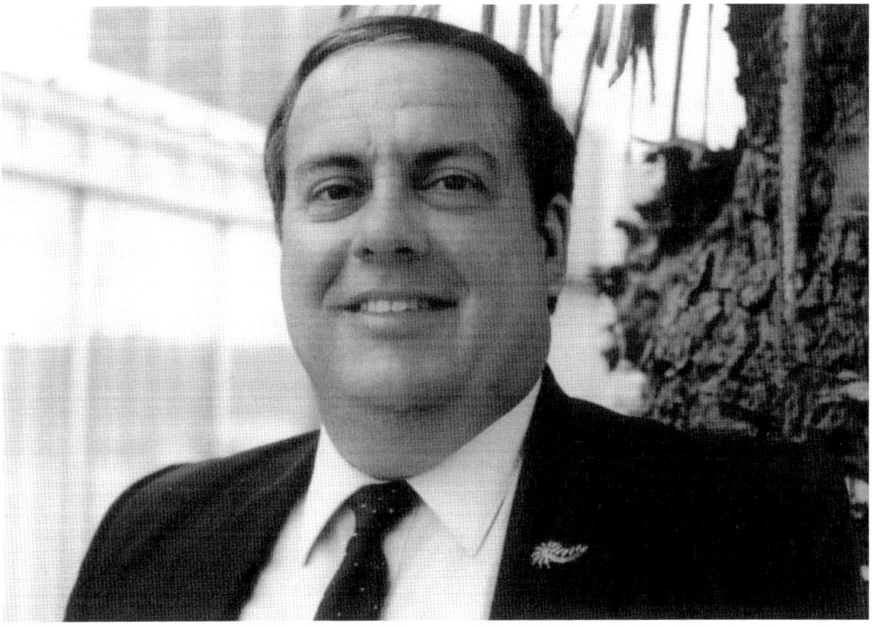

Alan Hale

Hale was viewing comets in July 1995 when he spotted a fuzzy anomaly. He notified the International Astronomical Union, shortly before Thomas Bopp, in Arizona, did likewise. By 1997, Comet Hale-Bopp was bright enough to see with the naked eye. Hale visited countries such as Iran as a goodwill ambassador. To that end, Hale now runs the Earthrise Institute, which advocates the use of astronomy and space science to bridge the gaps between nations. Hale, a graduate of the US Naval Academy, worked on spacecraft projects at the Jet Propulsion Laboratory, Pasadena, California. For a time, he hosted an Alamogordo radio program playing eclectic music from several decades. (Above, courtesy Alan Hale; below, courtesy Michael Shinabery.)

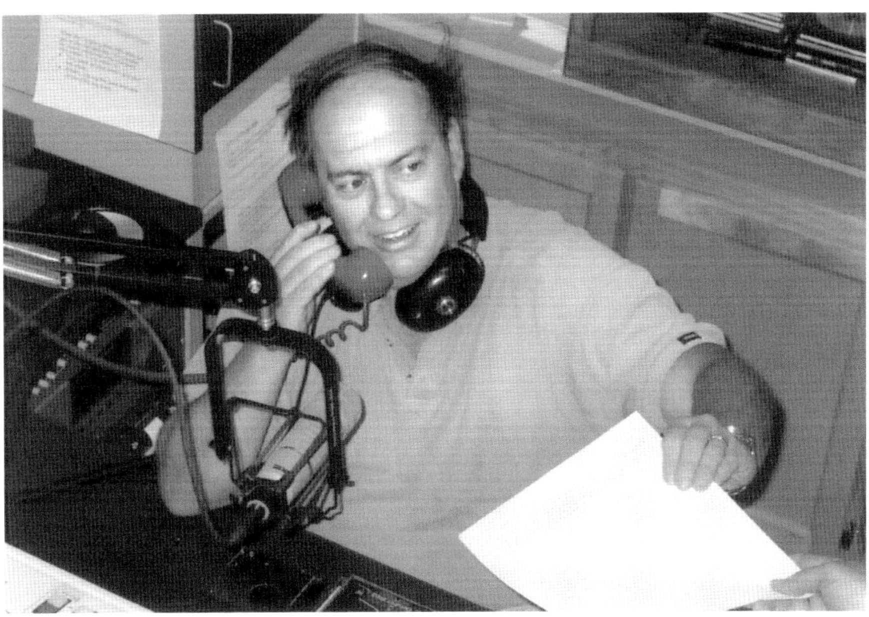

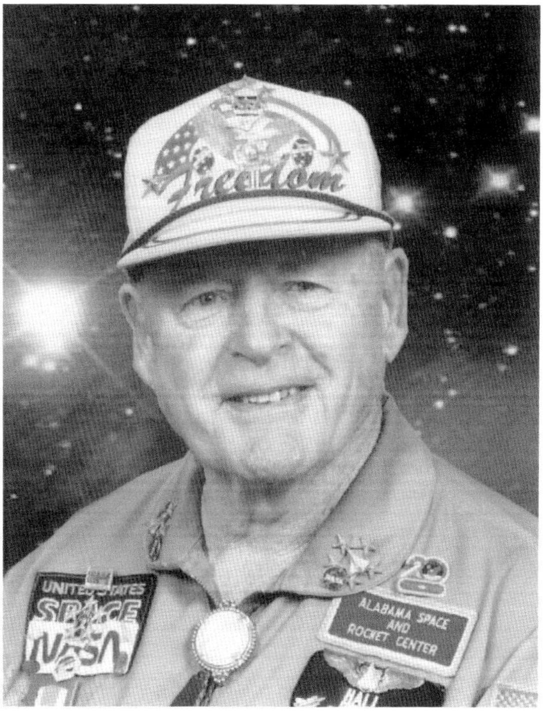

George Hall

Hall waited his entire life to fly to space. Airsickness initially stalled his dream while he was undergoing pilot training. So Hall joined the Marines and survived Pearl Harbor and Midway Island. He eventually came to Alamogordo to teach Spanish at Alamogordo High School and oversee the audio-visual program. As an International Space Hall of Fame docent, he touted space to visitors and applied to NASA to be a Teacher in Space on the ill-fated shuttle *Challenger*. Hall finally rocketed skyward on May 22, 2012, a decade after his death. His ashes were flown aboard an unmanned Space-X Falcon 9, along with those of astronaut Gordon Cooper and Star Trek's James Doohan. (Courtesy Tiffanie Owen.)

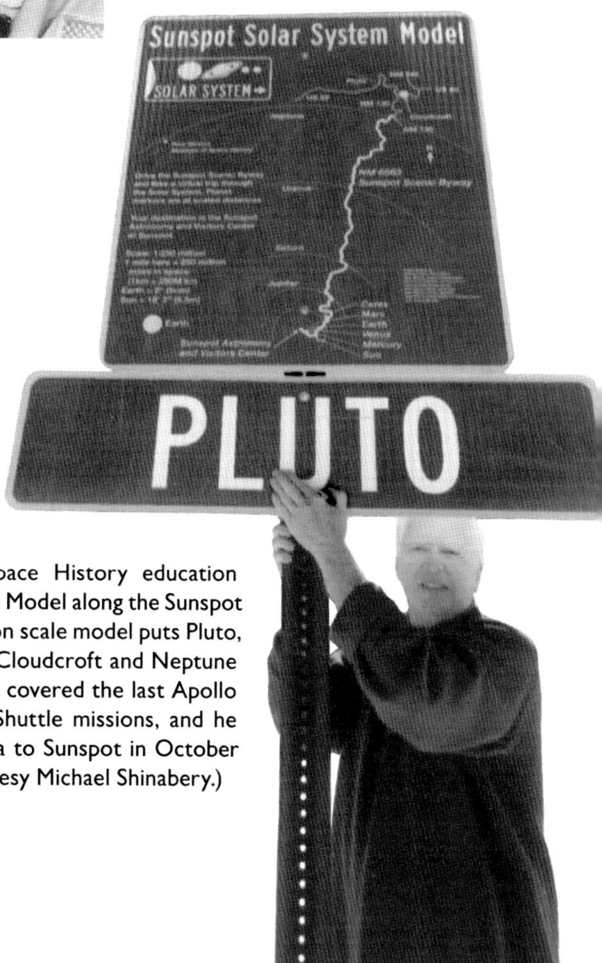

Dave Dooling

Dooling, the New Mexico Museum of Space History education director, developed the Sunspot Solar System Model along the Sunspot Scenic Byway (NM 6563). The 1-to-250-million scale model puts Pluto, which has a lopsided orbit, passing through Cloudcroft and Neptune at the museum. As a science writer, Dooling covered the last Apollo launches to the Moon and the first Space Shuttle missions, and he worked for NASA. He moved from Alabama to Sunspot in October 2002 and joined the museum in 2012. (Courtesy Michael Shinabery.)

CHAPTER FIVE

Business and Politics

When Charles Bishop Eddy and his brother John Arthur Eddy cofounded Alamogordo with William Ashton Hawkins in 1898, business was a driving force. While the first residents, mostly railroad workers, lived in tents, a hotel with electric lighting soon went up. A year later, 150 buildings stood, 29 of which were commercial businesses, including an ice plant and a Baptist college.

Early businessmen were active in the community and in government. That attitude of service has never changed, except for the fact that, today, there are as many prominent businesswomen as there are businessmen. Many of the leaders of commerce have served as city and county commissioners, as mayors, and as state representatives and senators. They hold membership in either the Rotary Club of Alamogordo or the White Sands Rotary Club, which is not historically uncommon. A look at the Rotary Club of Alamogordo's roster finds such familiar names as Alister McTavish, Walter Wade, Albert Menger, and R.A. McCleskey.

Decades before the big-box stores hit town, Jerry Yates owned the Ink Well, an office-supply store in a unique Southwestern adobe that today is an antique mall. Jim Griggs's construction company built many familiar businesses, including McDonald's, Pizza Hut, and Otero Federal Credit Union. He also taught driver's education in the public schools and coached baseball, football, and basketball. Griggs founded the award-winning building trades program that evolved into the high school's vocational education program. He served 16 years as a city commissioner and was on the Alamogordo Chamber of Commerce Transportation Committee, which brought the relief route to Alamogordo.

Mike Espiritu was a command chief master sergeant in the Air Force. After retiring, he became president and CEO of the Alamogordo Chamber of Commerce and the Otero County Economic Development Council. He also created Alamogordo High School's Air Force JROTC, which, quickly became the largest such program in New Mexico.

Many of the community's businesses have prospered over the decades, surviving in good and bad economies because they offer good, old-fashioned service that harkens back to the founders' era. Some companies are owned by second and third generations, and some have even brought national and international attention to Alamogordo—all because, one day, a businessman literally sowed a seed. Small business helped build the community, and small business continues to sustain and preserve the town's life.

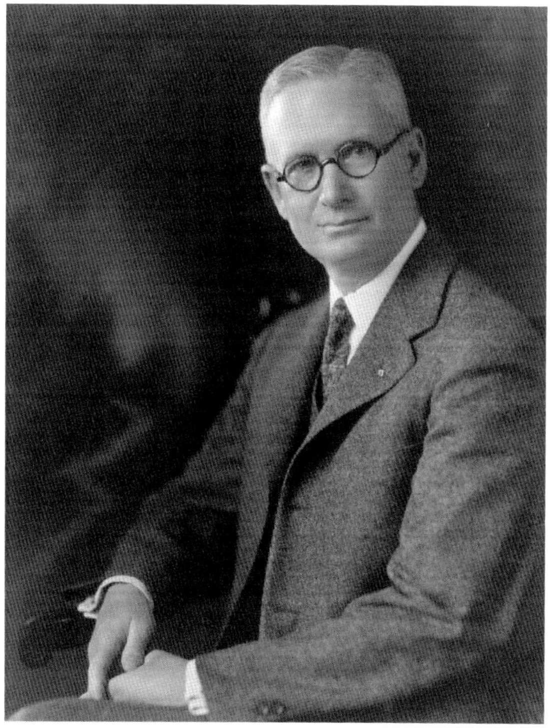

Dr. Fred Evans

Evans was a major in World War I, and military records show that he was in the 2nd Division Sanitary Train, identified as ambulance companies and field hospitals. He was Alamogordo Chamber of Commerce president in 1924 and 1934. Evans died on February 13, 1952, and he is buried in Monte Vista Cemetery. (Courtesy Alamogordo Chamber of Commerce.)

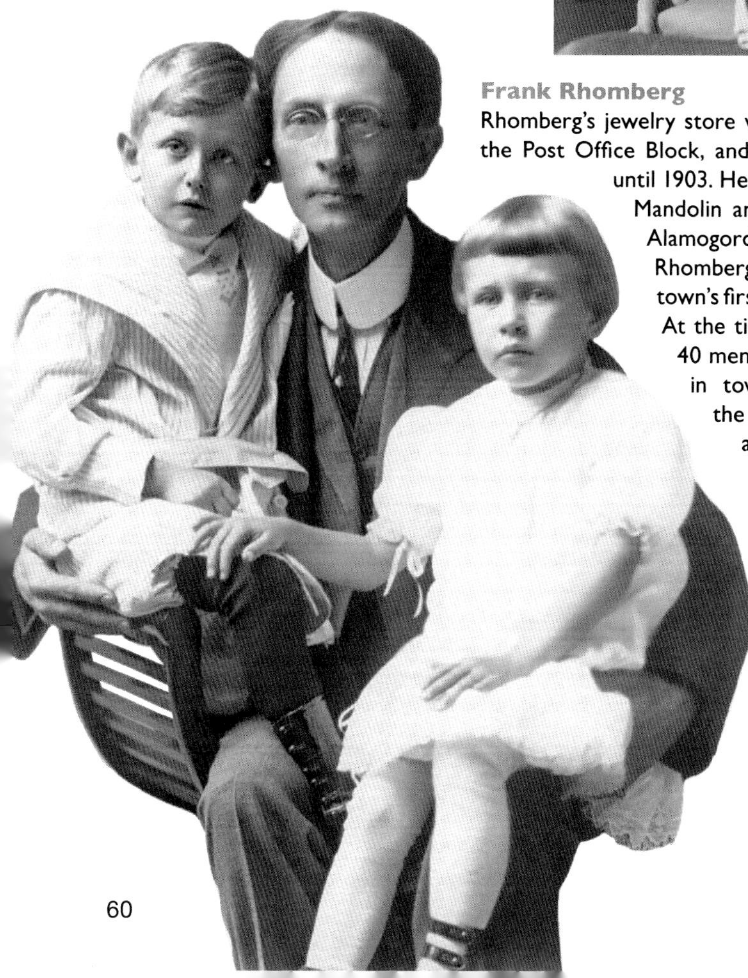

Frank Rhomberg

Rhomberg's jewelry store was located in what was known as the Post Office Block, and Frank Rhomberg was postmaster until 1903. He played with the American Amateur Mandolin and Guitar Club and wrote "March Alamogordo," or the "Alamogordo Two Step." Rhomberg conducted the orchestra at the town's first church dedication, in August 1899. At the time, First Presbyterian, with nearly 40 members, had the largest congregation in town. Rhomberg was secretary of the Alamogordo Commercial Club and, in 1903, was a delegate to the Republican Convention in Socorro. He sold his business six years later and moved to Hollywood. He was only 53 when he died in California in 1925. Rhomberg is shown here with his niece and nephew in 1912. (Courtesy Tularosa Basin Historical Society; photographer, Prietauer Studio.)

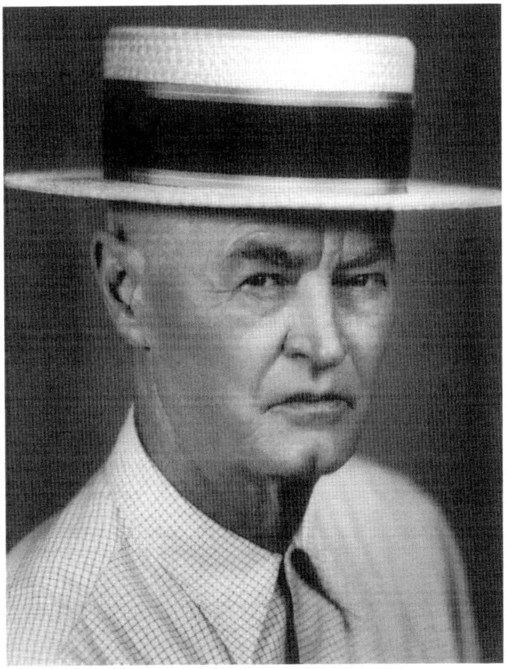

H.H. Stevenson
In spite of his stern appearance, Stevenson was described by those who knew him as a generous man. He employed many youth at Stevenson's Hardware & Furniture, including Bob Hamilton (who later founded Hamilton O'Dell Funeral Home) and Willie Estrada. When he was 11, Estrada was in the store looking at bicycles when Stevenson offered him a job. Estrada worked there until he was drafted by the Army and was subsequently killed in Korea. (Courtesy Alamogordo Chamber of Commerce.)

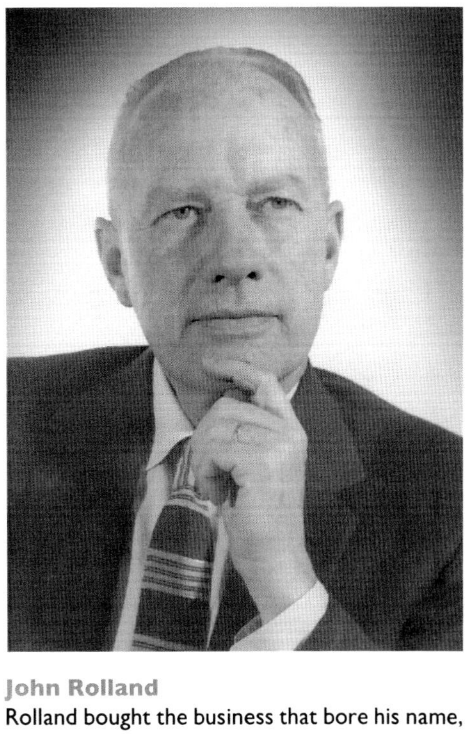

John Rolland
Rolland bought the business that bore his name, Rolland Drugs, from the Aragon brothers. The store provided prescriptions, developed film, and did photo finishing. Rolland also served as a county commissioner, was director of schools, and was on the New Mexico School for the Blind and Visually Impaired Board of Regents. He also organized the volunteer fire department. (Courtesy Alamogordo Chamber of Commerce.)

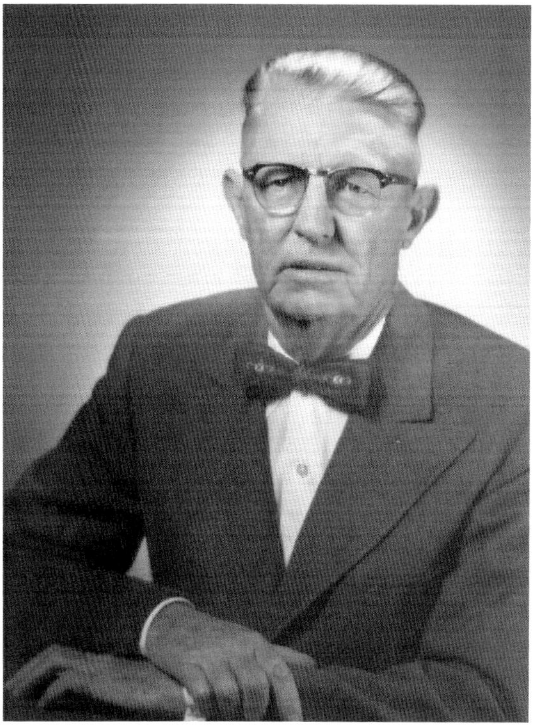

Mose Cauthen
Cauthen, the chamber of commerce president and a World War I veteran, was having coffee at the Plaza Pub on December 7, 1941, when news of Pearl Harbor came over the radio. Cauthen sent a telegram to US senator Dennis Chavez asking who was in charge of establishing military bases. Over several days, Cauthen coordinated with the Army Corps of Engineers, found suitable land and water with Mayor Eber McKinley, and asked rancher Sam McNatt to relinquish the land that soon became Alamogordo Army Air Field. (Courtesy Alamogordo Chamber of Commerce.)

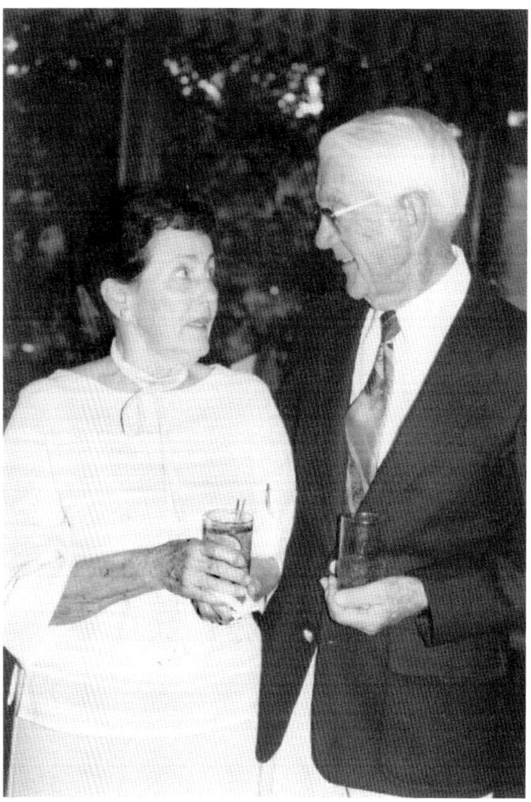

George Rapier Abbott
A lifelong Alamogordo resident, Abbott helped start First National Bank in 1956, serving as board chairman until 1987 and as chairman emeritus until his death. He was Otero County treasurer, on the board of education, and on New Mexico State University's board of regents. Besides owning Pioneer Title & Abstract, in 1954, Abbott chaired the committee to build the Otero County Courthouse. He is seen here with his wife, Revis, in 1985, on their 50th wedding anniversary. Abbott was 98 when he died in 2006. (Courtesy Wyatt Atkins.)

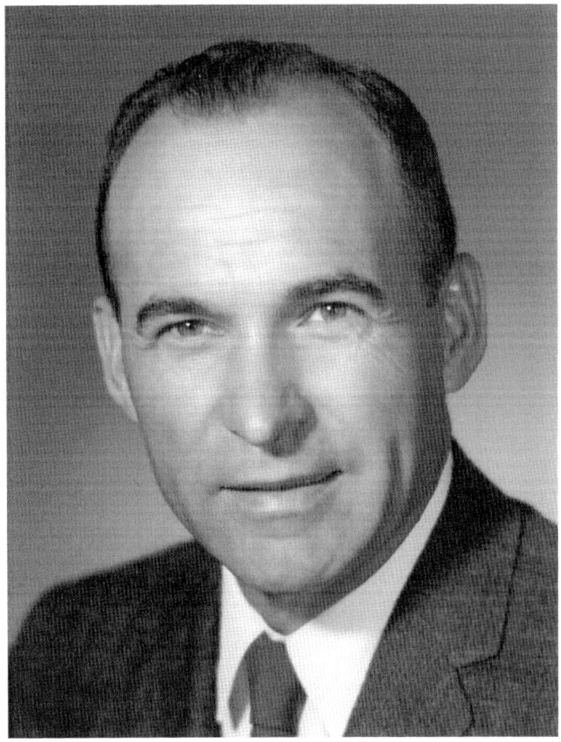

Ken Garland
Garland came to Alamogordo to manage Sprouse Reitz and made the community his home for the next 72 years. During World War II, he served in the Coast Guard, and in 1958, he became a partner in the Tom Charles Insurance Agency, which he eventually owned. Garland served on First National Bank's board for 38 years. He served on the school board, was chair of the White Sands Boy Scout District, and had 54 years of perfect attendance at the Rotary Club of Alamogordo. (Courtesy Alamogordo Chamber of Commerce.)

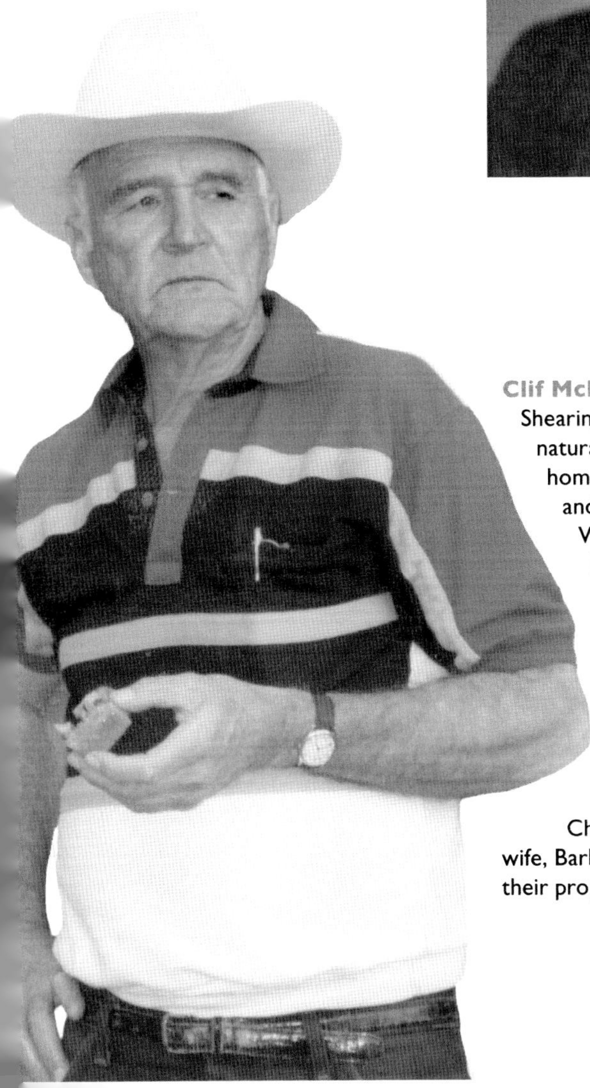

Clif McDonald
Shearing sheep while growing up made McDonald a natural to be a World War II Navy barber. Returning home, he opened his own shop, as well as real estate and landscaping businesses, and he helped found Western Bank. Named a Citizen of the Year by the Alamogordo Chamber of Commerce, McDonald chaired the Democratic Party of Otero County for 12 years and served two terms as a county commissioner and four as assessor. As a member of the Alamogordo Chamber of Commerce Transportation Committee, McDonald helped secure funds to widen US 54 and 70 to four lanes, and he spent a quarter-century working to build the Charlie T. Lee Memorial Relief Route. He and his wife, Barbara, are retired. They keep a herd of goats on their property. (Courtesy McDonald family.)

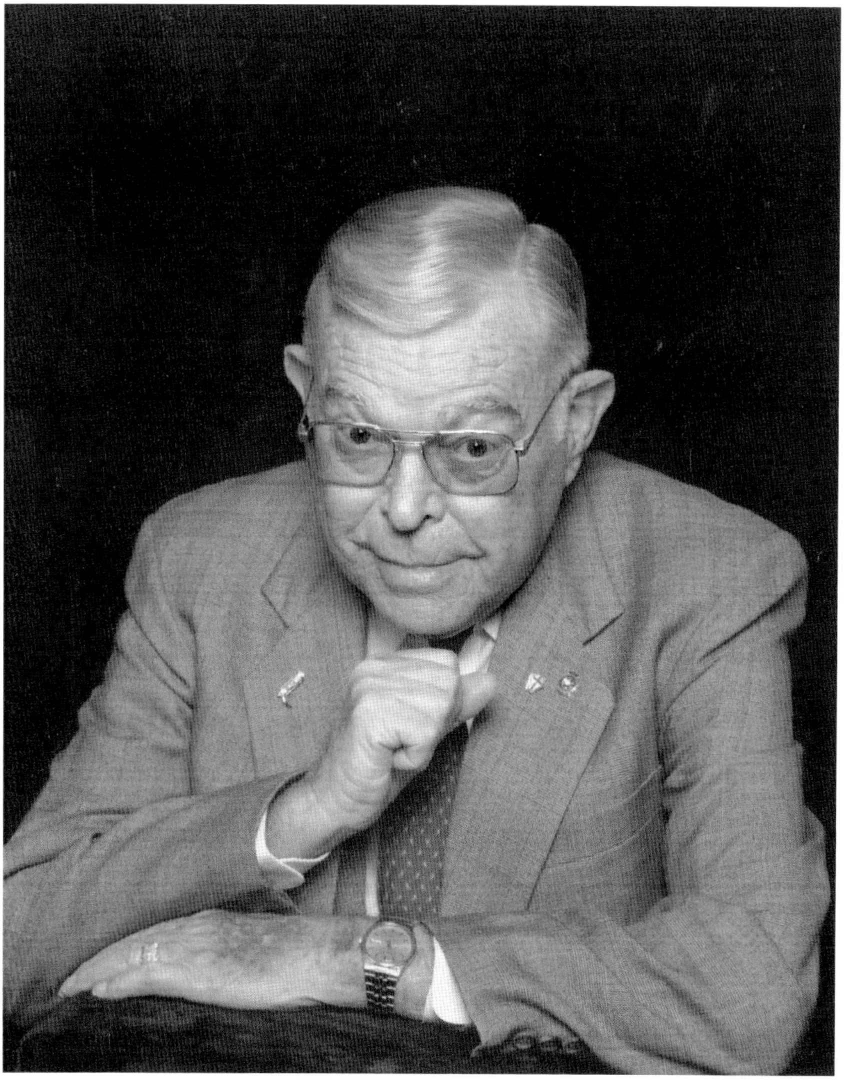

Billie Holder

When he needed his 21st Boy Scout merit badge to earn Eagle rank, Holder chose printing. That meant spending time at a newspaper in his native Oklahoma, where the ink got into his blood. Holder was 37, working in Kansas, when he bought the weekly Alamogordo paper in 1954 and reformatted it into the *Daily News*. When the nation was embroiled in the Cold War–era space race, frenzied activity toward that effort was taking place at Holloman Air Force Base and White Sands Missile Range. The town may have been small, but the pool of stories was large. Holder's popular weekly column, The Wailing Wall, written under the pseudonym "Weepin' Willie," delved into the community's rich social, artistic, and professional activity. Holder served as state chairman for the National Newspaper Association and was president of the New Mexico Press Association. In 1963, as part of an American Newspaper Study group, he toured the Iron Curtain nations and interviewed communist officials. The Rotary Club of Alamogordo elected him president in 1968, and he went on to be District 5520 governor from 1973 to 1974. Holder and Aubrey Dunn, who bought into the *Daily News* in the late 1950s, sold the paper in 1983. After Holder died in January 1994, the Rotary Club began awarding an annual Billie Holder college scholarship. (Courtesy Genie Harshey.)

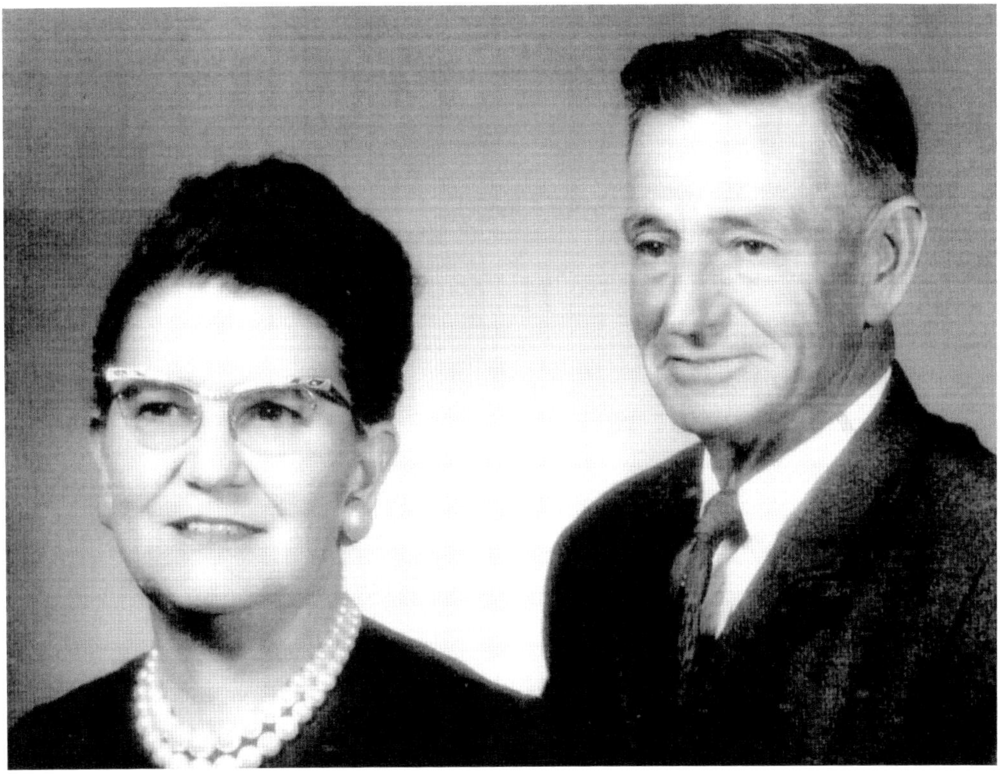

G.B. Oliver Sr.
Oliver Sr., seen here with his wife, opened Alamogordo's first theater during the silent-film era on Tenth Street and New York Avenue. He served on the town board and owned New Market Foods. Then, in 1940, he became a full-time rancher. Oliver was six months old, in 1901, when he came to Alamogordo on the area's first passenger train. He told his daughter, Maude Oliver Rathgeber, that he remembered his mother helping a young, blind Elizabeth Garret write "O Fair New Mexico." The New Mexico Legislature adopted it in 1917 as the state song. (Courtesy Rathgeber family.)

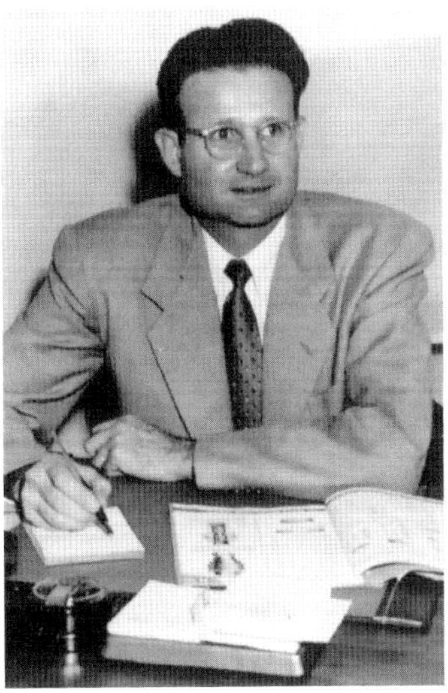

Joe Shyne
In 1957, Shyne came to Alamogordo with his family to oversee construction and become the first administrator at the new Gerald Champion Memorial Hospital. In 1959, he and his wife, Millicent, opened Shyne Realty, as Holloman Missile Development Center was closing. The exodus of personnel left 600 vacant houses. It was a difficult time to be in real estate. So Shyne developed a modern subdivision, Robin Hood Park, east of Cloudcroft. The development was named after a popular television show. The Shynes were intrigued by the residential subdivisions extending up the side of Camelback Mountain in Phoenix, Arizona, so they brought the idea to Alamogordo, building the first subdivision on the western escarpment of the Sacramento Mountains. (Courtesy Michael Shyne.)

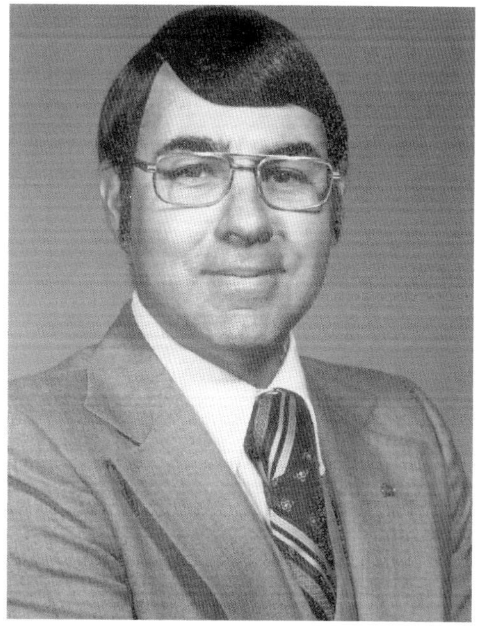

Ken Eaton

While visiting family in Alamogordo, Eaton and his cousin decided to partner in a television and radio repair shop. His last name began with an E; his cousin was Bud Zufelt; thus the name EZ. Eaton bought out Zufelt in 1964 and eventually opened a store in Ruidoso, two in Las Cruces, and one in El Paso. After 36 years in the business, Eaton passed the keys to his son, Mark. When he was younger, Eaton played drums in Calvin Boles's band. An avid hunter, he has traveled all over the world, and 53 trophies adorn his wall at home. (Courtesy Alamogordo Chamber of Commerce.)

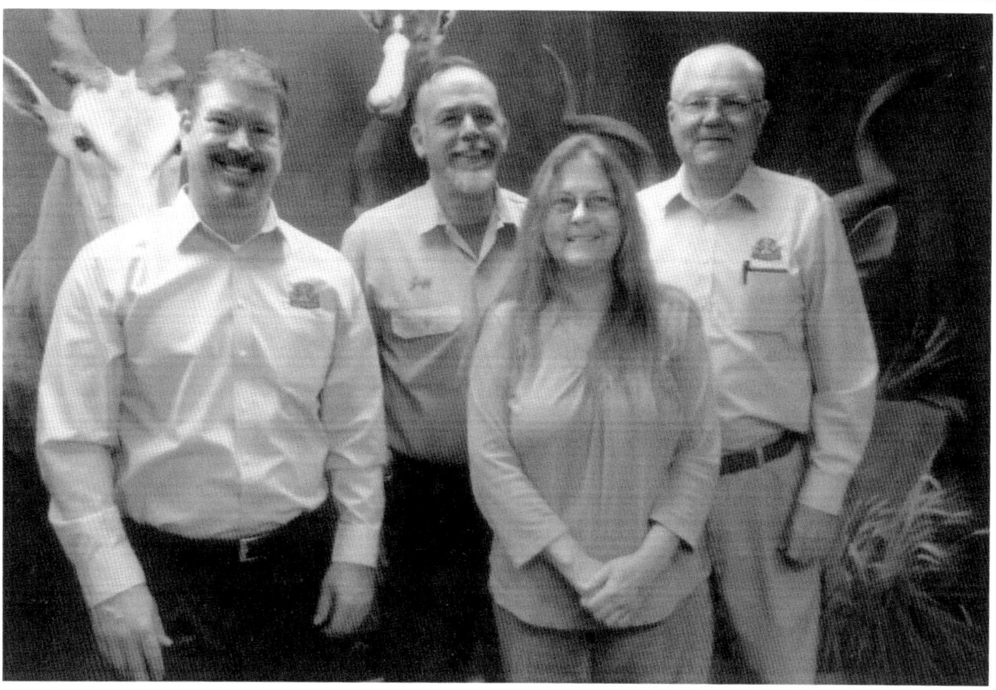

Mark Eaton

He may have been the boss's son, but, for his first 18 years at EZ TV & Appliance, Eaton (right) worked in the warehouse, drove the delivery truck, and learned customer service. Then, five years after Eaton became manager, his father passed him the keys to the business. Eaton kept the name and the commitment to quality, both in the products and in terms of customer treatment. The staff includes, from left to right, John Quinn, Jeff Cook, and Karla Cotton. An avid hunter, Eaton has traveled all over the world, and his trophies adorn the office wall. (Courtesy Michael Shinabery.)

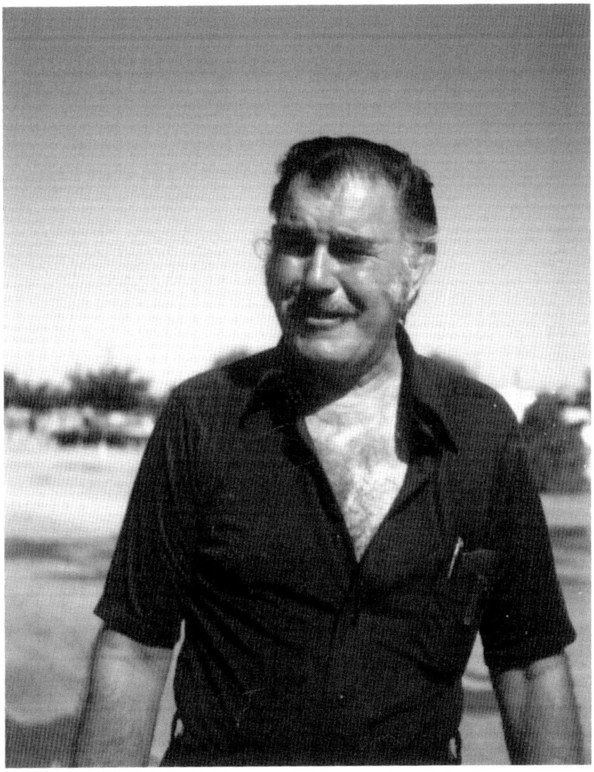

Edward Saulnier

Saulnier was one of those responsible for creating RAT SCAT (Radar Target Scatter Facility) at Holloman Air Force Base. In 1970, he and his wife, Frankie, built the KOA, which became one of the largest in the country and consistently won the award for best campground. Saulnier is seen here in 1975. The couple sold the business and retired two years later. (Courtesy Marcia Stirman.)

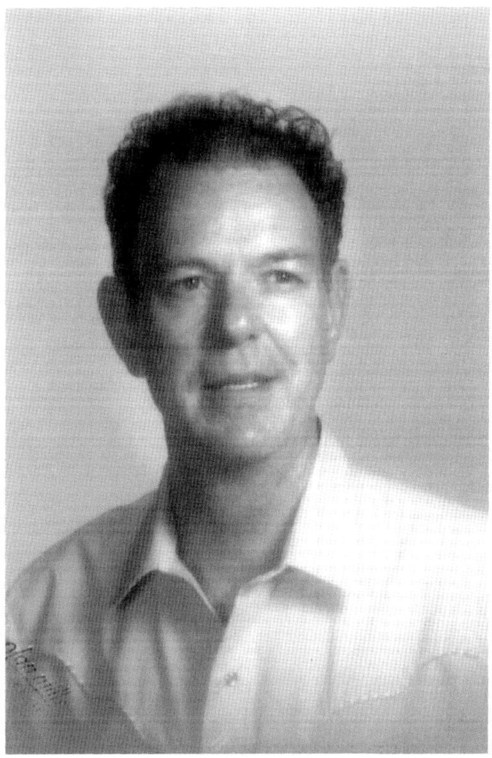

Arley Robinson

Robinson was 19 when he came to Alamogordo as the new owner of the Mountain View Inn. At the time, that was pretty much all there was north of Indian Wells Road. A decade later, the business burned down, and Robinson eventually moved to California. There, he would own four Denneys, a vineyard that sold grapes to Sun-Maid, a farm that sold fruit to Del Monte, and a hotel in the seaside resort of Morro Bay. Growing up near Gran Quivira instilled in him a love for the natural land. In California, he participates in a project that preserves the Central Coast, which he considers his most notable accomplishment. (Courtesy Arley Robinson.)

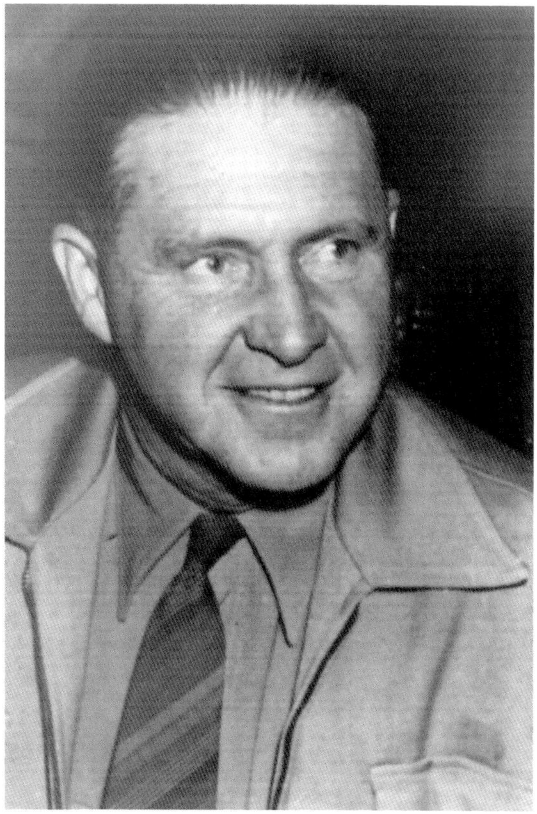

Gerald Champion
Champion, for whom the Champion Regional Medical Center is named, was considering running for governor when he was killed on February 4, 1948. He was a passenger in an airplane piloted by his brother-in-law H.M. Denney when it crashed near Cloudcroft. Champion was president of the Otero County State Bank and chairman of the Otero County Hospital Association. (Courtesy Gerald Champion Regional Medical Center.)

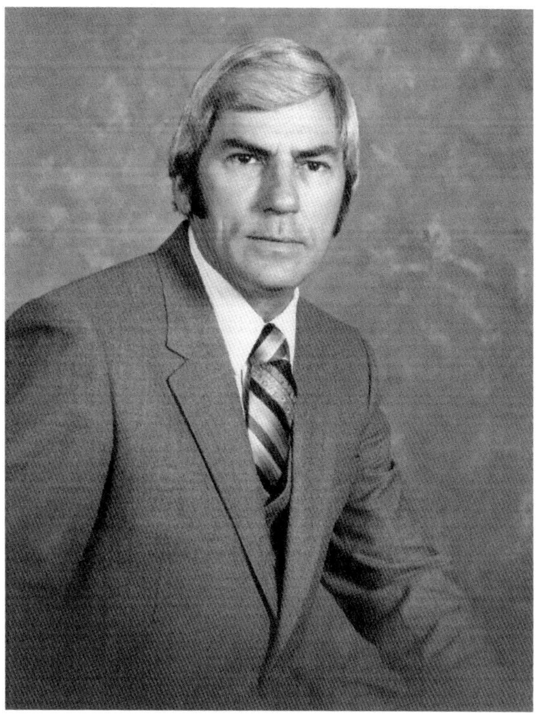

Jim Randall
A teenage Randall cooked at Holloman Air Force Base and assisted his dad selling cars at Sacramento Motors. When Sacramento offered full-time employment in October 1975, Randall responded that he made more cooking, so the business upped the ante. He bought his first stock in the company two years later, and in 1965, he attended GM's dealership school. Randall continued buying stock until he owned the business in 1984. Today, he is a successful auctioneer and has been a Citizen of the Year, so named by the Alamogordo Chamber of Commerce. (Courtesy Alamogordo Chamber of Commerce.)

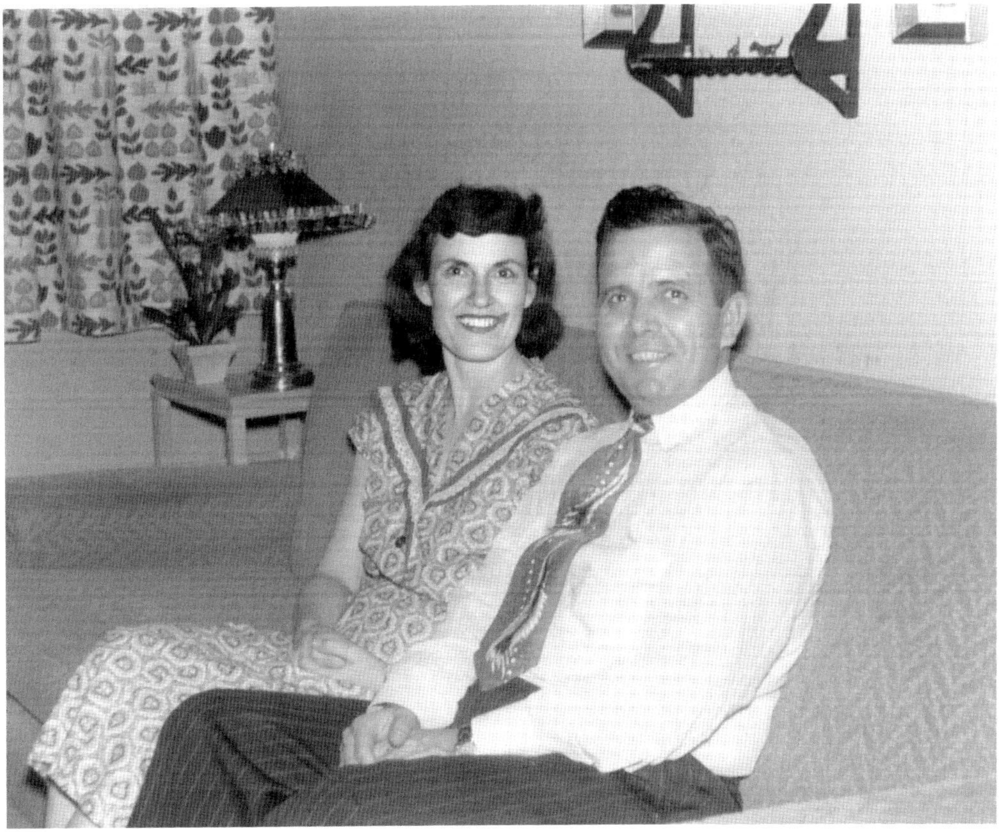

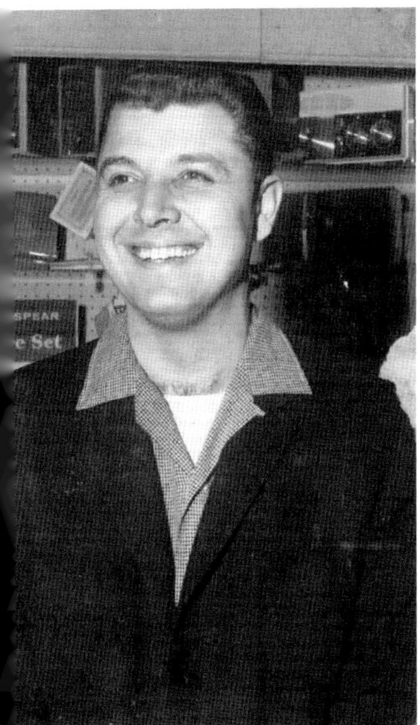

Wade Maupin

White's Auto Stores founder Earl White one day mentioned to Maupin, in El Paso, that Alamogordo needed an auto store. Gerald Champion's father loaned Maupin the money, and, to make ends meet, the family lived above the New York Avenue store. After hours, Maupin delivered, which was the beginning of the customer service for which the business has become known. Maupin, seen here with his wife, Edna Mae, died in 1968, but today, his son Wadell and grandson Kerry continue the family tradition with Home Furniture Company and Western Auto. (Courtesy Maupin family.)

Wadell Maupin

When his father, Wade, died at age 52, Maupin become owner of the family businesses, White's Auto and Home Furniture. In 1957, Maupin moved from New York Avenue to Ninth Street, where the store currently stands. By then, the family had opened White's stores in Tularosa, Farmington, and Tucumcari, as well as Levelland, Texas. Eventually, Maupin sold them all, except for the Alamogordo and Tularosa stores. In 1987, he changed the franchise to Western Auto True Value, which his son Kerry manages. Maupin continues to manage Home Furniture. (Courtesy Maupin family.)

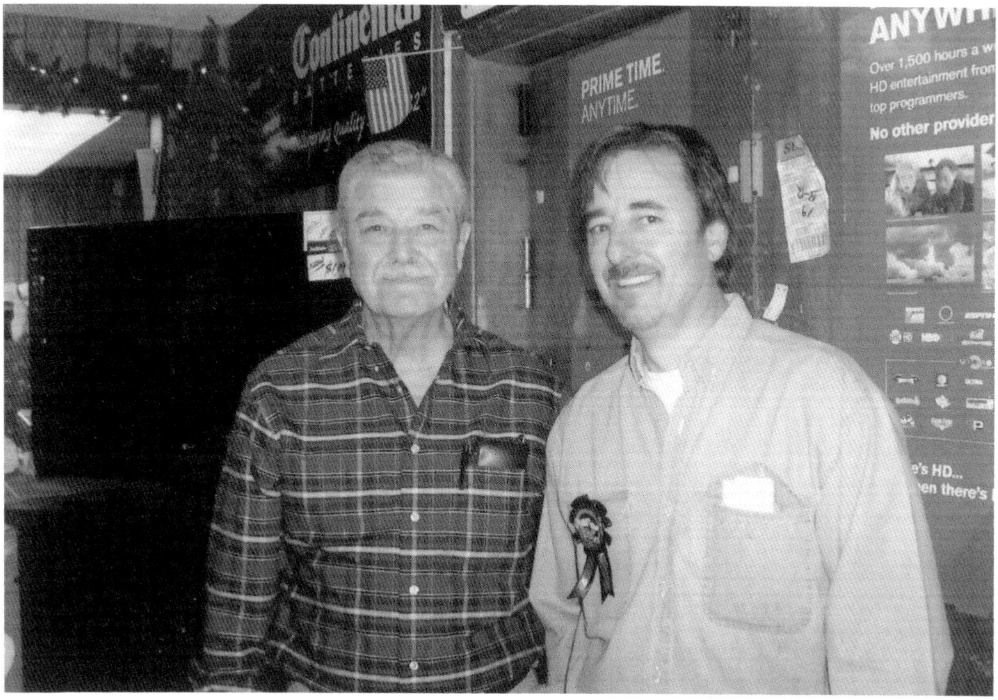

Kerry Maupin

Kerry Maupin's father, Wadell, gave him an opportunity to manage the family's oldest business, Western Auto True Value. Under his leadership, the store has been feted as an Alamogordo Chamber of Commerce Business of the Quarter and Business of the Year. Maupin learned the importance of serving the customer from his dad. They are seen here together in 2007. Wadell learned from his father when Wade Maupin founded White's Auto in 1945. (Courtesy Maupin family.)

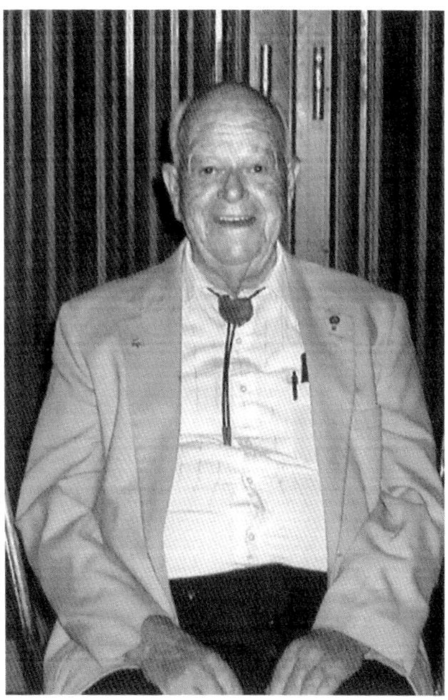

J. Marion Bell

The Capitol Christmas tree was harvested from the Lincoln National Forest in 1956, and Bell, head of the Alamogordo Chamber of Commerce, rode the train with the tree all the way to Washington, DC. He personally handed it over to Pres. Dwight Eisenhower. (Courtesy Norm Arnold.)

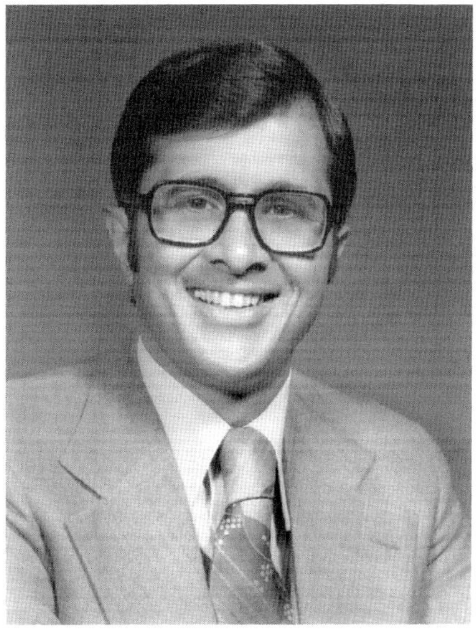

John Lattauzio

Whether the economy was up or down, Lattauzio's J&J Minimarkets were successful in Alamogordo from 1962 until Lattauzio's 2008 retirement. A staunch conservative, he served as chair for both the Republican Party of Otero County and the state party. (Courtesy Alamogordo Chamber of Commerce.)

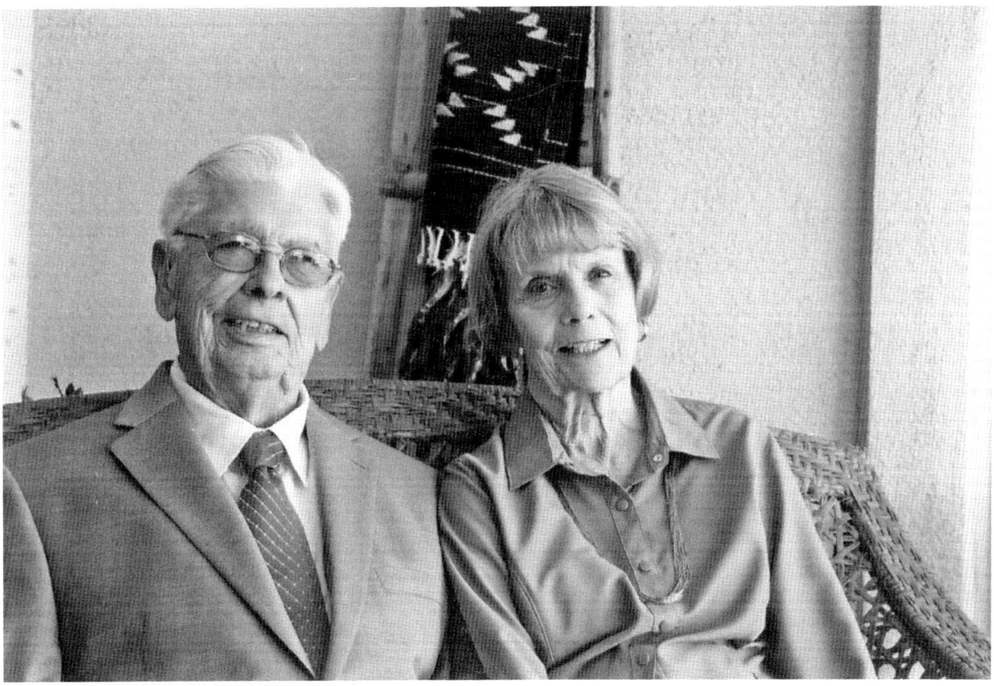

Ron and Gloria Burch

Ron and Gloria came to Alamogordo in 1956 after Ron's Army service. He worked for Land-Air (later DynCorp), and after his 1997 retirement, the couple started their contracting business, Pyramid Services, with no employees. Then, 11 years later, Pyramid had 700 employees with contracts in five states. During this stage, the management structure was changed, and the Burches' daughter Laura (now CEO) and son David were put in control. Ron and Gloria remained on the board. After Pres. Barack Obama signed Executive Order 1434 (Economy in Government Contracts) in January 2009, the contracting business changed, and Pyramid management decided they could not compete. It is slowly completing contracts and will eventually phase out the business. (Photograph by Tim Schultz; used with the permission of Ron and Gloria Burch.)

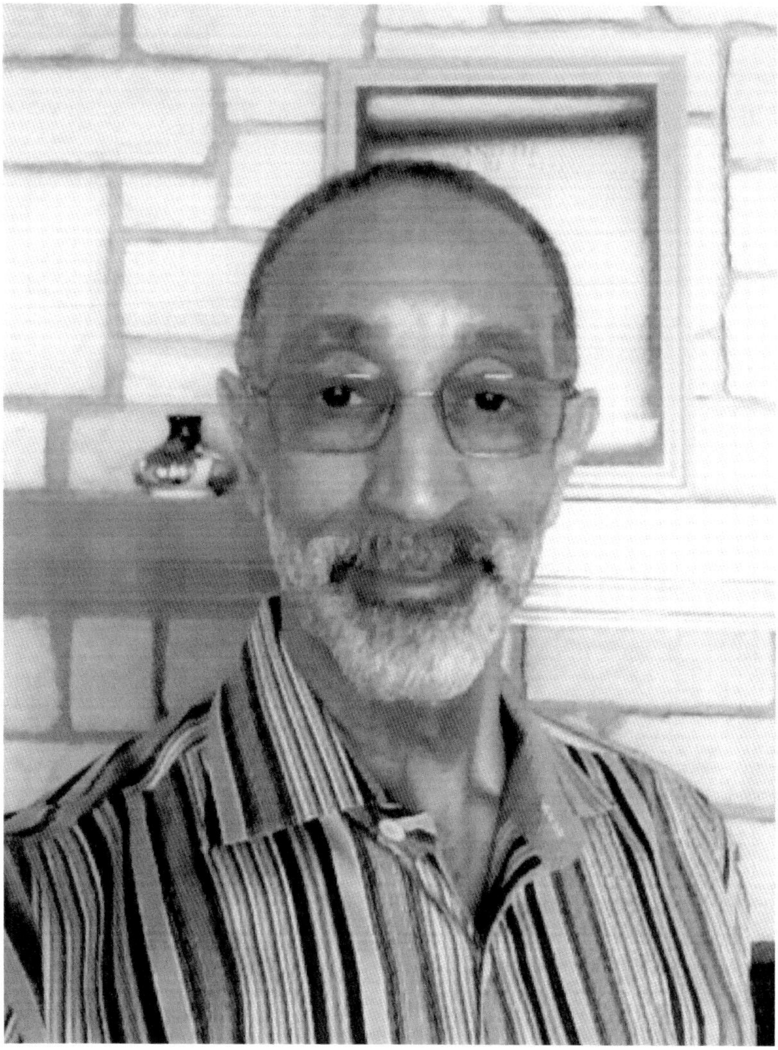

Wayne Martin

Martin was lead singer with the El Paso group the Inspirations and selling cars when he had the chance to buy Alamogordo's Ford dealership. Martin had to spend $500 to fly to Denver to convince corporate bosses he could make the business work in a small town. Martin became owner in 1989, alongside his wife, Millie, whom he had met when she was lead singer of El Paso's Fabulous Fabulettes. By 1999, Vision Ford employed 70 people and was number 49 in New Mexico's top 100 privately owned businesses. In 1995, Gov. Gary Johnson presented Wayne Martin with the Viva Award, and two years later, Martin was the first African American in Alamogordo's history to be named Citizen of the Year by the Alamogordo Chamber of Commerce. *Ebony* magazine has featured him, Ford's *Dealer World* magazine put him on the cover, and *Black Enterprise* magazine consistently names his company one of the nation's top black-owned businesses.

As Martin's success increased, he increasingly blessed the community. He sponsored Special Olympics and the annual Vision Ford Easter Party, which hosts 1,200 kids at the Alameda Park Zoo. He opens Vision Ford to numerous organizations, including churches, for meetings. He also owns Paradise Ford, in Florida. His son Michael Martin, Vision's business manager, owns four dealerships. (Courtesy Wayne Martin.)

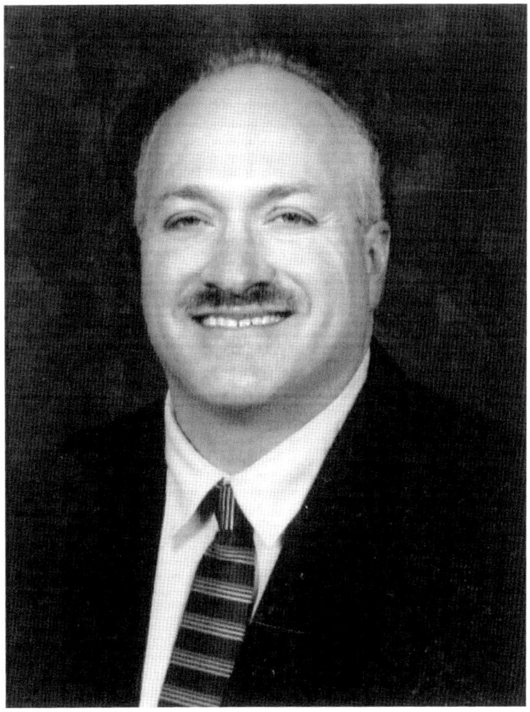

Kent House

House owns Hamilton O'Dell Funeral Home and Alamogordo Funeral Home. He started at Hamilton as an intern in 1980 after graduating from Alamogordo High School. While at the University of Central Oklahoma, he interned at homes in Sayre and Oklahoma City. House returned to Hamilton in 1991. The list of his community involvement is longer than his resume and includes United Way, Crimestoppers, the White Sands District Boy Scouts, and serving as fundraising chair for Kids Kingdom. (Courtesy Alamogordo Chamber of Commerce.)

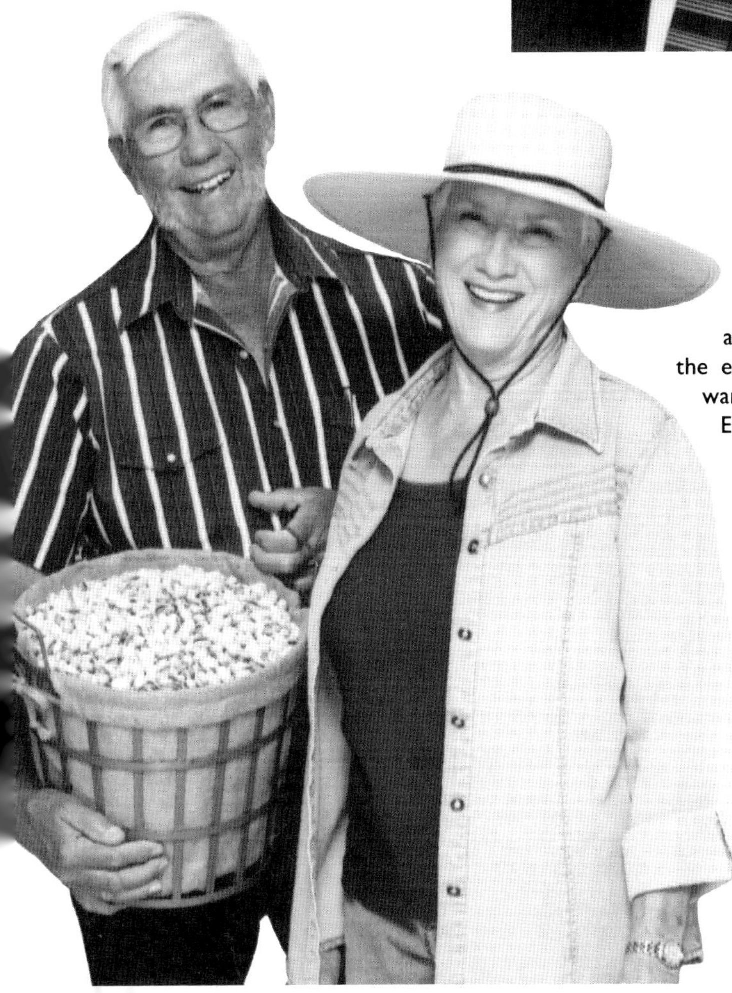

The Schweers

While an Air Force officer at Holloman Air Force Base in the early 1970s, George Schweers wanted to get into agriculture. Eagle Ranch was born when he bought 400 pistachio trees. He and his wife, Marianne, and their three children worked the land before developing their own machine-processing operation. Today, they own 12,000 trees, and their 24,000 grapevines produce Heart of the Desert wines. (Courtesy Schweers family.)

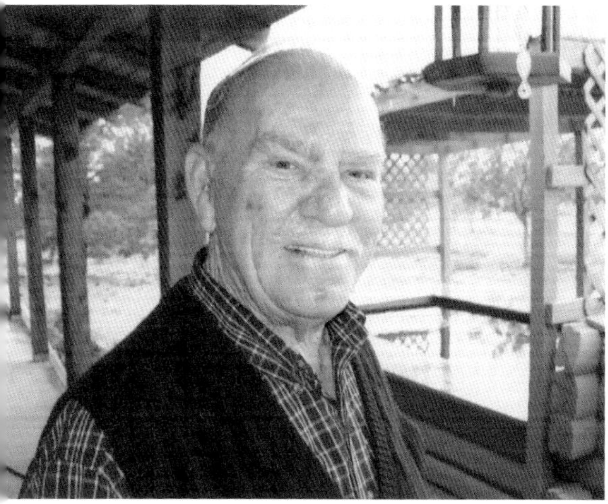

Thomas McGinn

McGinn worked for Thomas English Muffins in the 1970s when he came through Alamogordo and saw a future for desert agriculture. He bought 90 acres of land and, after he retired in 1980, opened Pistachio Tree Ranch. A three-story cement pistachio has been featured in travel magazines and is a tourist draw. McGinn's son Tim erected the monument in 1980 to honor his father's foresight. Ernest Martinez, who owns Bar M Construction, built the *World's Largest Pistachio* in 2008. (Courtesy McGinn family.)

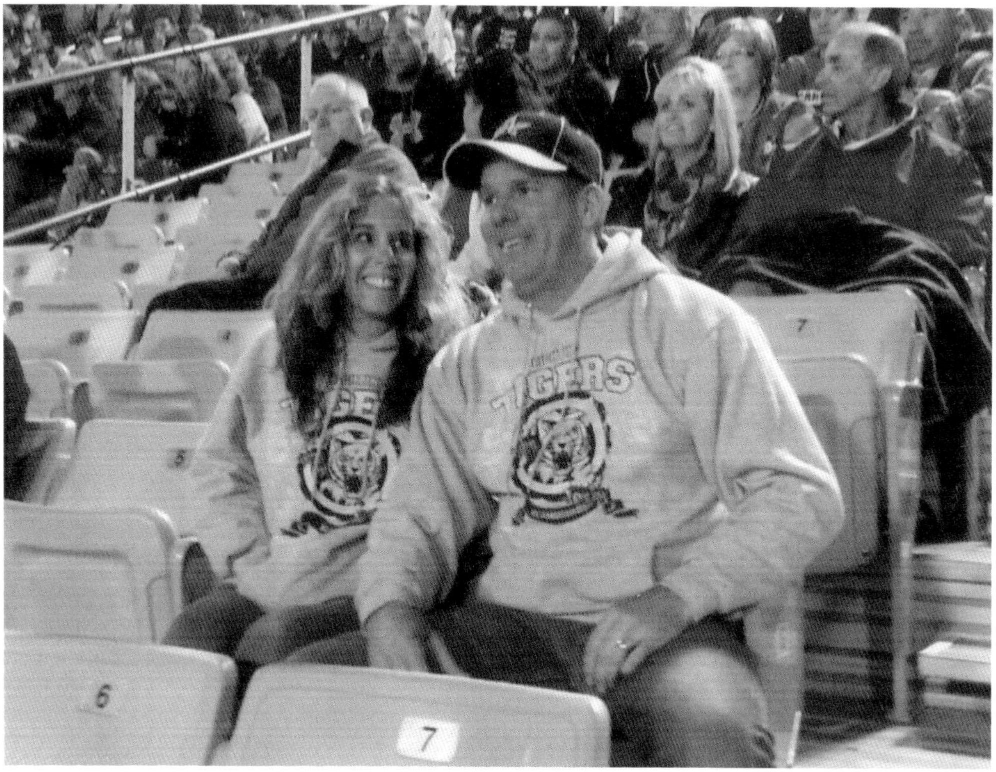

Tim and Clarissa McGinn

The McGinns own the Pistachio Tree Ranch and Arena Blanca Winery, which Tim's father founded in 1980. Tourists ride through the orchard aboard an electric trolley and sample flavored pistachios and award-winning candies and wines, all made on the property. Visitors can also have their photograph taken with the *World's Largest Pistachio*, a three-story cement monument in homage to McGinn's father, Thomas McGinn, who founded the business. Tim, a 1986 Alamogordo High School graduate, spent a year in Denmark as a Rotary exchange student. In 1995, he began his first of two consecutive terms as county commissioner, after which Clarissa served two terms. Both fiscal and social conservatives, they promised no new taxes, and stuck to their guns. (Courtesy McGinn family.)

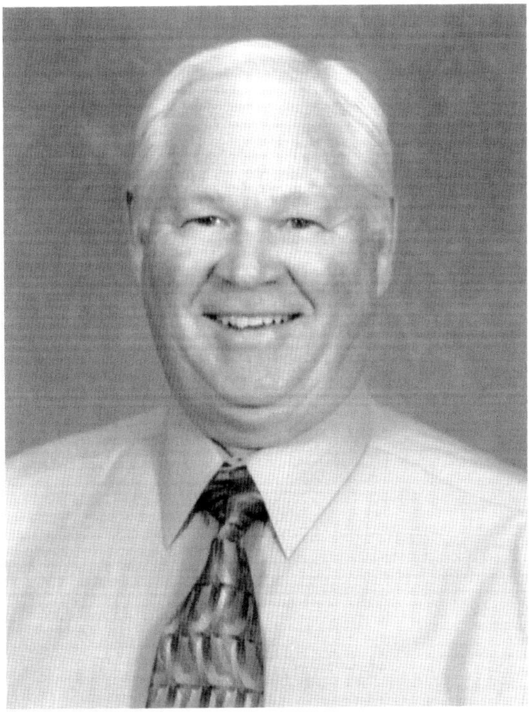

Phillip Runnels

The son of US representative Harold Runnels, Phillip Runnels was a flight instructor during Vietnam. In 1997, he came to Alamogordo as owner of radio stations KRSY AM and FM. He bucked the syndication trend four years later, beginning local morning talk, which still airs. Runnels, a barbecue cook, owned the popular Phat Phil's and Uncle A's. In 2014, he carted his business to Paris, Texas, to be nearer his family. (Courtesy Alamogordo Chamber of Commerce.)

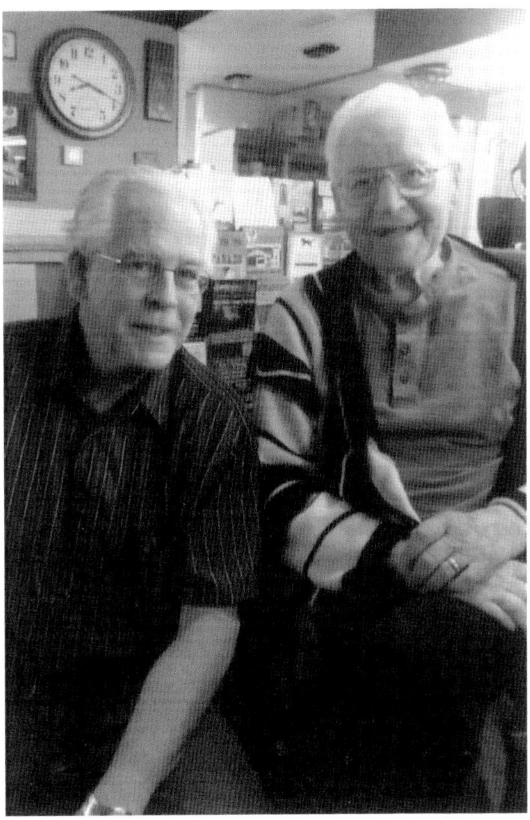

George and Steve Brockett

The Waffle and Pancake Shoppe serves great food and food for thought from George Brockett (right). He acquired the business in 1987. Harold Welch, First Lady Laura Bush's father, gave Brockett his first job. He came to Alamogordo in 1969 and opened his first restaurant, It's Burger Time. Then, from 1977 to 1992, he owned George's Restaurant and Rib Room, the city's largest dining establishment. Brockett created thousands of jobs and took an active interest in his employees, helping fund college and vocational tuitions. His son Steve (left) joined the family business in 1979, and he now owns the Waffle and Pancake Shoppe. His passion, though, is politics. A former Alamogordo mayor and city commissioner, and a moderate Democrat, he has consulted campaigns for both Democratic and Republican candidates in New Mexico and other parts of the country. (Courtesy Michael Shinabery.)

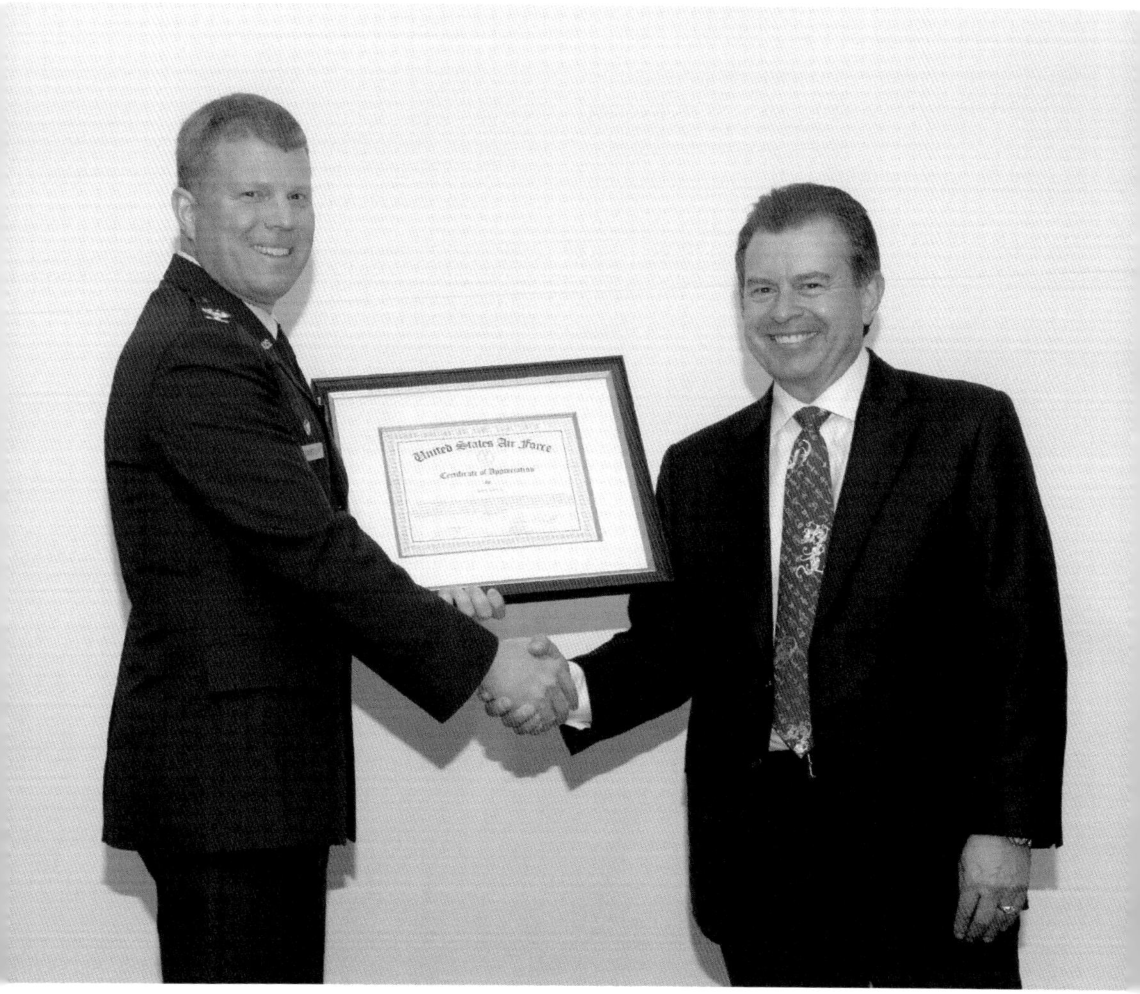

Bobby Martinez

The new owner of Desert Sun Motors came to Alamogordo in 1994. Martinez had begun selling cars in Espanola in 1981 after earning a bachelor's degree in finance, and four years later, he was promoted to sales manager, and then to general manager. Martinez paid off his Desert Sun loan from General Motors far earlier than expected. In the next 20 years, he opened two dealerships in Roswell and one in Espanola, and in Alamogordo, he added a Toyota dealership and Desert Suds carwash. His businesses have created 250 jobs, and 2014 sales totaled more than $13 million. Martinez was president of the New Mexico Automobile Dealers Association in 2005 and Citizen of the Year in 2012, so named by the Alamogordo Chamber of Commerce. As his success blossomed, Martinez has been equally generous, most notably with the Holloman Big Give, where teams of airmen compete while doing volunteer community projects. Through that, Martinez has contributed $65,000 to the team prizes and returned $1.3 million to the community. Here, the 49th Wing commander, Col. Andrew Croft (left), honors Martinez as a Holloman Air Force Base Wingman. (Courtesy Holloman Air Force Base.)

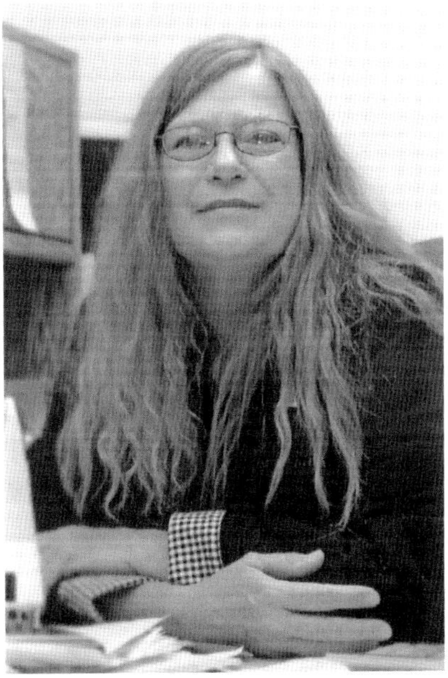

Cathy Harper

In the mid-1990s, Harper, sales manager for KZZX/KINN, brought Otero County's first Professional Rodeo Cowboys Association rodeo to Alamogordo. Later, at the *Alamogordo Daily News*, she created the annual Women of Merit award to recognize outstanding area women. Now the New Mexico Museum of Space History's marketing director, Harper was involved with the creation of Spaceport America, rekindling her childhood passion for space. (Courtesy Ron Keller.)

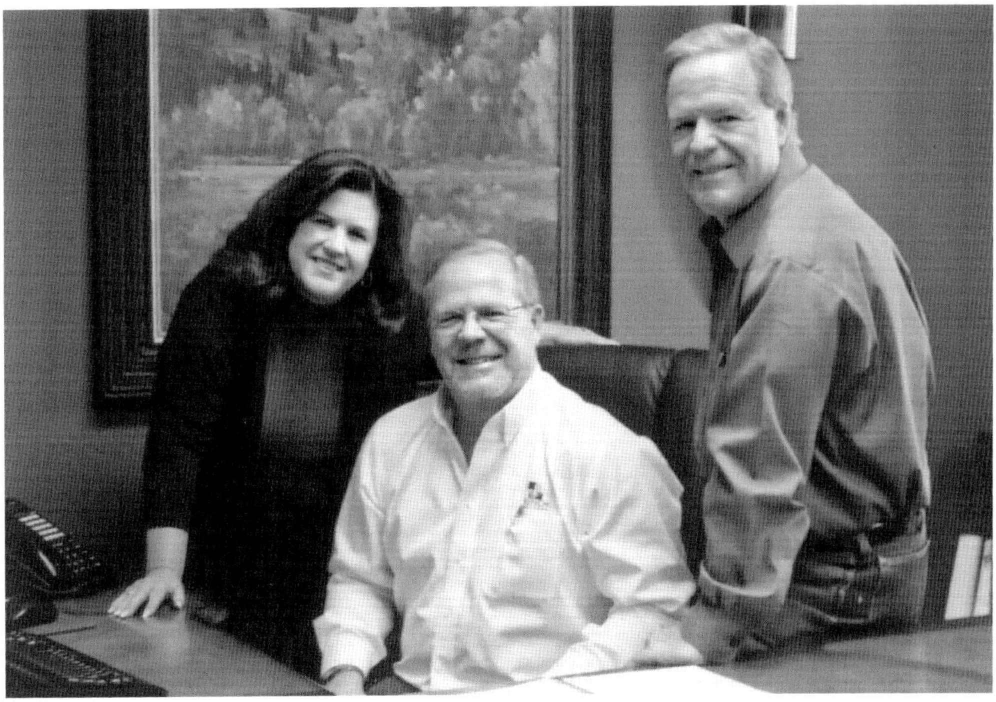

French Brothers

Jim (center) and Tom (right) started in construction when they were 15 and passed their state contractor tests at 18. In 2014, French Brothers became the first New Mexico builder to earn the industry's toughest honor, the National Housing Quality Bronze Award. The next year, the company earned the Silver Award. Energy-efficient homes are its specialty, and it has expanded into Roswell, Las Cruces, and Hobbs. Shown here with the brothers is their business partner and vice president of sales and marketing, Corrine Bachman. (Courtesy French Brothers.)

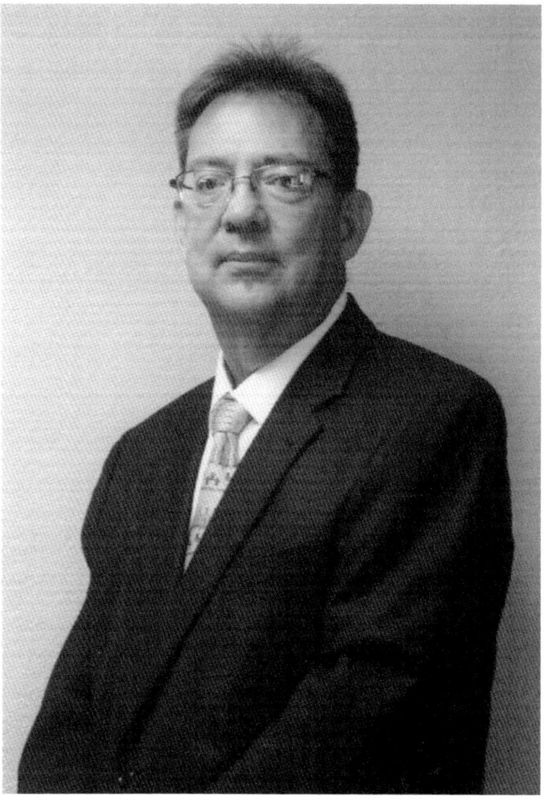

Kurt Lueck

Manager of the German moving company Ito Umzuege, Lueck knew US history and the Bill of Rights when America was still his dream. Lueck loved John Wayne Westerns while growing up in his native Germany. When he was 24, he proudly immigrated and eventually became a naturalized citizen. He continues to passionately study American and New Mexico history. (Courtesy Kurt Lueck.)

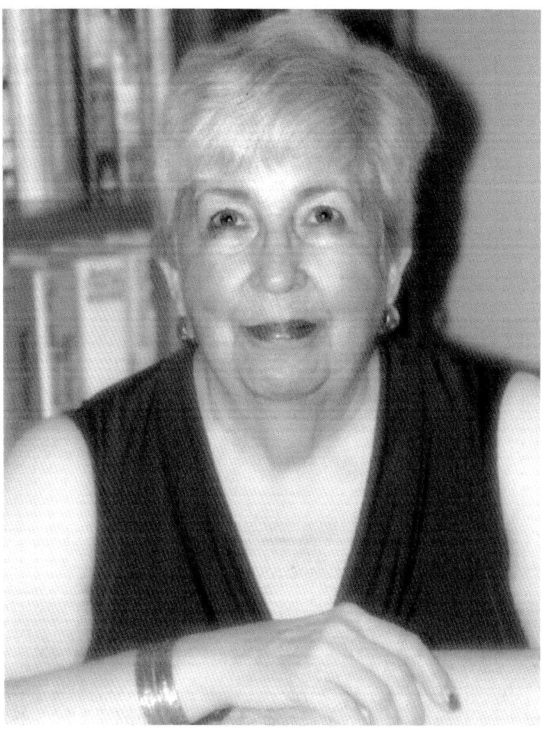

Pam Clarke

In 2004, Clarke became Otero County Habitat for Humanity's first full-time employee. She grew the organization from one that built just one or two houses annually to three to four. She helps with selecting the families, arranges mortgage lending, oversees environmental reviews required for land purchase, and secures grants. Clarke started the Owner Occupied ReHab Program and was instrumental in acquiring from the Department of Housing and Urban Development the designation of Community Housing Development Organization. (Courtesy Rudy Clarke.)

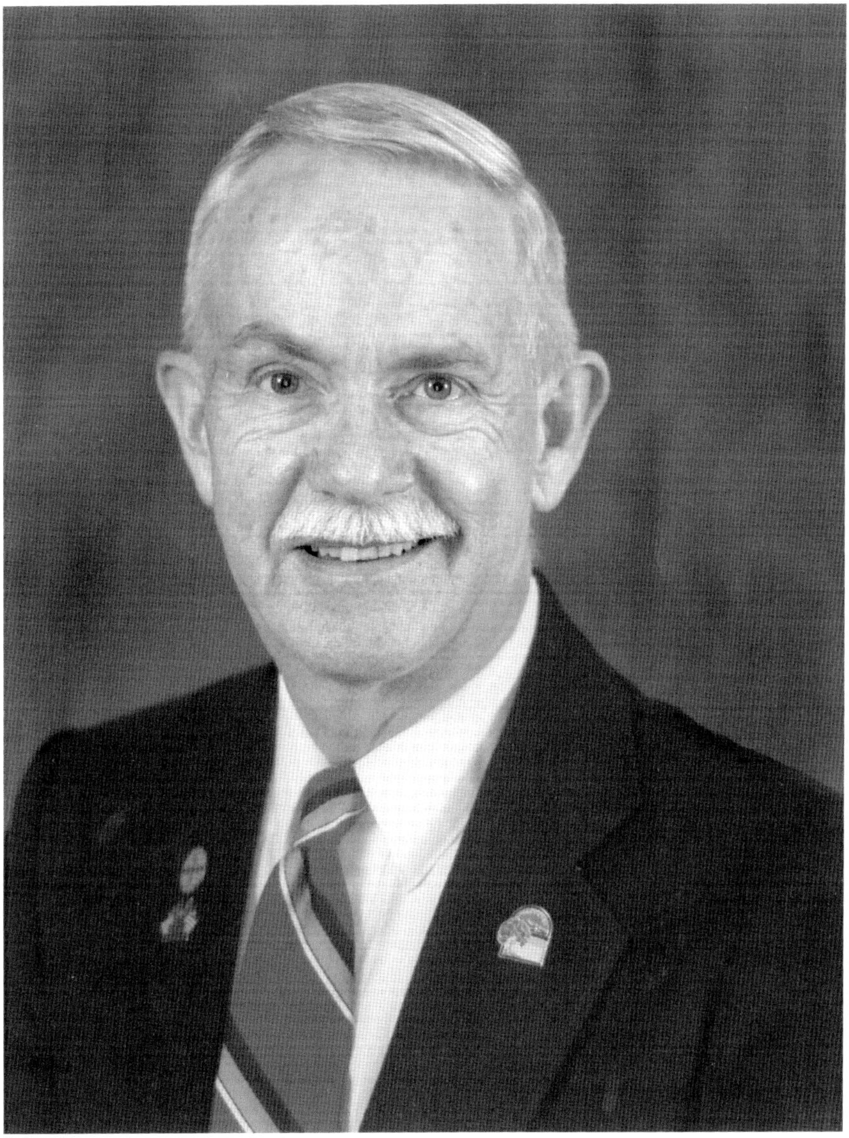

Dwight Harp

When Harp drove into Alamogordo in August 1989 to lead the new Small Business Development Center, his first task was to assemble the surplus desks from a local bank. Harp and his staff annually counseled more than 400 clients, and the New Mexico Legislature often recognized their success stories. Harp took his marketing expertise to Holloman Air Force Base 20 years later, where he was sponsorship coordinator with the 49th Wing's Marketing Department. Major Command selected it as Best Marketing Office, and, subsequently, he and his staff were named Best in the Air Force. Harp served in the Army. During the Vietnam War, he broadcast for the Armed Forces Radio and Television Service. In civilian life, he worked in small-market radio. In January 2012, he achieved a personal goal when the Anglican Church of North America ordained him a deacon. Harp leads a Sunday service in Cloudcroft, is an Alamogordo Police Department chaplain, and serves as a Wingman at Holloman. The Wingman designation denotes him as a community member who wholeheartedly supports the men and women who maintain the base's mission. (Courtesy Alamogordo Chamber of Commerce.)

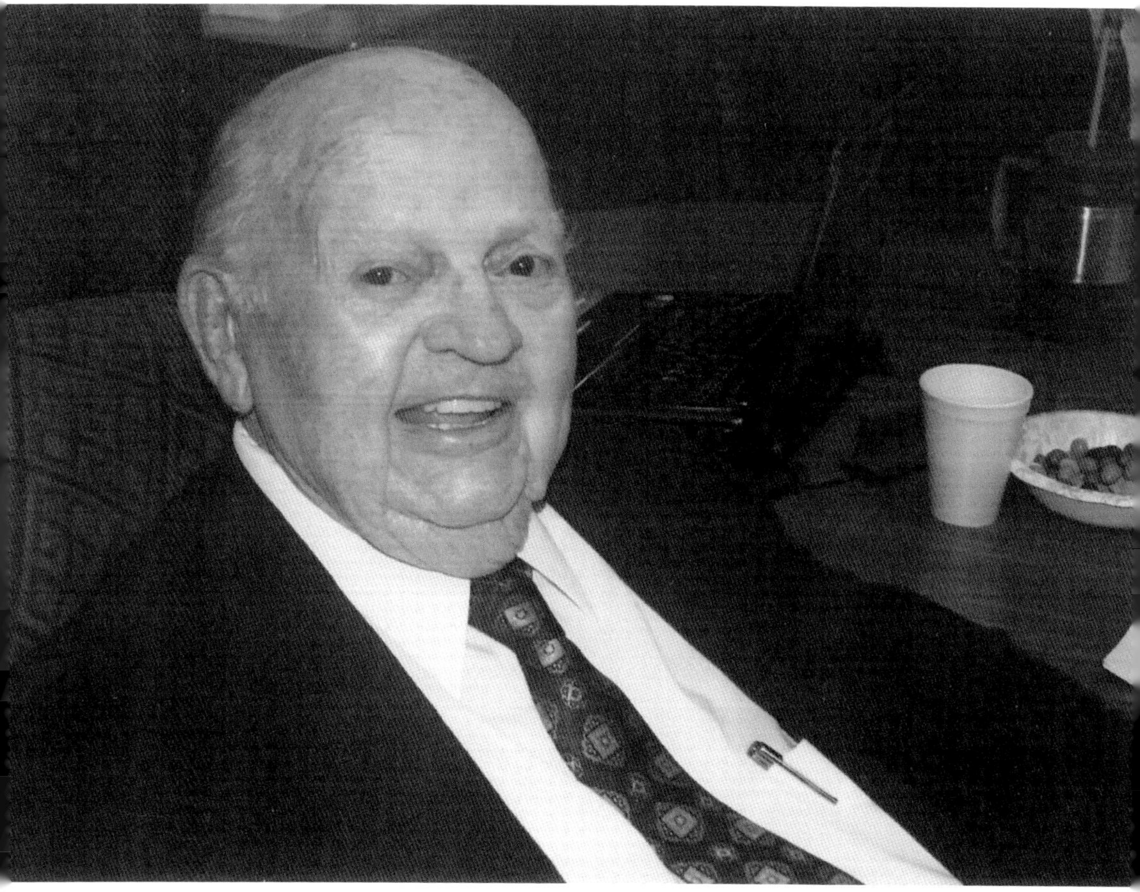

Wyatt Atkins

He thought he was only driving the truck from Arcadia, Louisiana, to Fort Worth in 1943. Atkins did not even have a driver's license and had to stop in Shreveport to spend $2 for a chauffeur's permit. Arriving in Fort Worth and anxious to go home, Atkins was frustrated to learn he was to continue on to Alamogordo to deliver concrete to pour a slab for the power company, Community Public Service. The rural roads were awful, the truck had electrical problems, and Wyatt, who was not even 21, had little money. Limping into Alamogordo, he spent his last thin dime on a sandwich and coffee and was dumbfounded to learn he was now a CPS employee and expected to help build the new plant. So Atkins went about setting down roots. Over the years, he owned car dealerships, such as Missile Motor Company, which sold Studebakers, Dodges, and Edsels. Politically, he became a Democratic dynamo. Atkins served as a state senator for five years, was a county commissioner for two terms, and, for 12 years, was the city police judge. He was a delegate to the national convention that nominated Adlai Stevenson for president. While there, Eleanor Roosevelt invited Atkins to tea. Atkins insists he never saw any tea, but did mingle with a lot of VIPs. In 1956, First National Bank was formed. Soon thereafter, he joined the board, where he helped to guide the institution for decades. Ted Kennedy once came to Alamogordo, and Atkins personally escorted him around the community. In 1963, when Pres. John Kennedy visited Holloman Air Force Base and White Sands Missile Range, Atkins secreted Kennedy's limousine in his business garage. (Courtesy Wyatt Atkins.)

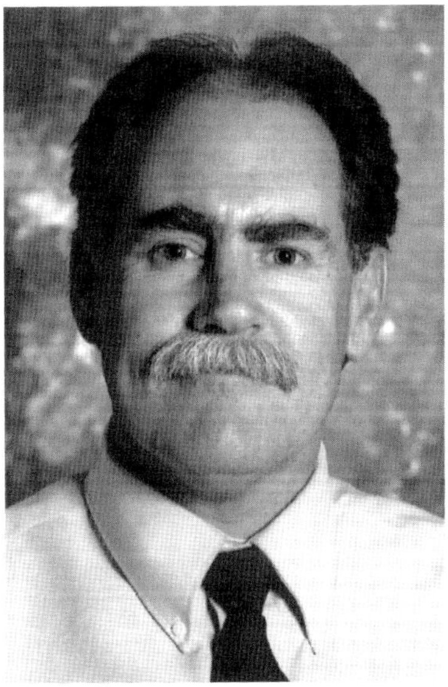

Darrell Pehr

The terrorist attacks of September 11, 2001, hit the *Alamogordo Daily News* editorial staff hard when they learned that a retired Alamogordo policeman, whom reporters knew, was aboard United Airlines Flight 175. Pehr, the editor, kept the staff on deadline and coordinated information from Holloman Air Force Base. Pehr is now director of news at New Mexico State University and owns Cloudcroft's *Mountain Monthly.* (Courtesy Darrell Pehr.)

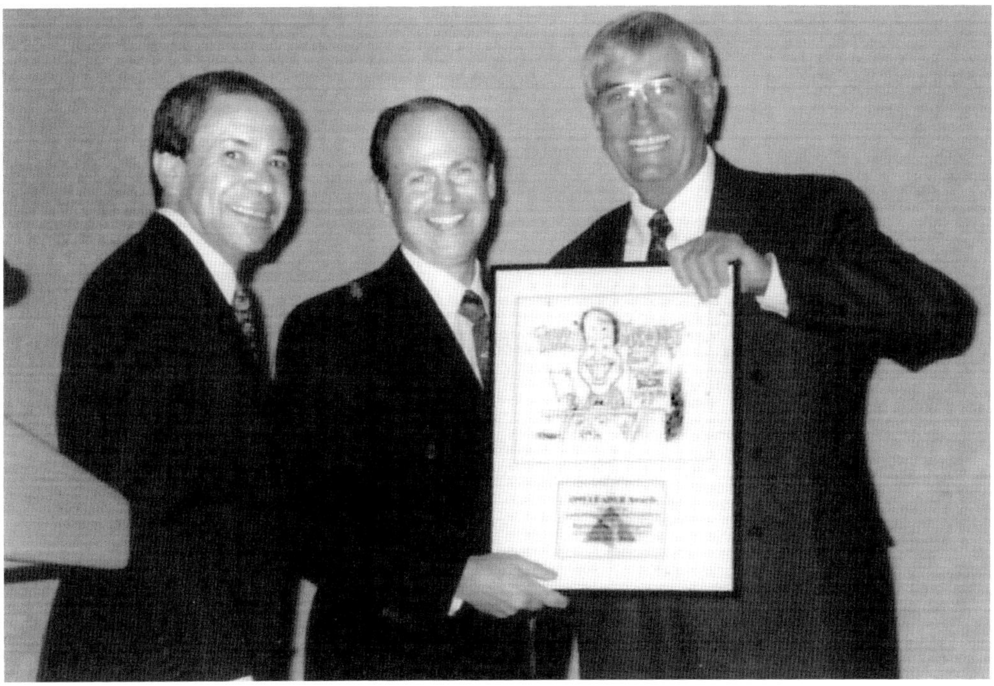

Dr. Terry Marquardt

Marquardt (center) was state representative from 1994 to 2007, serving as Republican caucus chair and minority whip. The American Legislative Exchange Council and the New Mexico District Attorney Association honored him as Legislator of the Year. Former governors Toney Anaya (left) and Garrey Carruthers (right) presented him with the New Mexico Business Leader Award. Marquardt chairs Alamogordo Main Street, which is revitalizing the historic downtown area, an idea spearheaded by retired colonel Pam Lee. His business, Marquardt Eye Associates, has been in a historic building along New York Avenue since 1974. Marquardt is a board-certified specialist, a diplomate of the American Board of Optometry. (Courtesy Terry Marquardt.)

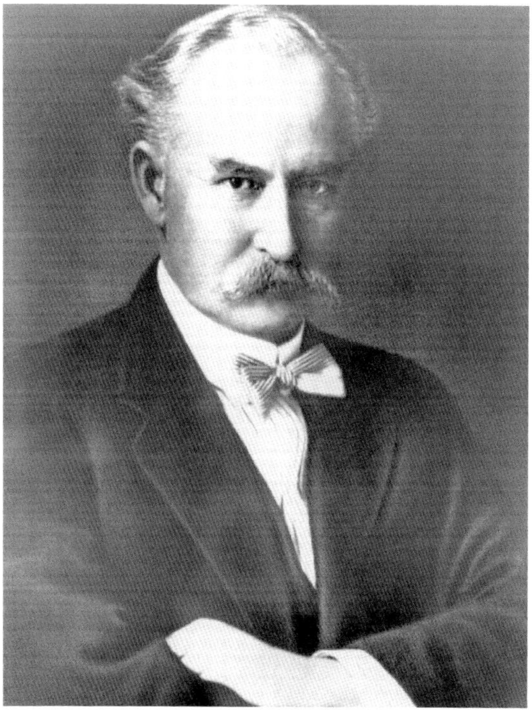

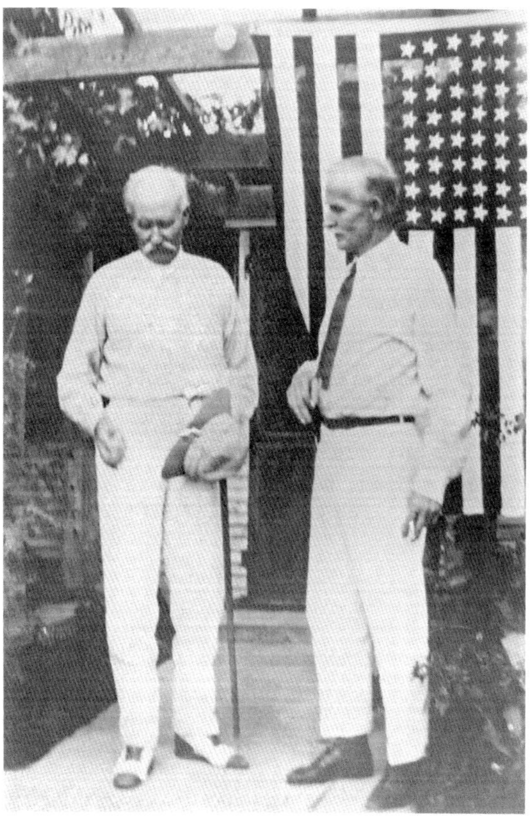

Albert Fall

His career was stellar. At one time, he was William Ashton Hawkins's law partner. Among Fall's many political accomplishments, he went to New Mexico's Territorial House of Representatives while still in his 30s, was appointed judge of the Third Judicial District, was associate justice of the New Mexico Supreme Court, and served as the state's attorney general. When New Mexico was granted statehood in 1912, Fall went to Washington, DC, as a Republican senator. In 1921, Pres. Warren Harding named him secretary of the interior. In what became known as the Teapot Dome Scandal, Fall was eventually convicted of accepting a bribe to lease federal lands to oil companies, and he went to prison. In the below photograph, Fall (left) is with Eugene Manlove Rhodes in 1938, six years before Fall died. (Both, courtesy the Tularosa Basin Historical Society.)

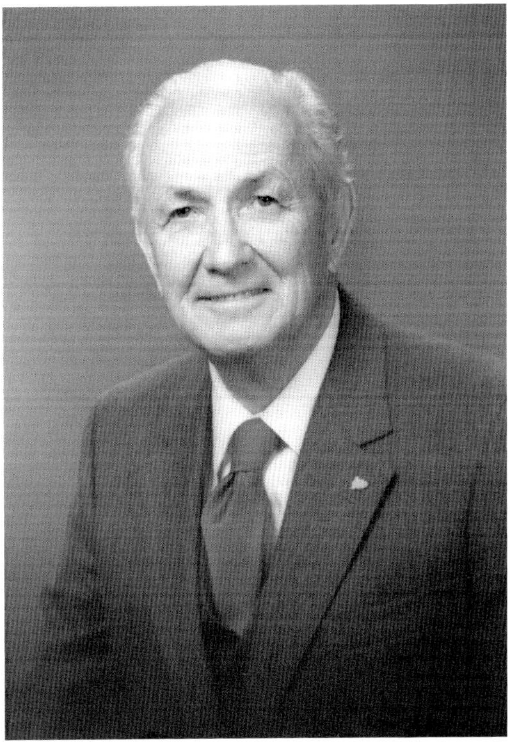

John Mershon
Mershon served from 1959 to 1982 in the New Mexico House of Representatives. A Democrat, he chaired the powerful Legislative Finance Committee and the House Appropriations Committee. At home, he helped found First National Bank and the Otero County Electric Cooperative, and he secured funding to pave US 82 from Alamogordo to Cloudcroft. Before his death, he bequeathed his lifelong collection of family and political memorabilia to the Sacramento Mountains Historical Society. (Courtesy Mershon family.)

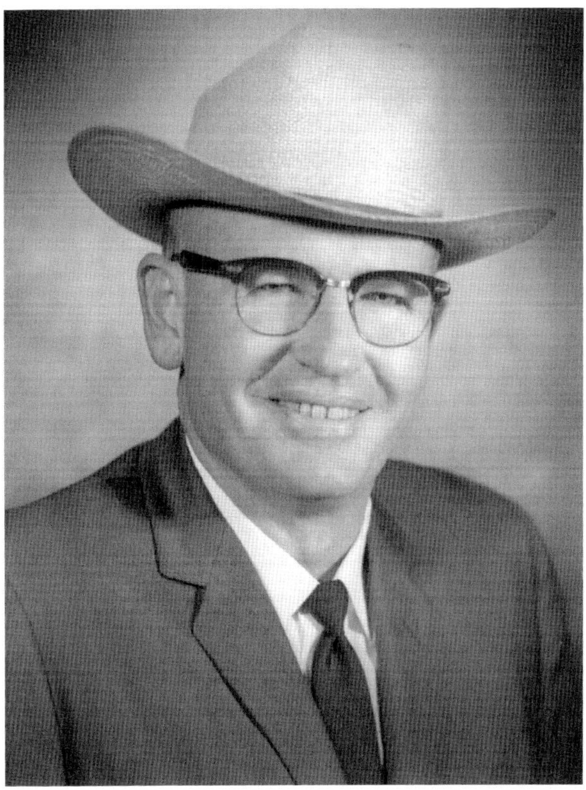

Aubrey Dunn
In 1954, Dunn became Otero County assessor, but he left to be the *Alamogordo Daily News* bookkeeper and business manager and, eventually, the co-owner. In 1965, Dunn began 15 years in the New Mexico Legislature, where he was chairman of the Legislative Finance Committee. He helped ensure that small schools received adequate funding and helped establish the severance tax fund. The Alamogordo Chamber of Commerce visitor center is named in his honor. Dunn fought cancer for one year more than he served in the New Mexico Legislature, and he lifted the spirits of other sufferers with his One Day at a Time cards. (Courtesy Alamogordo Chamber of Commerce.)

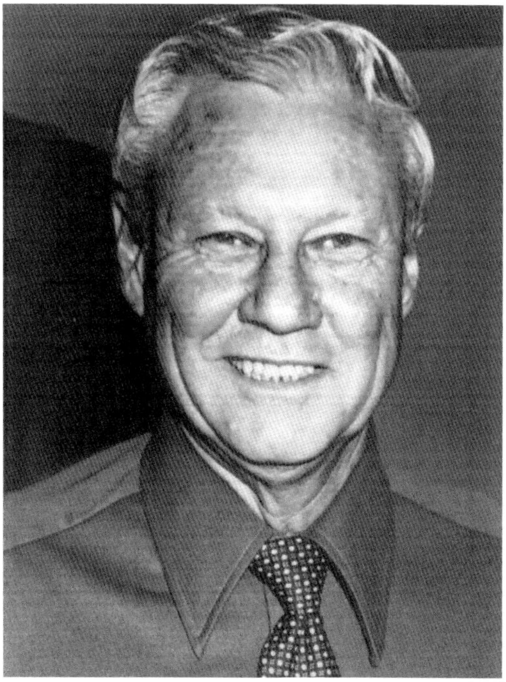

Eddie Olsen
When Standard Oil informed Olsen that he was transferring to Montana, Olsen resigned and became a banker. He was a city commissioner and then mayor from 1972 to 1974. Olsen and his wife, Jigger, are the only couple in which each spouse served as mayor, she from 1978 to 1982. Olsen joined the Coast Guard during World War II when a Fort Bliss soldier made a nasty comment about him remaining a civilian. Olsen served in both the European and Pacific theaters, and he was aboard a ship near Iwo Jima when a photographer snapped his photograph for the December 17, 1944, *Parade* magazine. (Courtesy Alamogordo Chamber of Commerce.)

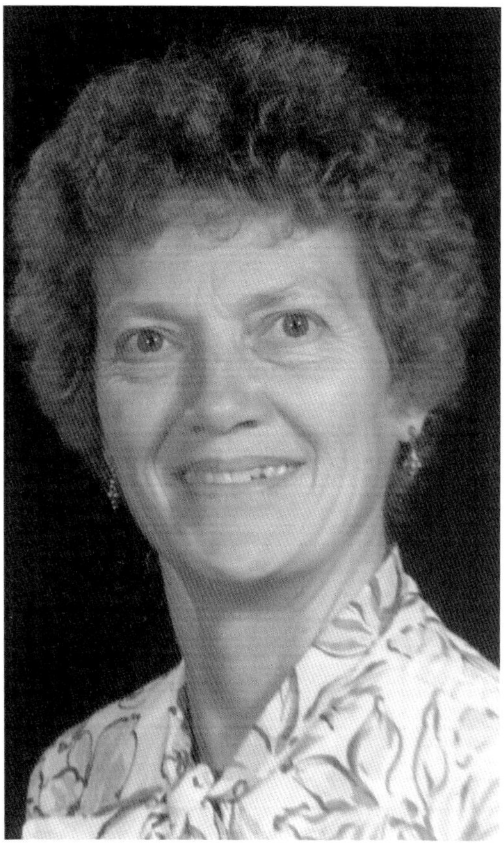

Jigger Olsen
A childhood friend called Mary Virginia Olsen "Jigger," and eventually, Olsen had her name legally changed. Olsen was Alamogordo's mayor from 1978 to 1982 and the town's first female mayor and commissioner. She and her husband, Eddie, are the only couple in which each spouse served as mayor, he from 1972 to 1974. She was a teacher and counselor at Chaparral Junior High School for 21 years. (Courtesy Olsen family.)

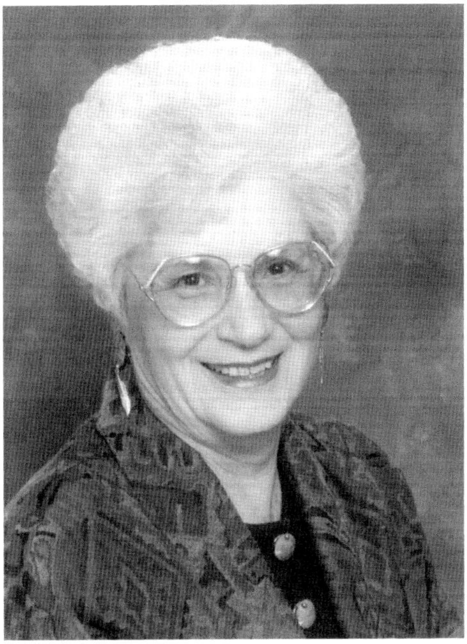

Toots Green
Chief executive officer at Loco Credit Union and president of the New Mexico Association of Credit Unions, Green served six years as a state representative. As a Committee of 50 member, Green represents Holloman Air Force Base on the Air Combat Command, Commander's Support Group. She has also been chair of the annual Thanks Team Holloman event, which gives a thumbs-up to the Air Force men and women supporting the base's mission. (Courtesy Alamogordo Chamber of Commerce.)

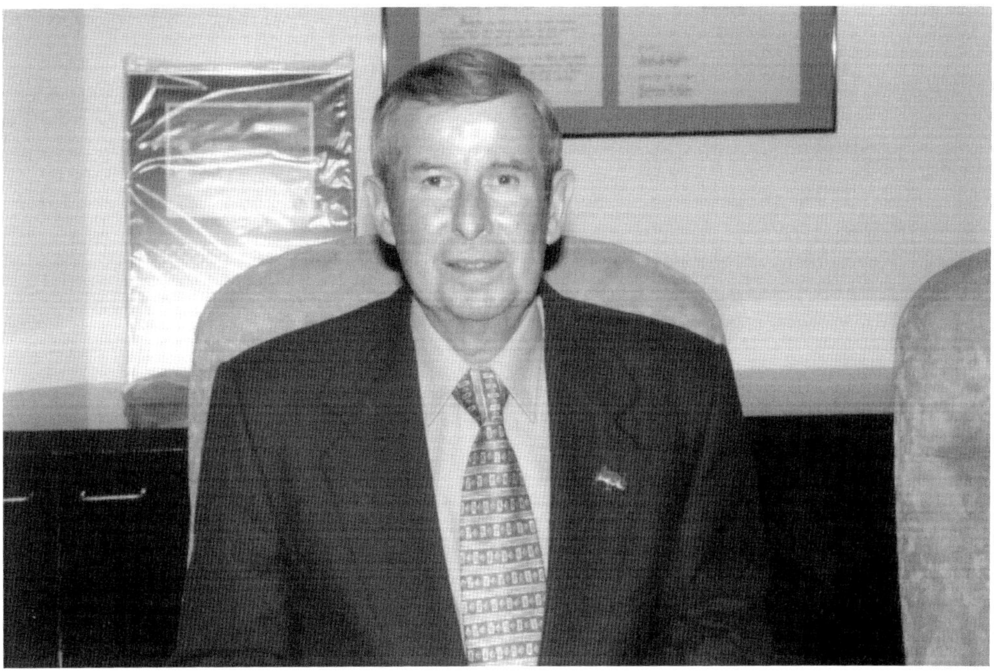

Don Carroll
Carroll is Alamogordo's longest-serving commissioner and mayor. His service started as an at-large commissioner from March 1982 to March 1984. He was mayor pro tem from March 1984 to January 1985 and then mayor from January 1985 to July 1987. He was out of office until his election as a district city commissioner in 1988, served in that position until 1992, and was mayor pro tem from 1992 to 1996. Carroll was then mayor from March 1996 to March 2008. An Air Force veteran, he spent 35 years in military research and development. (Courtesy Don Carroll.)

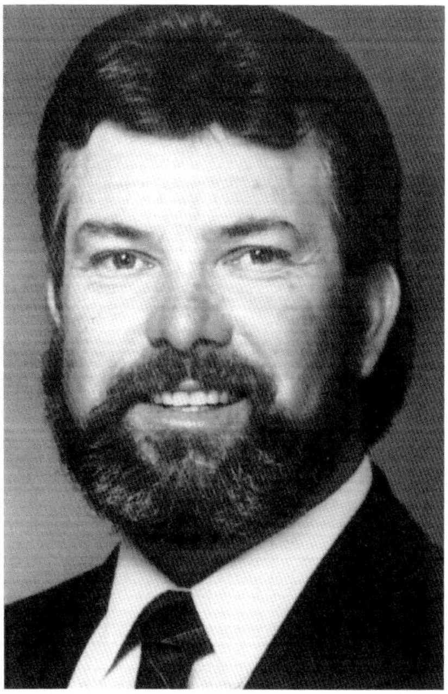

Ronny Rardin

Property rights were paramount when Rardin became an Otero County commissioner in 1993. He did not back down from confrontations with agencies such as the US Forest Service and face-offs with environmentalists and lawmakers in Washington, DC. Rardin served two terms, and he was again elected in 2008 and 2012. A man of great Christian faith, Rardin pastors Saving Grace Baptist Church. (Courtesy Ronny Rardin.)

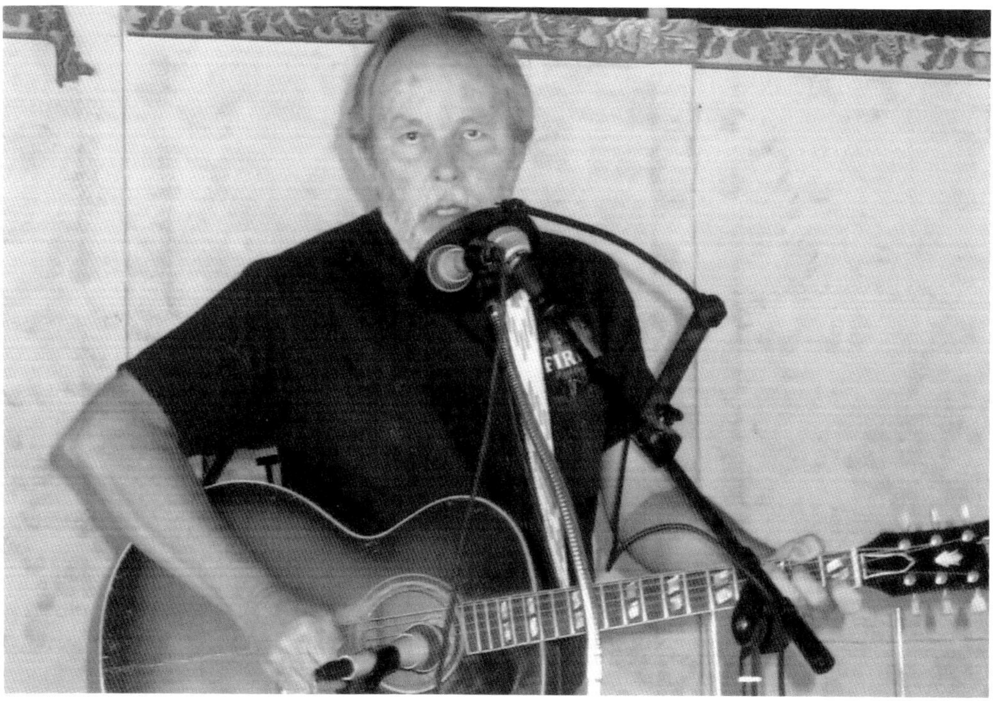

Michael Nivison

In the late 1990s, Nivison joined the battle against the federal government infringing on property and water rights in the West. A two-term county commissioner, his priority was maintaining New Mexico's custom and culture. Nivison testified in Washington, DC, and traveled throughout the country, advising other communities on similar issues. He is also a talented musician who has released his own songs on CD. (Courtesy Michael Shinabery.)

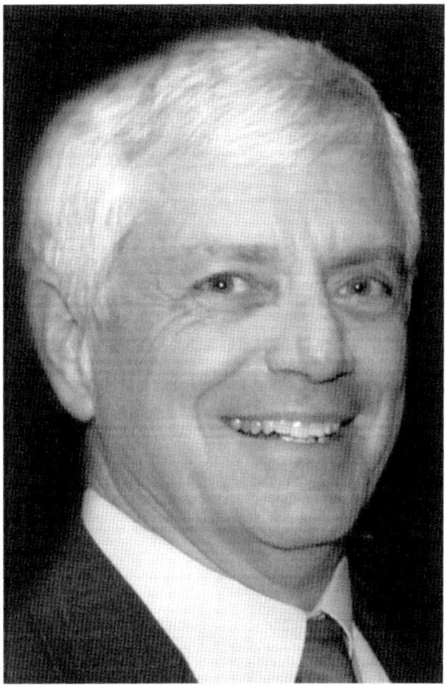

Ron Griggs
Griggs was only two years old when he came to Alamogordo. After college, he worked for his father, Jim Griggs, in construction, then in Denver, Colorado, and subsequently for Texaco in Midland, Texas. In 1994, Griggs and his wife, Joan, bought Alamogordo Title Company, which they owned until 2002. He has been an Alamogordo city commissioner, mayor, and is now a state senator. (Courtesy Griggs family.)

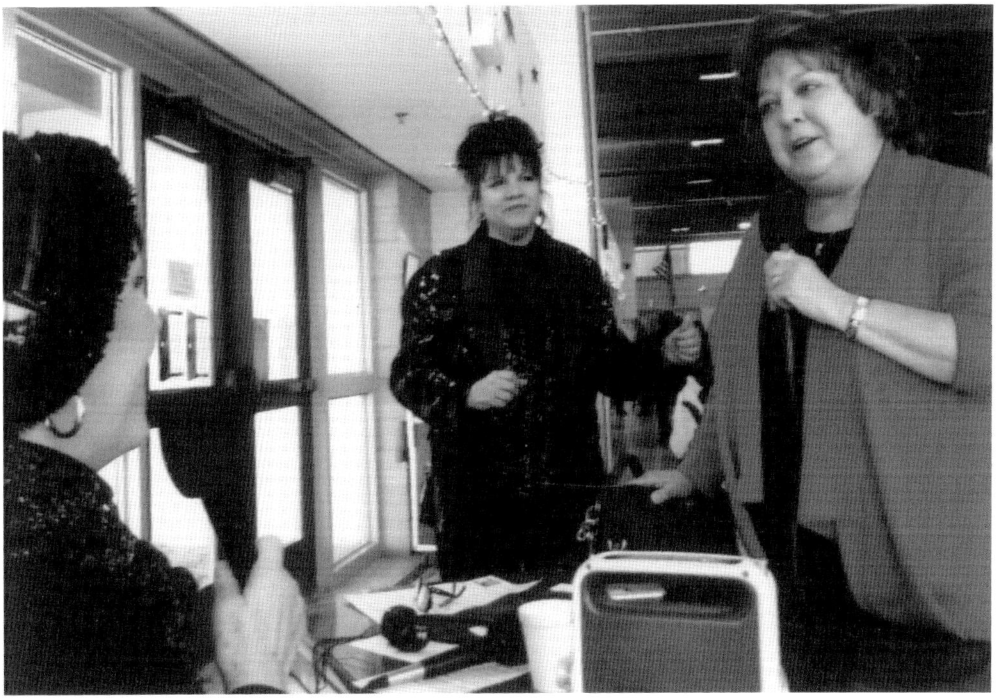

Dianna Duran
The first Republican in the job since 1928, Duran became New Mexico's top election official when she took the oath of office in January 2011 as the 24th secretary of state. She was reelected in 2014. Duran began as an Otero County deputy clerk before being elected clerk and then state senator. Here, Duran (right) is being interviewed on KRSY by Marcia Stirman (left) at the 2014 Legislative Prayer Breakfast. Joann Reynolds, Stirman's cohost, looks on. (Courtesy Michael Shinabery.)

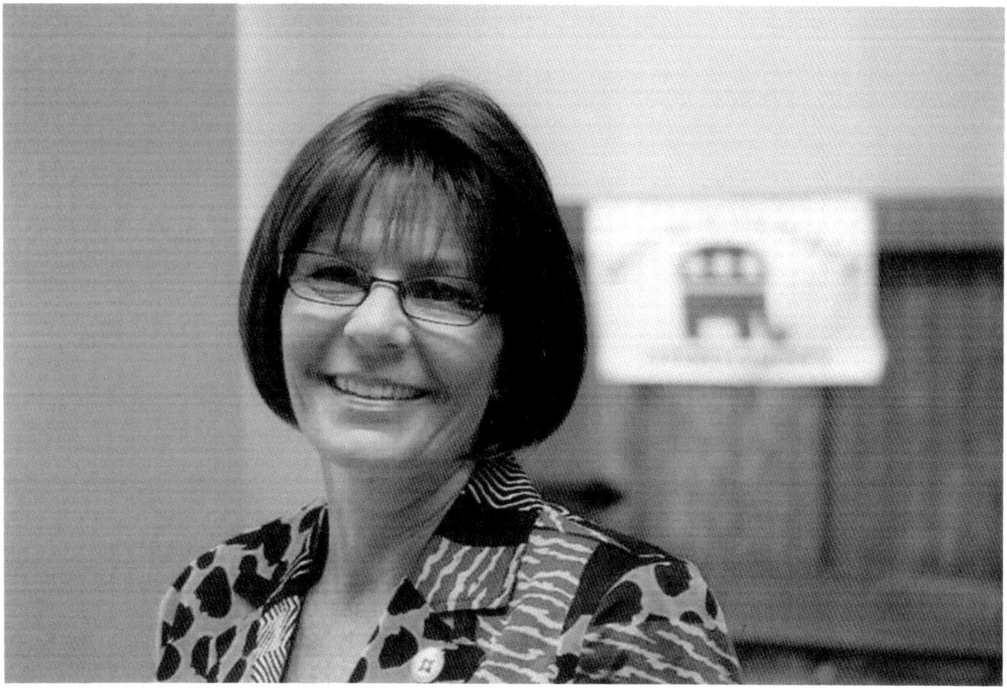

Yvette Herrell

After voters in 2010 elected Herrell the District 51 state representative, the Rio Grande Foundation soon named her the top woman legislator and number two overall. Her voting record reflects federalism, limited government, and conservative values. Herrell, a cofounder of the Balanced Budget Amendment Task Force and the Article V Caucus, is on the American Lands Council board. (Courtesy Yvette Herrell.)

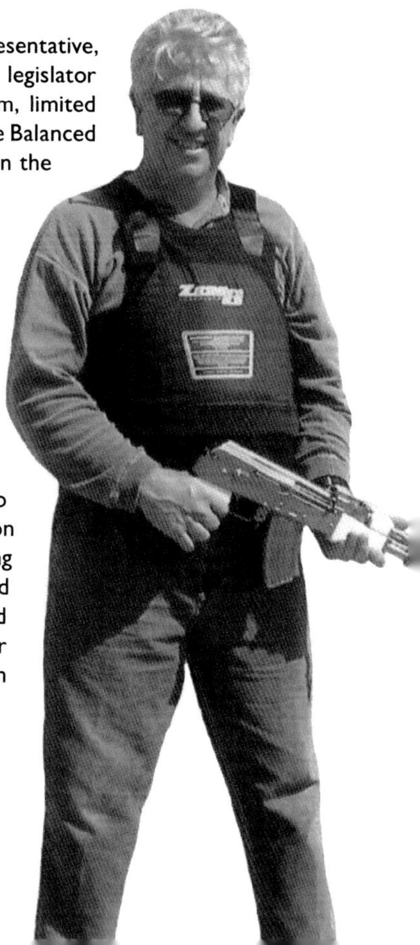

David Weitzel

When Saddam Hussein's regime fell, Weitzel, a former Otero County manager, went to Iraq to teach government reorganization and municipal operations. That meant holding classes on using electronics equipment, setting up a satellite Internet system and e-mail, public safety, and even sports and recreation. Weitzel said "teaching the rule and respect for law is the ultimate solution for their problems, but also the toughest and most patient solution to come." (Courtesy David Weitzel.)

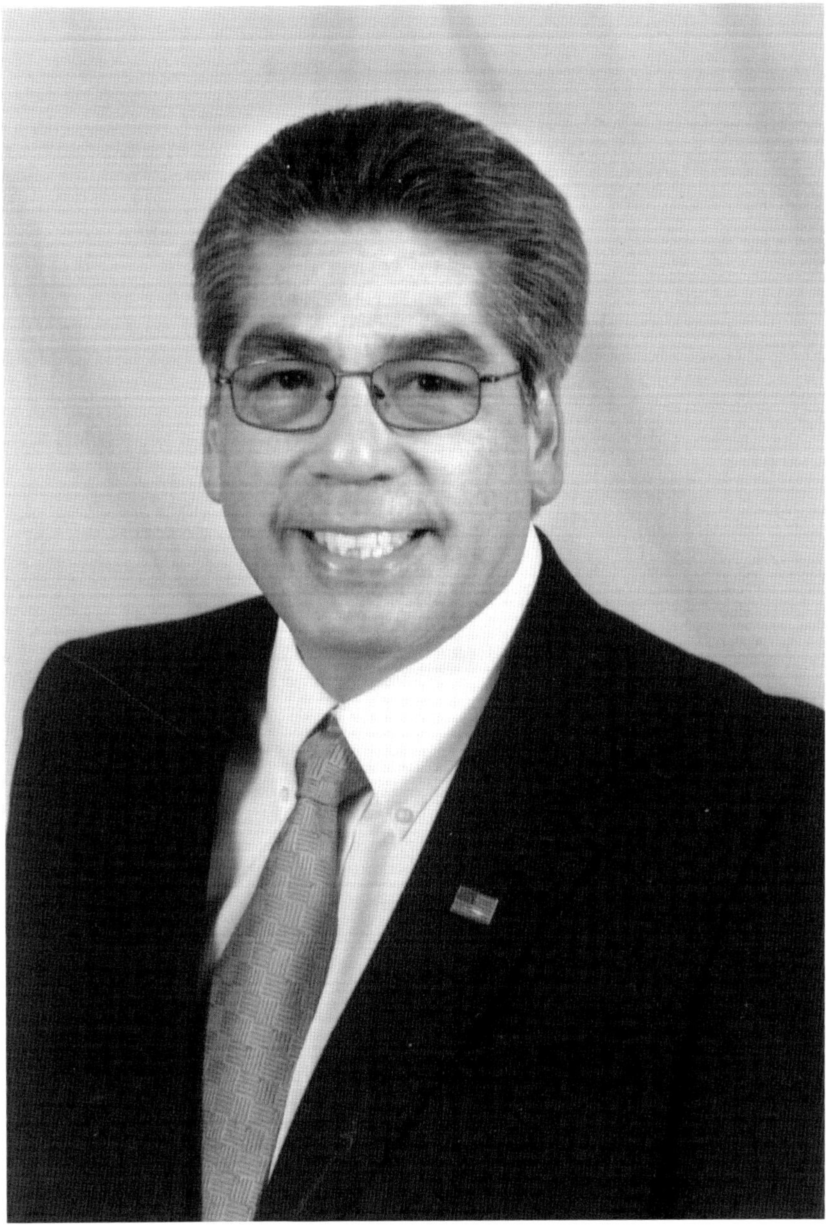

Manny Gonzales
Gonzales is Alamogordo's logistics expeditor when high-level Republicans visit. He was master of ceremonies for Pres. George W. Bush's two campaign appearances. He hosted Vice Presidents Dick Cheney and Dan Quayle; Senators Bob Dole, John McCain, and Pete Domenici; Representatives Steve Pearce and Heather Wilson; and Lt. Gov. John Sanchez. He was a member of Pearce's congressional staff, Sanchez's campaign director, and advisor to state legislators Maurice Hobson, Dianna Duran, Terry Marquardt, and Bill Burt. For more than a quarter century, Gonzales has been a successful insurance practitioner, currently affiliated with Charles, Garland & Harris. He has chaired the New Mexico Commission for the Blind and the Alamogordo High School Tiger Sports Boosters Club, and he was founding chair of Otero County Big Brothers/Big Sisters. (Courtesy Manny Gonzales.)

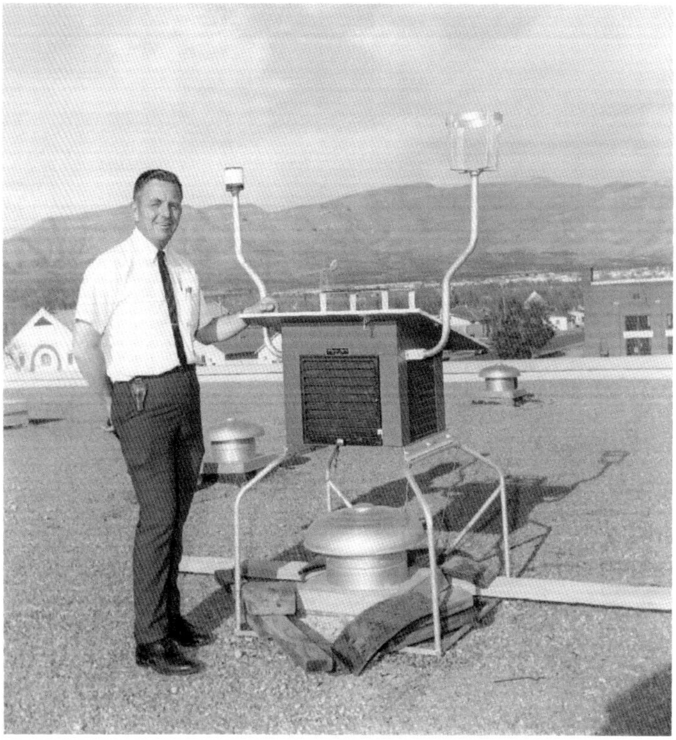

Fred Wood

The New Mexico Public Health Department officer for Otero County from 1968 to 1985, Wood was responsible for overseeing hazardous waste and ensuring water and air quality. In 1983, Wood cautioned against burying thousands of Atari ET games, which contained lead solder, in the landfill. Those games were dug up in 2014 in a nationally publicized event. In 1970, Wood ordered buried 10,000 pounds of grain that had been tainted with organic methylmercury. Members of a local family had died after eating hogs that ate the grain. (Courtesy Helen Wood.)

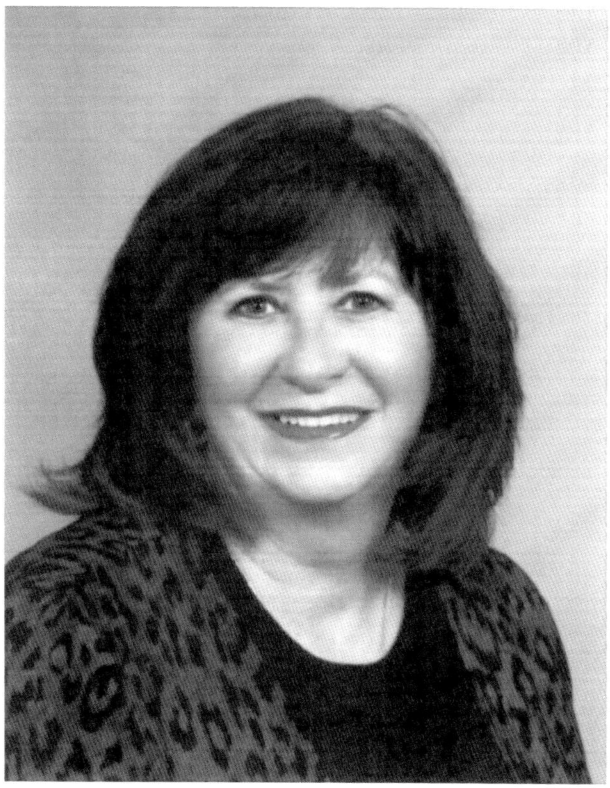

Nadia Sikes

When Sikes and her husband came to Holloman Air Force Base in 2004, she plunged into community service. A former marketer with a Fortune 500 company, Sikes was elected city commissioner, and she promotes community activities on her KRSY AM radio program. She has sat on the boards of the Center of Protective Environment, the Public Library Foundation, Friends of the Library, CAPPED, and the NAACP. (Courtesy Nadia Sikes.)

CHAPTER SIX

They Made a Difference

Veterinarian Dr. G.L. Wiley arrived at his office in July 2004 to find that one of his employees had brought in a sick fawn found sitting in the middle of the road. Wiley called the New Mexico Department of Game and Fish and treated the animal. When the officer arrived, Wiley refused to identify the employee, so the officer handcuffed the doctor and carted him off to jail. The charge was unlawful possession of a deer and obstructing an officer. The district attorney for the 12th Judicial District, Scot Key, declined to prosecute. The officer attended counseling on how to better interact within the community.

Alamogordo residents make a difference in a lot of ways. Sometimes, that means solving a problem; other times, it means highlighting a problem. There is no lack of activists who are willing to step up and tackle an issue, whether it is social, religious, political, or educational.

Some saw fellow residents going without basic necessities and acted to provide sustenance. Others encountered what their belief system told them was wrong and set about righting it. Ken Nicholson and Denise Lang founded Peace and Justice of La Luz. Their public protests unite the like-minded and publicly draw attention to issues, ranging from what they feel are unjust wars to intrusions on personal rights.

In the mid-1990s, in reaction to what many called Pres. Bill Clinton's "War on the West," grassroots groups in Alamogordo sprang up and grew up. People for the West and People for Otero County were active. Their burgeoning memberships were fed up with such actions as the Mexican spotted owl "endangered" listing in the Lincoln National Forest. These organizations declared that the endangered designation severely curtailed logging, cost jobs, eventually shut down the industry, and contributed to overgrowth and fire danger.

Dr. John Jones, a busy family physician, mentored youth as a Boy Scout Scoutmaster. Because of his support, many achieved their Eagle rank.

Maude Rathgeber, who founded the New Mexico chapter of the conservative Eagle Forum, staged annual Sovereignty and Your Rights Seminars. She brought national figures to Alamogordo to speak, including Alabama chief justice Roy Moore (the "Ten Commandments Judge"), Congresswoman Helen Chenoweth-Hage, Henry Lamb of the Environmental Conservation Organization, and the father of Michael New, the American soldier who refused to serve under a UN commander.

A common thread runs through all those who step up, whether young or old, no matter their personal beliefs: they are selfless with their time, energetic with their actions, and do not seek a pat on the back.

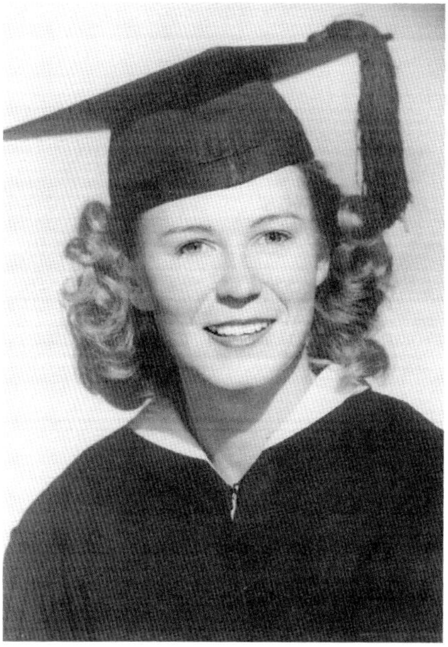

Maude Oliver Rathgeber

After earning her bachelor's degree in music education from UCLA in 1946, Rathgeber taught music in Alamogordo Public Schools. Then, 12 years later, she left to marry the boy she had not paid a bit of attention to in school. But by that time, Jack Rathgeber was a handsome naval aviator. A Democrat, she was opposed to the Equal Rights Amendment and reregistered as a Republican, then founded Eagle Forum–New Mexico. In the mid-1990s, after 20 years of Rathgeber promoting conservatism, registered Republicans exceeded Democrats for the first time in Otero County history. Rathgeber helped start the Community Concert Association, which brought artists such as pianists and recording artists Ferrante and Teicher to Alamogordo, and the Alamogordo Public Library, where she spearheaded the Children's Storybook Wall. She also served on the State Library Board and once rode the bookmobile. Rathgeber is shown here on her UCLA graduation day. (Courtesy Rathgeber family.)

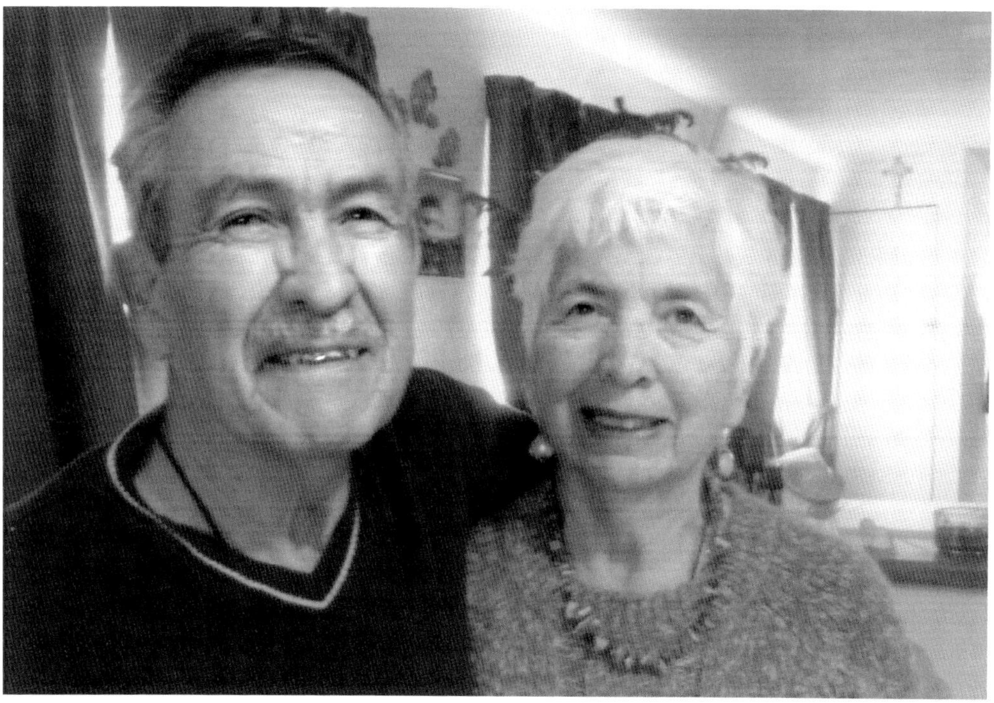

The Estradas

Pete and Virginia Estrada's lifetime of volunteering was a positive example to their seven children. He was a postal carrier who coached Little League and Babe Ruth baseball. Virginia was a receptionist for Murray Morgan at the *Alamogordo Daily News* and then for Billie Holder when he bought the business. Aubrey Dunn was her supervisor. The Estradas have given time over many years, as well, to the Veterans Administration, Zia School, New Mexico School for the Blind and Visually Impaired, and the Alamogordo Senior Center. (Courtesy Michael Shinabery.)

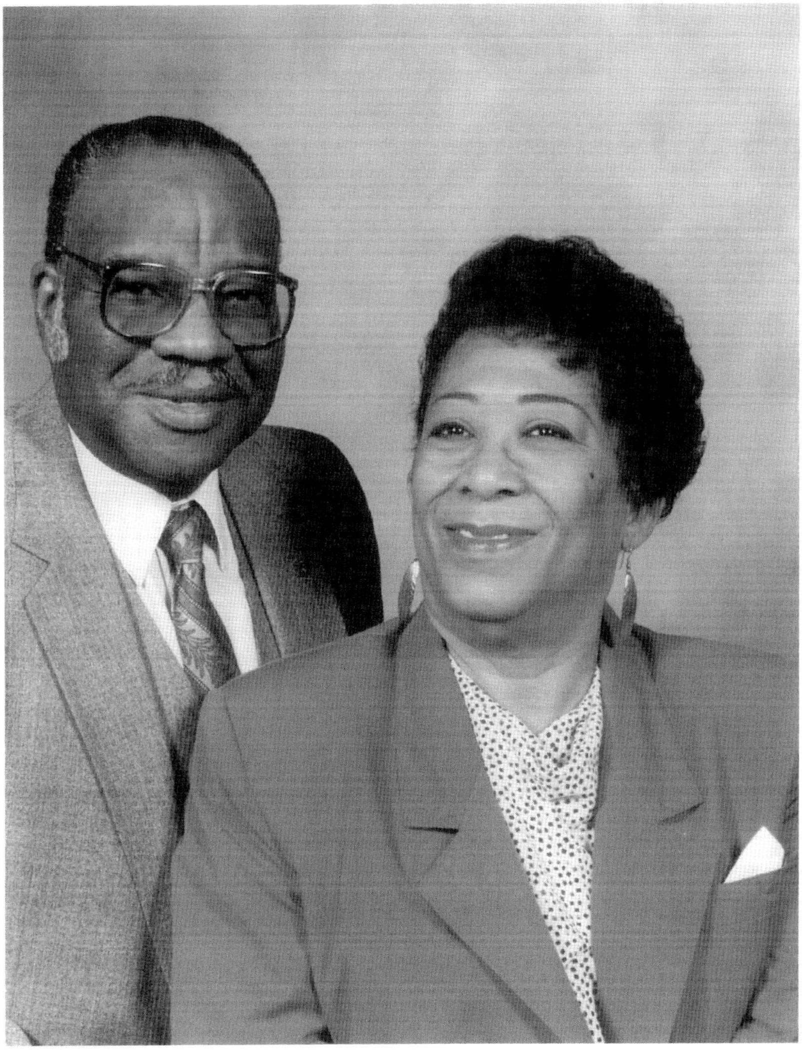

The Scotts

Isaiah was a senior master sergeant when, in 1971, he retired at Holloman Air Force Base. Before long, he was the new guidance counselor at Alamogordo Public Schools, then director of the guidance and counseling department, and he became a counselor at New Mexico State University–Alamogordo. His community activity included service on the board of directors and as president for the New Mexico chapter of the American Lung Association and the New Mexico School Counselors Association. He was on the NAACP board and was commander of American Legion Post 34. He also published articles on the Buffalo Soldiers in New Mexico.

Johnnie was the first paid teacher and director at the Zia School and Therapy Center. She taught at Holloman Elementary and Buena Vista Elementary, was principal of North Elementary in Alamogordo, and completed her career teaching the Gifted Program at Alamogordo Public Schools and Holloman. Her many honors include the New Mexico Governor's award for Outstanding New Mexico Women and Business and Professional Women's Woman of the Year. Among her community service was Black History chairperson, City of Alamogordo and New Hope Baptist Church, and the Zia Girl Scout Council Board of Governors. Johnnie also authored several articles on Southern New Mexico pioneers. (Courtesy Scott family.)

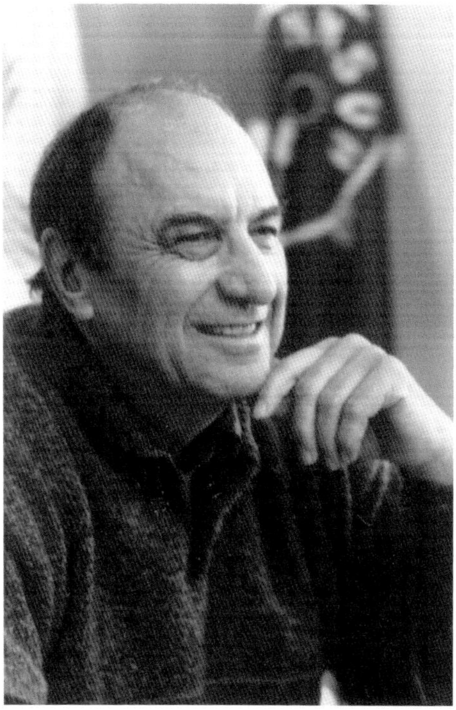

Jerry Watkins
In 1973, Watkins became superintendent of the New Mexico School for the Blind and Visually Impaired. In a story on his 1996 retirement, the *Alamogordo Daily News* said he "set academic standards of innovation and superiority that are now in use across the nation." Watkins fought to remove obstacles for his students. On campus, his constant companions were his beloved Great Danes, Golden Bear and Oso. Dr. David Townsend, in his eulogy at Watkins's funeral, pointed out Watkins's faith that life works out for the best. Watkins's many honors and professional memberships attest to the success of that belief. (Courtesy Alamogordo Chamber of Commerce.)

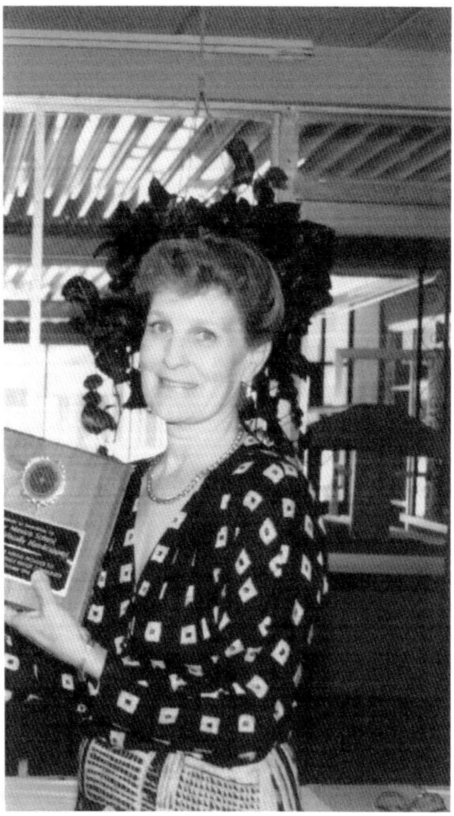

Barbara McDonald
When her youngest daughter was born blind, McDonald began substitute teaching at the New Mexico School for the Blind and Visually Impaired. In 1970, she became a full-time teacher, and in 1985, Gov. Toney Anaya appointed her to the Governor's Committee on Concerns of the Handicapped. When she retired in 1998 as assistant superintendent, McDonald wrote *A Tapestry of Time: The History of the School for the Visually Handicapped* for the school's 2003 centennial. Named a Citizen of the Year by the Alamogordo Chamber of Commerce, she became New Mexico's first female Rotarian in 1989, after Rotary International voted to admit women. (Courtesy McDonald family.)

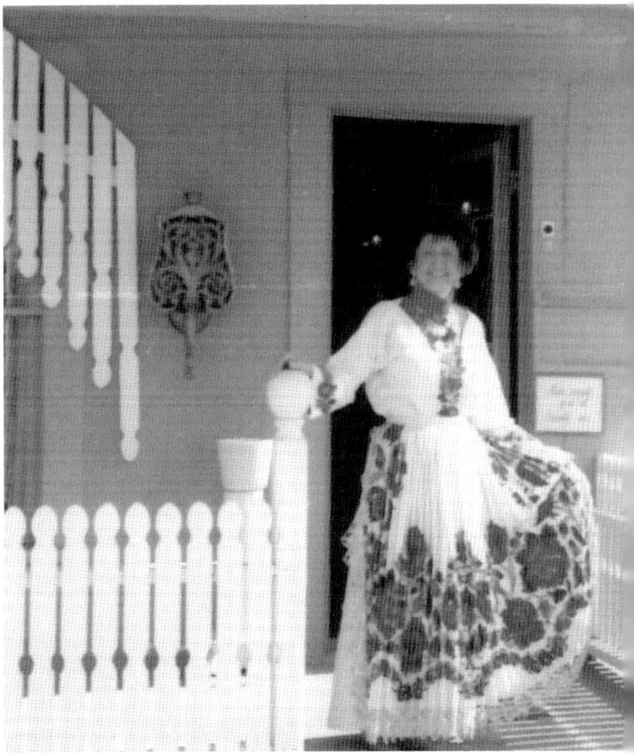

Millicent Shyne

Shyne was 65 when she bought and restored houses along Ohio Street. These unique structures would have been demolished. She saved Eugene Manlove Rhodes's home, and, in another structure, opened The Serbian Peasant (pictured), an antiques shop named in honor of her heritage. Shyne's father, an inventor, brought the family from Canada to St. Louis in 1920. She chronicled those delightful years in her autobiography, *2943*. During World War II, Shyne was a "Rosie the Riveter" at McDonnell Aircraft. She came to Alamogordo in 1957 with her family. The next year, she and Laura Lee Borgeson founded Gerald Champion Memorial Hospital's Auxiliary, while Shyne's husband was administrator. Later, they opened Shyne Realty, currently Westsource Realty, operated by their son Michael. Shyne died in 2010 at age 95. (Courtesy Michael Shyne.)

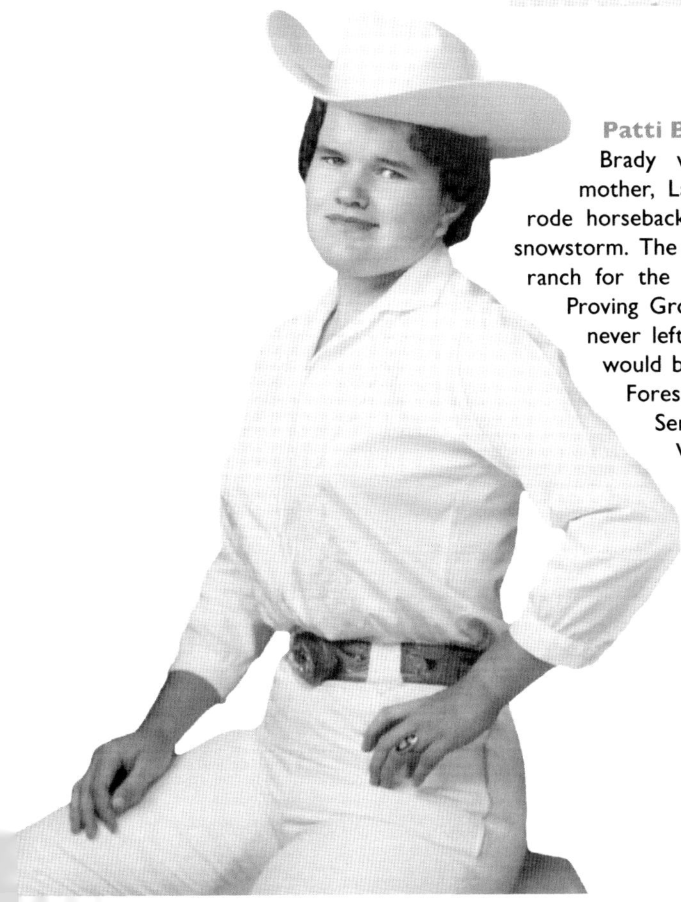

Patti Brady

Brady was still in the womb of her mother, Laura Burris, when, in 1942, Laura rode horseback to herd cattle through a raging snowstorm. The government had taken the family's ranch for the war effort to build White Sands Proving Ground. Cowboy custom and culture never left Brady. A teenage rodeo star, she would be a postmistress, work for the US Forest Service, and found the Cloudcroft Senior Center. Her passion is telling the White Sands ranchers' story so that their sacrifices are never forgotten. (Courtesy Patti Brady.)

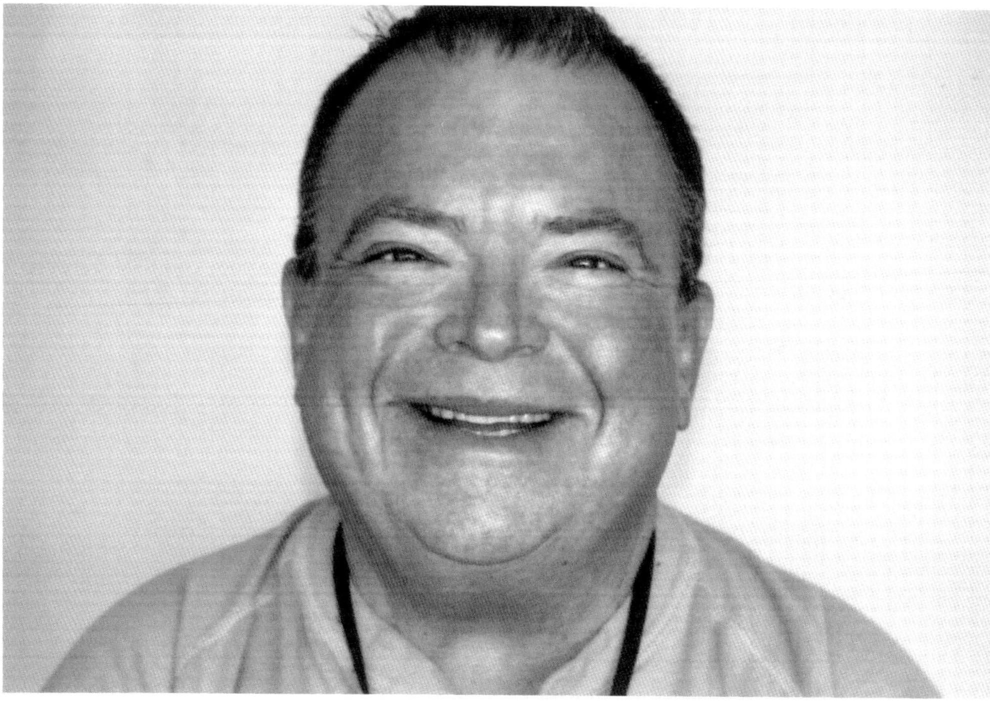

Ronny Diaz

Abused and neglected youth have stable homes thanks to Diaz, parent and foster recruiter for the New Mexico Children, Youth, and Families Department. Diaz joined the Peace Corps in 1979 to connect with his Latino roots in Central America. He studied soil conservation to teach to farmers, and he met his future wife there. Returning to Alamogordo, Diaz, who had been a disc jockey at age 15 on KINN, was KPSA's newsman and talk-show host until 1993. His mother, Evelyn Diaz, hosted KPSA's *Senior Scene*, addressing issues pertinent to older residents. (Courtesy Ronny Diaz.)

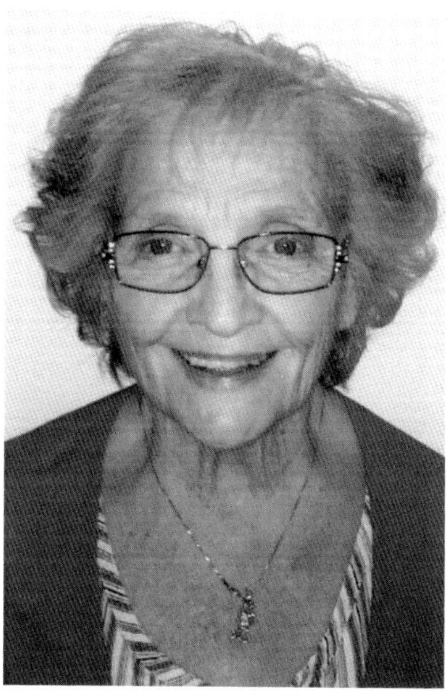

Barbara House

When House's daughter Johnietta was diagnosed with autism, there were no facilities for the developmentally disabled. So House, along with eight other mothers, started Zia Therapy Center. She drove the bus, helped start Zia's adult services, wrote grants to provide caregivers with a respite, and served on New Mexico's Association of Retarded Citizens. House retired after 54 years. Doctors said that Johnietta would not live past her teen years. She died in 2015 at age 58. (Courtesy House family.)

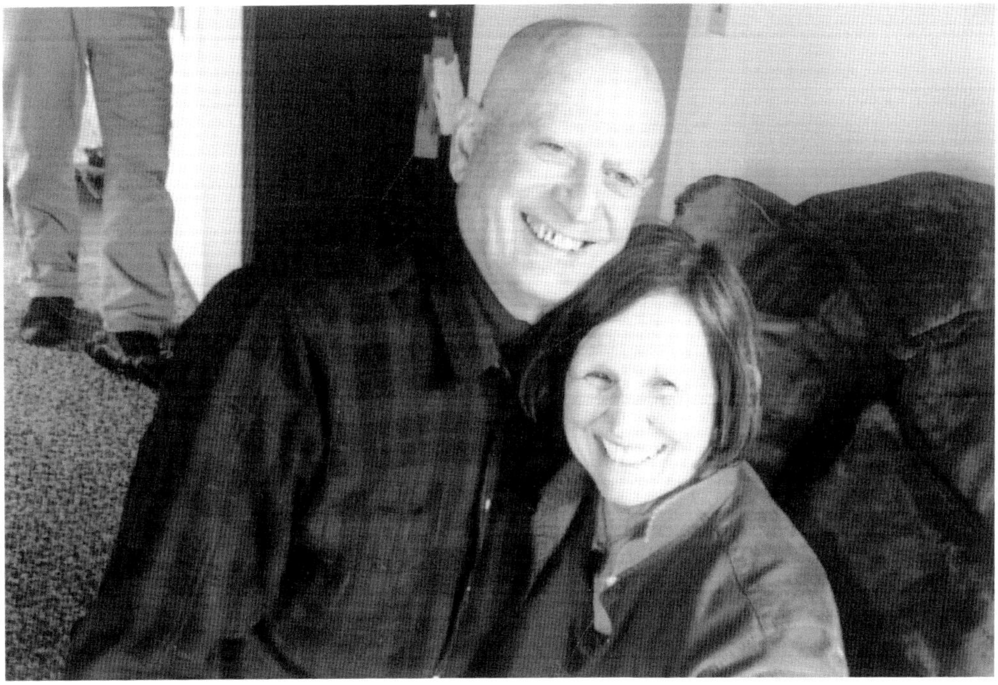

Jake and Carol Meyer
New Mexico State University wanted someone to run a program, Children in Need of Supervision, in 1982 and contracted with Amigos de los Niños, which hired Carol Meyer. Her husband, Jake, joined the next year. The couple, more interested in serving, changed the name to Children in Need of Services (CHINS) and then formed a nonprofit in 1986. Under CHINS, the Meyers started Big Brothers–Big Sisters, the Court Appointed Special Advocates, the Full House daycare, and a program to educate children on the dangers of tobacco. Jake died in 2015. (Courtesy Meyer family.)

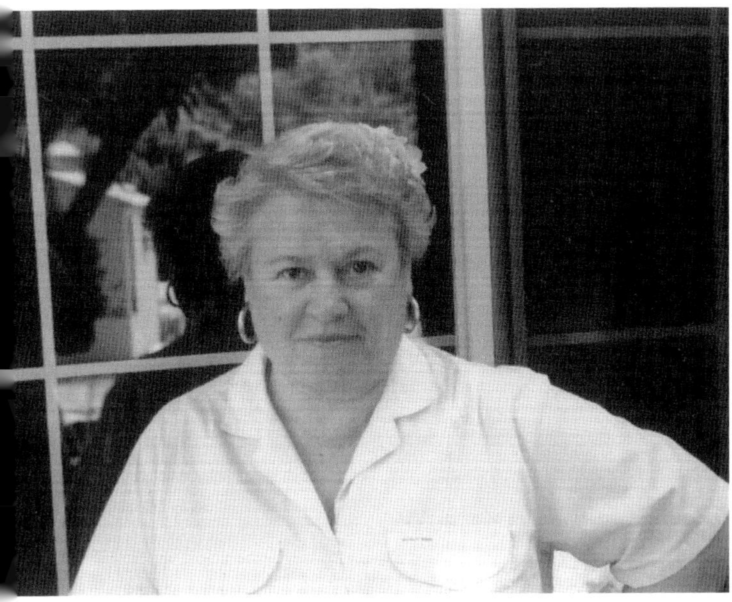

Betty Boles Johnson
Johnson was the daughter of Luther Boles, who provided water to early Holloman Air Force Base before the government confiscated his land and who founded Boles Acres. Without that water, Holloman might have ceased to exist. In 1981, when Betty learned that Diana, Princess of Wales, was expecting, she sewed a quilt. Diana's lady-in-waiting responded with a personal thank you note written on royal letterhead. (Courtesy Ron Johnson.)

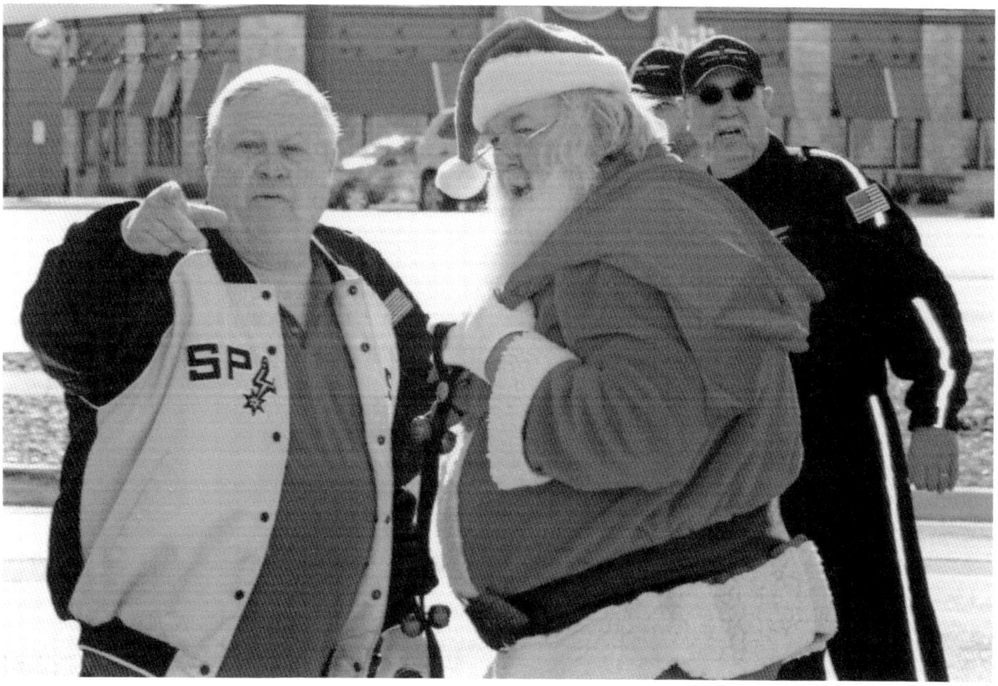

Wally Anderson

As a rookie policeman answering domestic calls during Christmas, Anderson (left) realized that children in those homes would not see any presents. In 1981, Anderson started Keystone Kops as the local Toys for Tots. Officers at peer agencies quickly signed on and were soon delivering gifts to homes. Now retired, Anderson raises funds and prepares for the next Christmas Eve, when youth arrive at the Willy Estrada Memorial Civic Center eager for Santa (Ed Thomas, right) to hand them a gift. (Used with the permission of Wally Anderson.)

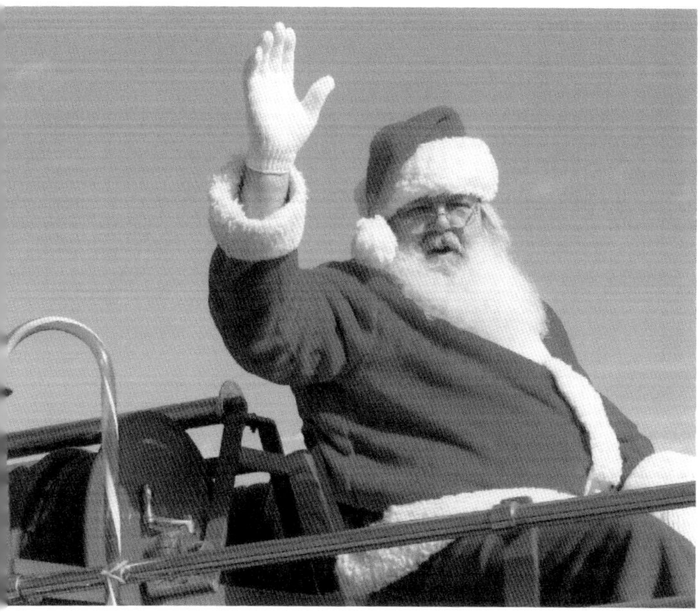

Ed Thomas

Kids around Alamogordo often catch a glimpse of Santa Claus throughout the year, because Thomas is St. Nick. Come Christmas, bedecked in a red coat with white fur trim and traditional stocking cap, he arrives at his appointed locations on fire trucks and in helicopters. In preparation for Christmas Eve, Thomas also sits behind radio microphones, taking calls from excited children. (Courtesy Ed Thomas.)

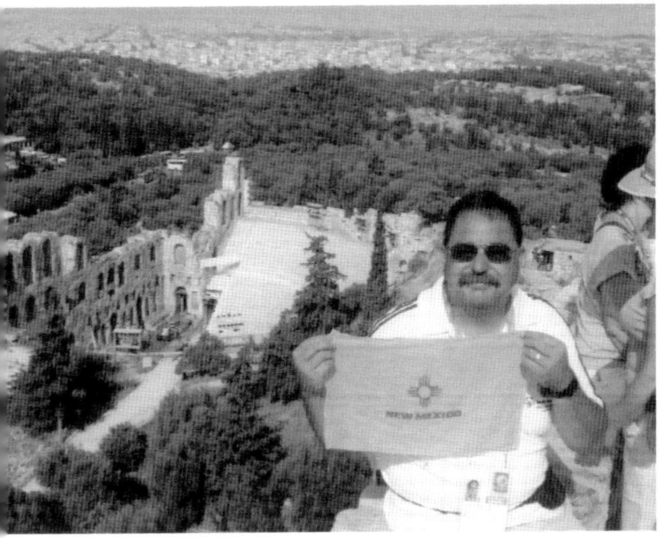

Charles Gonzales
In 2005, Gonzales became Special Olympics representative for the Otero County Sheriff's Department. The torch relay only ran from Alamogordo to Holloman Air Force Base until, as the South Region Torch Run coordinator, Gonzales expanded it through Ruidoso and on to Chaparral. In 2011, Gonzales ran the final leg in Athens, Greece, as New Mexico's representative. Special Olympics presented him with its highest honor in 2013: the Larry Willard Flame of Hope Award. (Courtesy Charles Gonzales.)

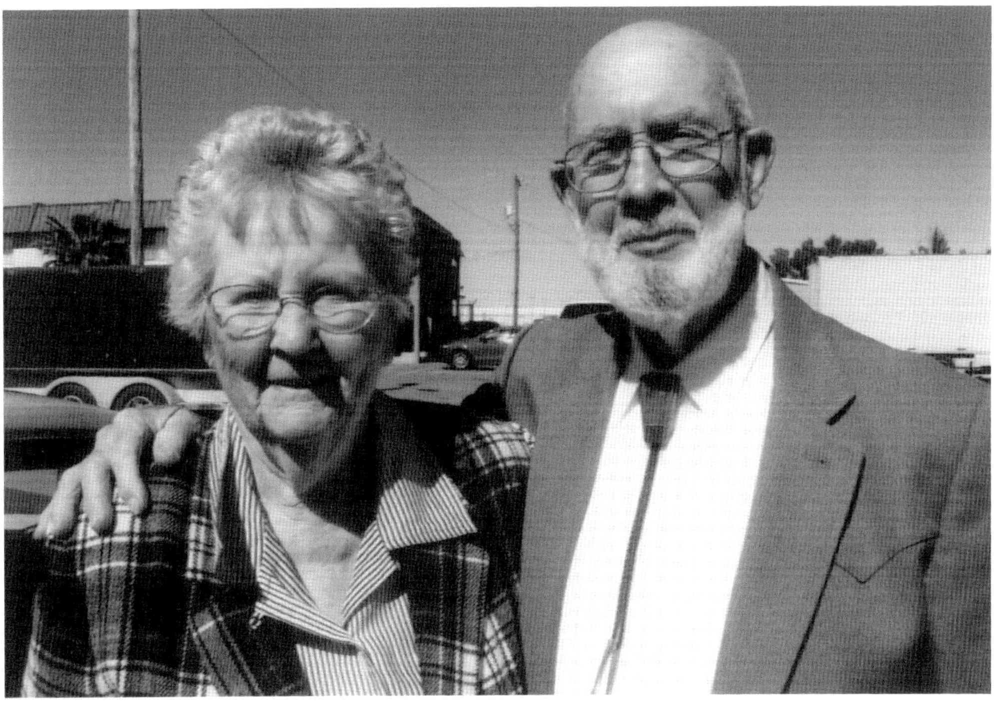

The Wards
Al and Charlene Ward were retired when they felt God calling them to Juarez, Mexico. In the late 1990s, they began making weekly trips to the orphanage Casa de Libertad. They have carried food and supplies to more than 100 orphans whose families cannot care for them or whose parents were killed in the drug wars. They only missed one scheduled trip, on September 11, 2001, but made the drive two days later. (Courtesy Michael Shinabery.)

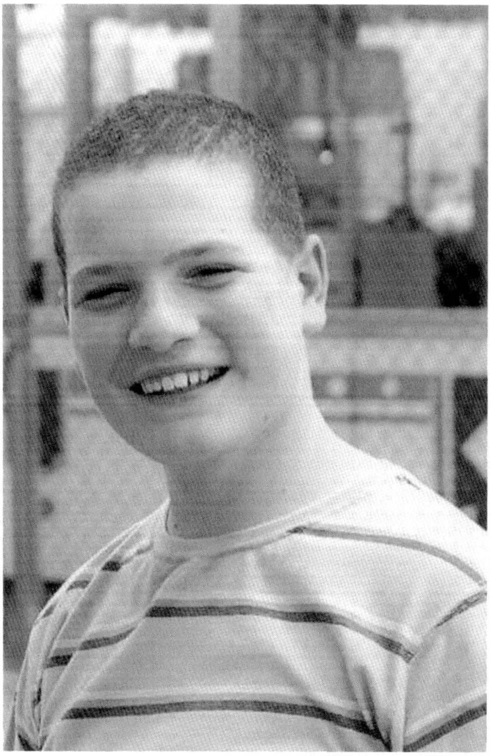

Gatlin Clark

Clark was only 11 in 2008 when he was diagnosed with Ewing's sarcoma. To save his life, doctors amputated a leg. Even with a prosthetic, he hoped to play football. When the cancer returned in 2009, Clark had his stem cells harvested for a bone marrow transplant. The next year, he got the worst news: medicine had no cure for the aggressive cancer. Clark, a dirt-bike rider, bravely made a difference before he died, starting Ride for the Cure. The annual event has raised $36,000 for organizations that help New Mexican children with cancer. (Courtesy Judy McGinnis.)

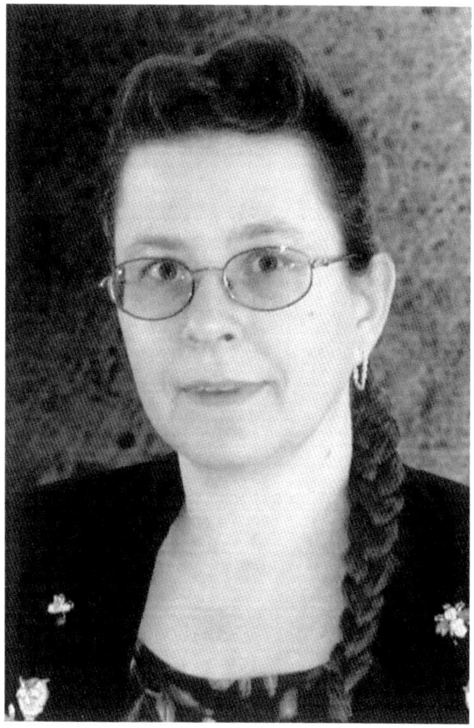

Teresa Van Winkle

When Van Winkle's sister was diagnosed with cancer in 1996, Teresa envisioned CAPPED (Cancer Awareness Prevalence Prevention and Early Detection) and a world without cancer and other preventable diseases. She wrote grants and touted her hopes to service clubs, finally raising the funds to open in 2003. CAPPED offers educational seminars, sun-safe hats for elementary-school students, and integrative health care services. (Used with the permission of Teresa Van Winkle.)

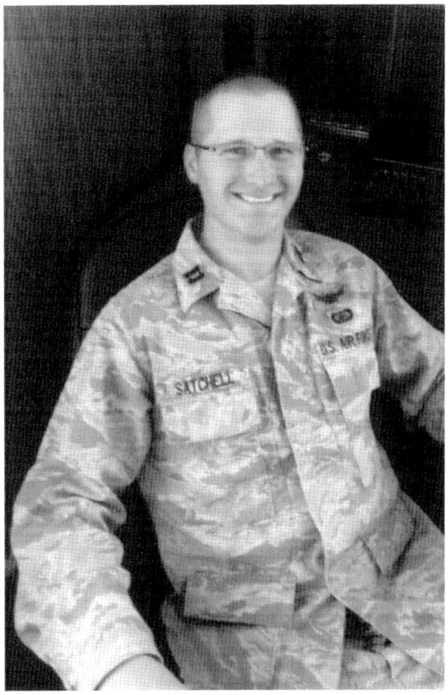

Capt. Matt Satchell

Satchell came to Alamogordo from Wright-Patterson Air Force Base in Dayton, Ohio. There, as an award-winning STEM fellow, he wrote curriculum and guest-lectured in the community's active STEM program (Science, Technology, Engineering, Math). Arriving at the Holloman Air Force Base High Speed Test Track, as deputy chief of engineering, he started OteroSTEM to provide mentoring, equipment, and funding for robotics competitions. He also brokered a STEM partnership between Holloman and Alamogordo Public Schools. (Courtesy Matt Satchell.)

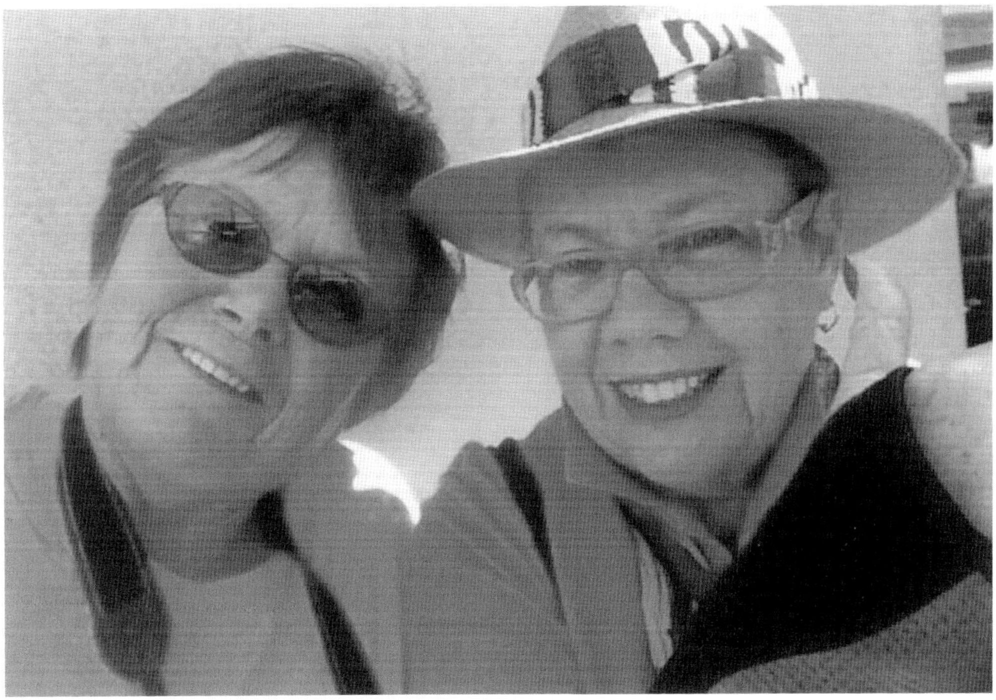

Lisa Blevins

In 2010, Blevins (left), an avid quilter, befriended Pam Holland (right) via the Internet. Blevins soon invited the world-renowned Australian quilter, photographer, artist, and author to Alamogordo. Holland now returns annually to host First National Bank's Southern New Mexico Festival of Quilts, which has raised more than $50,000 for local youth organizations. (Courtesy Pam Holland.)

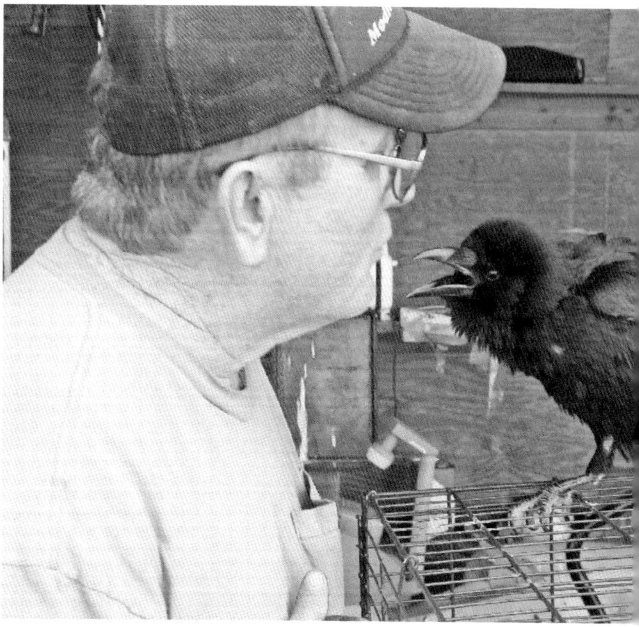

Tom Moore
Moore's Trading Post is popular among tourists. Crowds came to his gun and rattlesnake shows to see handlers crawl into sleeping bags with rattlesnakes. In 2001, federal agents arrested Moore. An undercover officer had befriended him a year earlier and eventually asked to buy a World War II machine gun. After the sale, agents battered down the doors, looking for underground tunnels that an informant said were rife with guns. There were none. Moore pleaded, was eventually released, and returned to the business. The raven seen here, which Moore named Igor, showed up one day and, for months, was his constant companion. (Courtesy Michael Shinabery.)

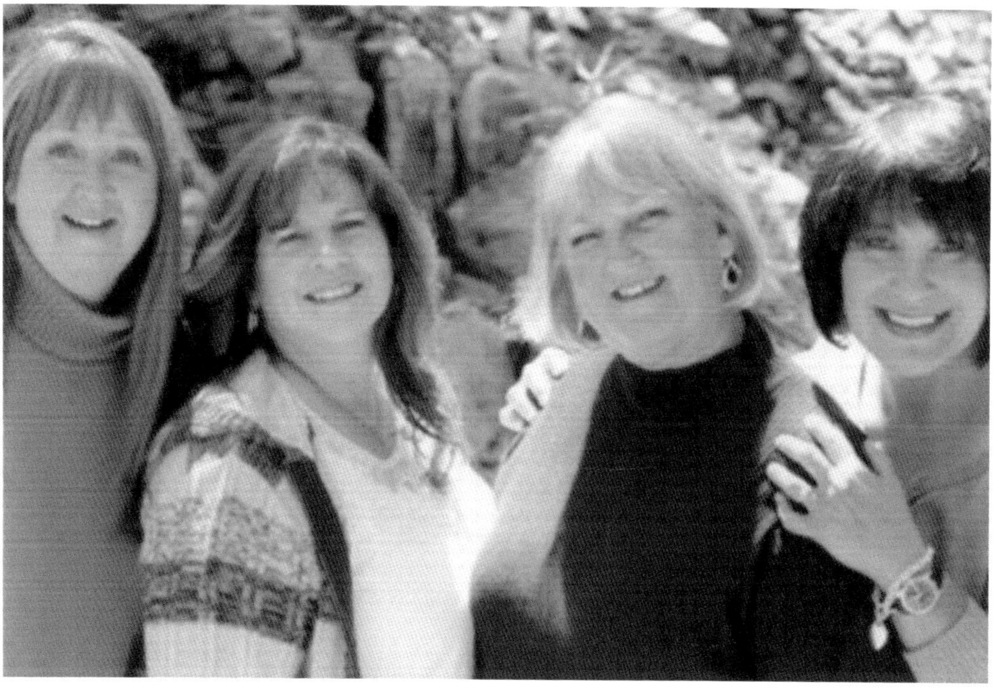

The Handmaidens
These women were members of a church choir when the pastor greeted them with, "How are the handmaidens of the Lord today?" Carla Thompson (right) thought that was a perfect group name. More than a decade and a half later, the Handmaidens continue to lift up the name of Jesus through worship in song. They have released the CDs *Wall of Fire* and *Your Presence for Christmas*. The members are, from left to right, Jeannine Oechsner, Samantha Parsons, Eileen Soffera, and Thompson. (Courtesy Carla Thompson.)

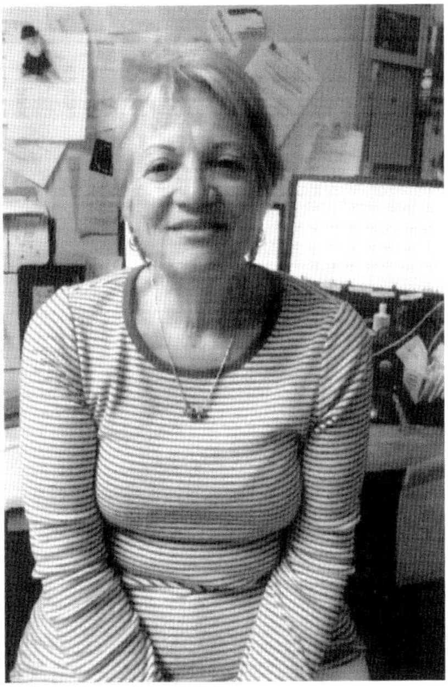

Dawn Provencher

She was Academy del Sol's counselor, social worker, and teacher of life. Students at the nontraditional high school might be single moms or completing court-ordered community service. Provencher helped them achieve academically and personally. She kept tabs on their home life and friends, was a trusted ear, and involved them in Optimist Club activities. Her satisfaction was knowing that their future was brighter. (Courtesy Michael Shinabery.)

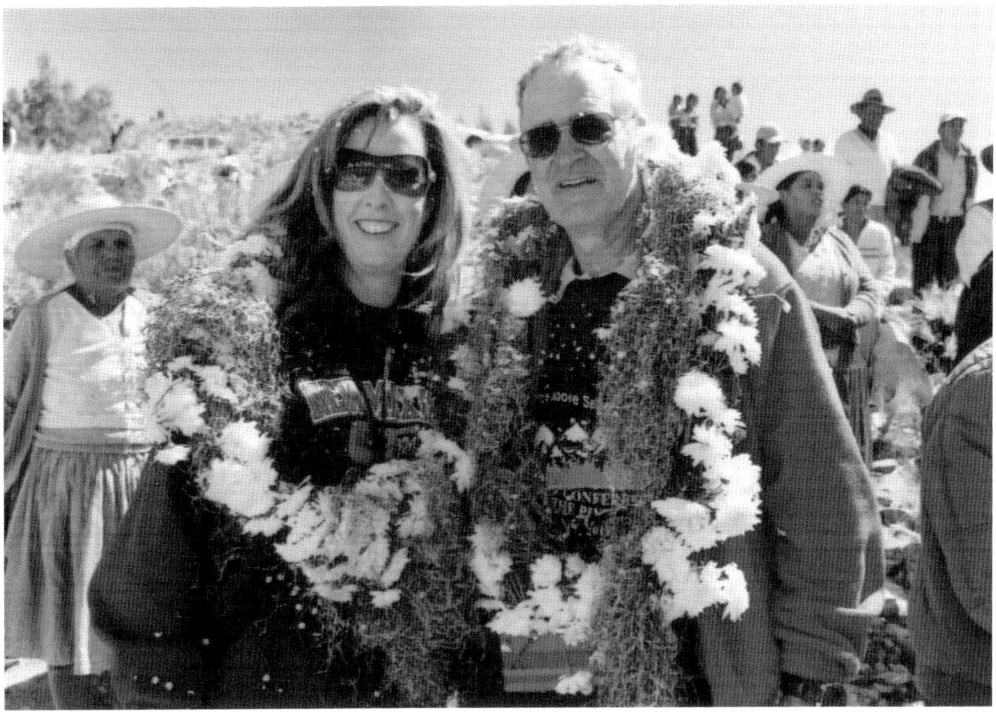

Norm Arnold and Robin French

When Norm Arnold and Robin French heard of Bridges to Prosperity, a program encouraging Rotarians to partner with engineers to build bridges in third-world countries, both began traveling throughout Rotary District 5520 asking others to be involved. French also writes Rotary Foundation Global Grants to purchase project materials. They have worked on-site in several countries. Here, they are in Bolivia, at the Herrera Cancha Bridge celebration. (Courtesy Norm Arnold.)

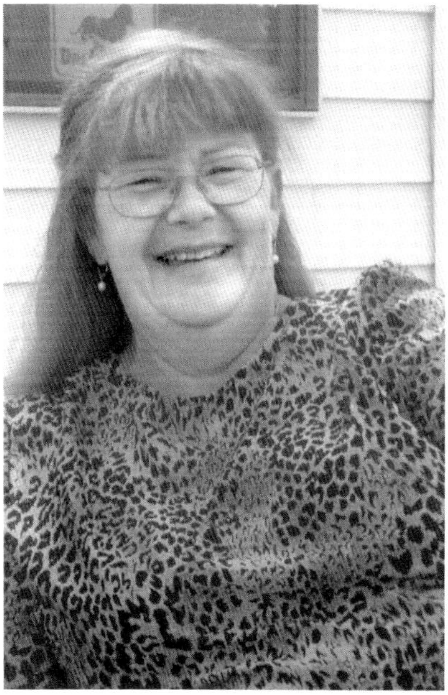

Debbie Raymond

Raymond speaks out for the handicapped, ensuring that the City of Alamogordo adheres to the Americans with Disabilities Act. Raymond, who suffers from multiple sclerosis, arrived in Alamogordo in 1999; three weeks later, she was on the mayor's committee for the disabled. She educated the community with her monthly newspaper column and KRSY radio program, both titled *Dialogue on Disability*. Her radio cohost was Robert Hawkins. (Courtesy Michael Shinabery.)

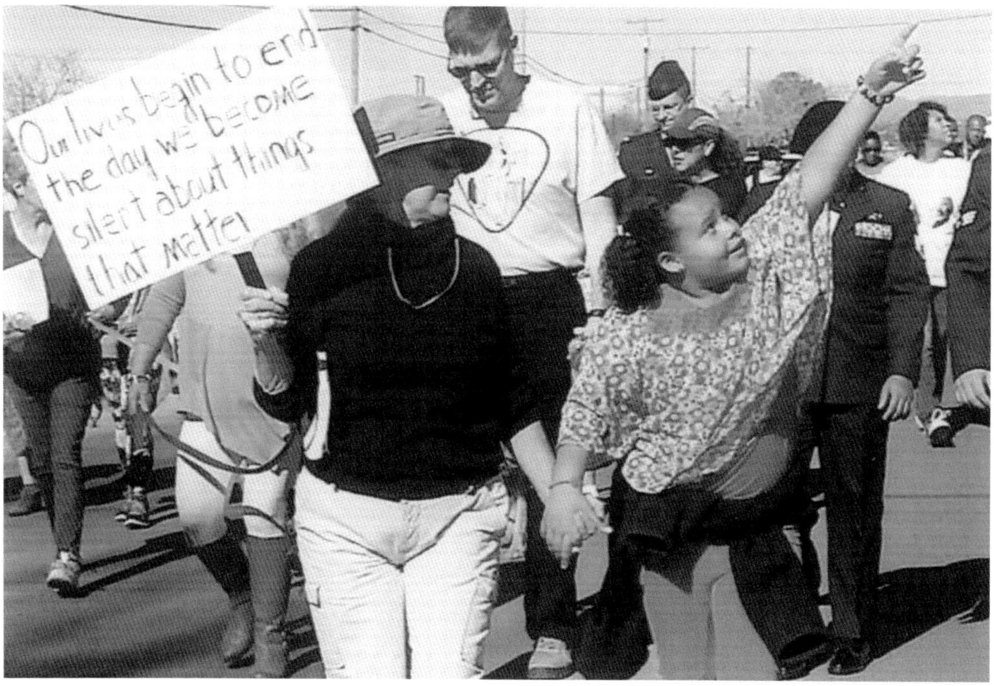

Denise Lang

Lang (carrying sign) made her stand against war when her late husband came home from Vietnam without his legs. She is a member of Peace and Justice of La Luz, cofounded with Ken Nicholson, whose liberal activism was born while working in social democratic Germany. Their public rallies call for an end to war and the war on drugs; the preservation of women's reproductive rights; and the fair treatment of undocumented residents. Otero County assessor Steve Boyle is seen behind Lang, who holds Kimora Riley's hand. (Used with permission of Denise Lang; photograph by Ann Bagby.)

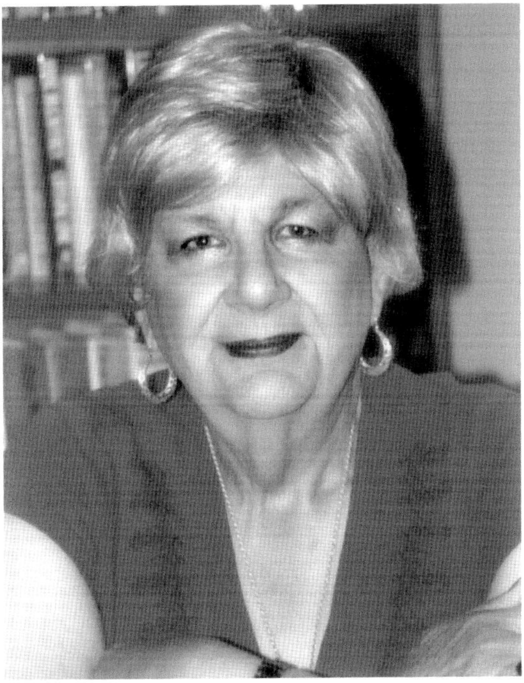

Rudy Clarke

A cross-dresser who has been taunted and snickered at, Clarke knows discrimination firsthand. In 2002, Gov. Bill Richardson appointed him to the Human Rights Commission. He travels New Mexico, adjudicating charges of workplace civil rights violations. Clarke has presented workshops on Diversity Training and Sexual Harassment in the Workplace to the state attorney general's office, college medical schools, and the medical staff of William Beaumont Army Hospital, El Paso. In 2002, when a local church held a Harry Potter book burning, Clarke spearheaded a Ban the Book Burning demonstration. Married, with three children—which he says is his greatest accomplishment—he has also managed airports in California, Arizona, and New Mexico. (Courtesy Rudy Clarke.)

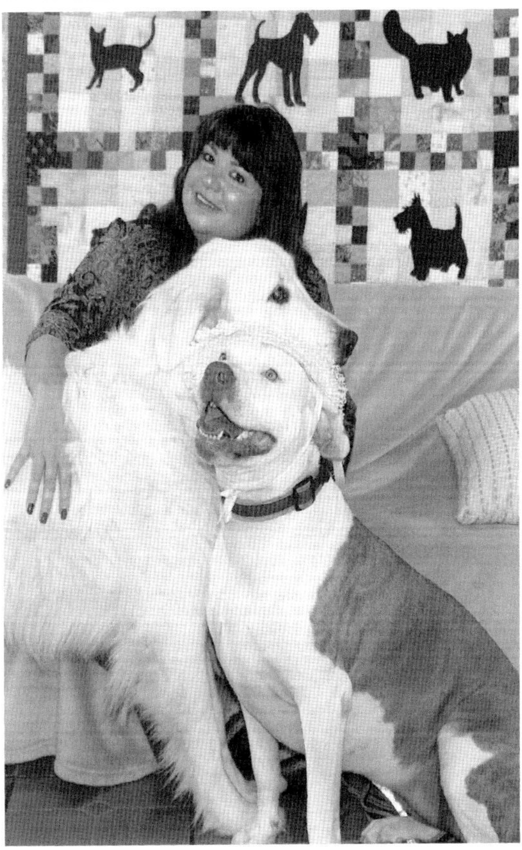

Sunny Aris

Aris is the executive director of Animal Village NM, the state's largest no-kill animal shelter, rescuing condemned dogs and cats from municipal facilities. Animals are fully treated and reside at AVNM until a responsible owner adopts. Animal Protection of New Mexico presented Aris the prestigious Milagro Award. She is an *Alamogordo Daily News* Woman of Merit and raises awareness about animal issues on KRSY AM's *Animal Village Radio.* (Used with permission of and photographed by Brent Michael, Light Fandangos Photograph, Tularosa.)

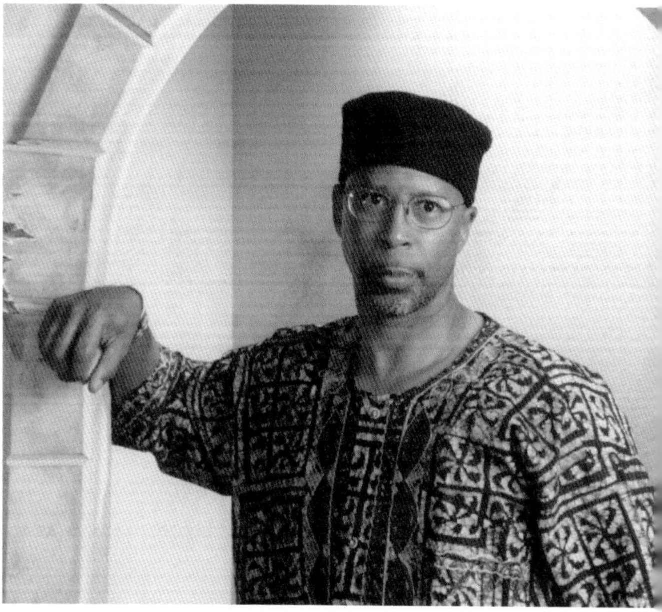

Warren Robinson
Not a day goes by when Robinson does not teach, counsel, encourage, or comfort. A teacher for 20 years, Robinson accepted his call to the ministry in 1979 while in Ohio. Ordained by the House of Prayer nondenominational church in Columbus, Ohio, and subsequently by the African Methodist Episcopal Church in Portland, Oregon, he received his first AME appointment in Chico, California. Robinson now pastors Alamogordo's Owen Chapel. In 2007, the USA Freedom Corps bestowed on him the President's Call to Service Award. (Courtesy Warren Robinson.)

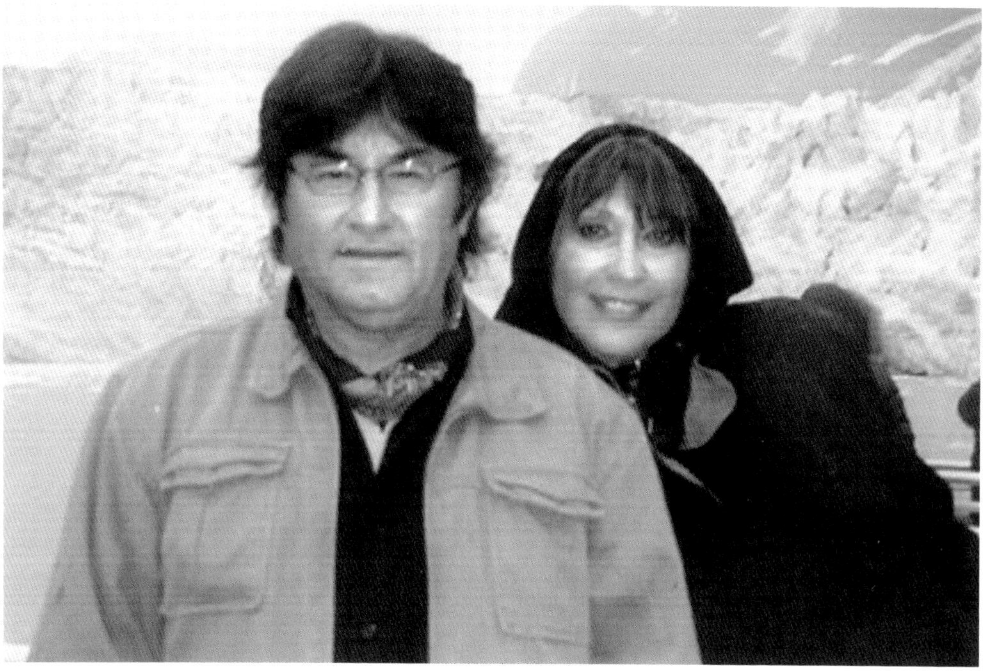

Rev. Carlos Davila
Davila came to Alamogordo in the summer of 1992, relocating to Holloman Air Force Base. He felt God's calling and, after retirement, planted Iglesia Triunfante, where he set up classes for English as a second language and a GED-orientation program to help first-generation Latinos obtain naturalization. His wife, Mery, brought together from the Central Latin District more than 300 lead intercessors, who annually participate in an intercessory prayer rally in Colorado Springs, Colorado. They hike into the Sacramento Mountains to ask God's intervention and blessings on the community they are grateful to call home. (Courtesy Carlos Davila.)

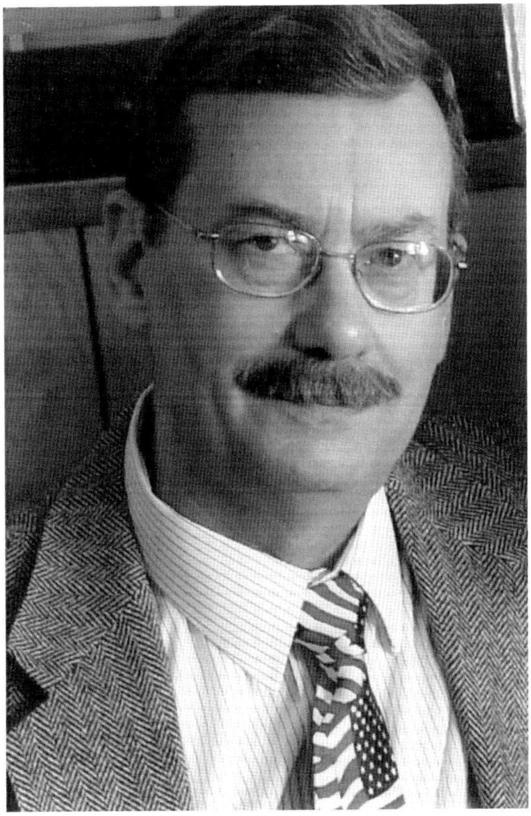

Al Maxey

Pastor Maxey spent six years counseling Terry Clark, preparing the convicted child killer for his 2001 execution. Maxey, senior pastor at Cuba Avenue Church of Christ, led Clark to Jesus Christ, baptized him, and, at Clark's request, was in the death chamber as chaplain for the execution. Maxey called the relationship "one of the most difficult choices God has called me to make." During Vietnam, Maxey served with the US Navy Special Forces. In 2014, he appeared with *Duck Dynasty* commander Phil Robertson at an Oklahoma conference. (Courtesy Al Maxey.)

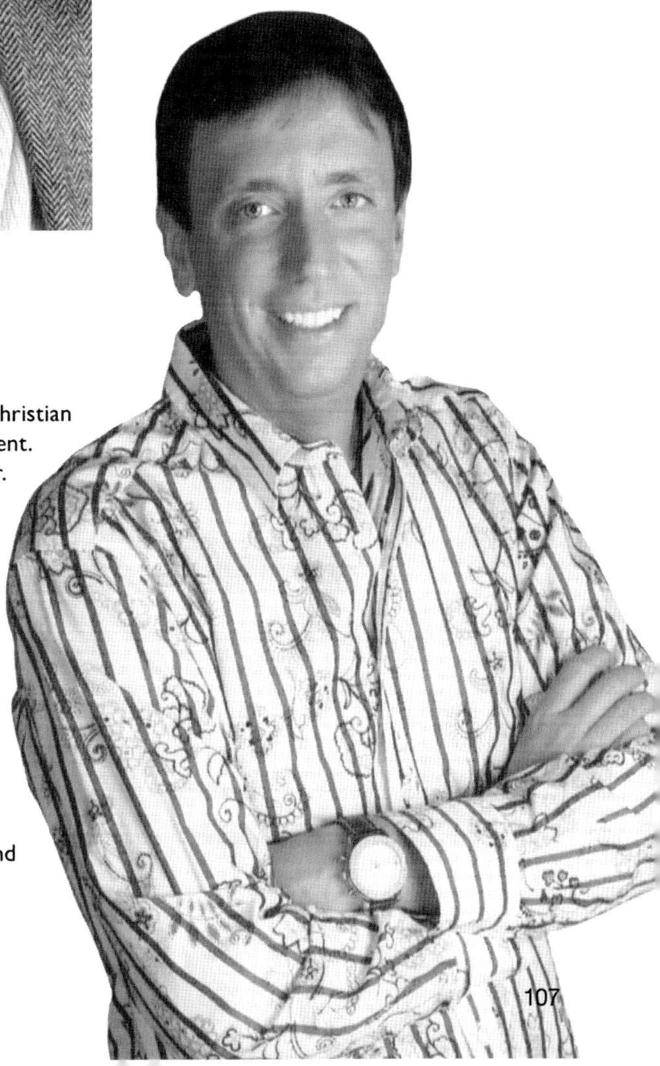

Dr. Stephen Swisher

Before he was one of America's foremost Christian leaders, Swisher was an Alamogordo student. The son of former Alamogordo pastor Dr. Lowell Swisher and his wife, Barbara, he launched Swisher Evangelistic Association in 1996. He is senior pastor of Epiphany United Methodist Church in Cincinnati, Ohio, and a faculty mentor in preaching and leadership in the doctoral program at United Theological Seminary in Dayton, Ohio. Swisher is married to Kellie Copeland, daughter of evangelists Kenneth and Gloria Copeland, and is father to daughter Emily. He has met and talked with the famous in all walks of life, including Hollywood, sports, politics, and music. (Courtesy Stephen Swisher.)

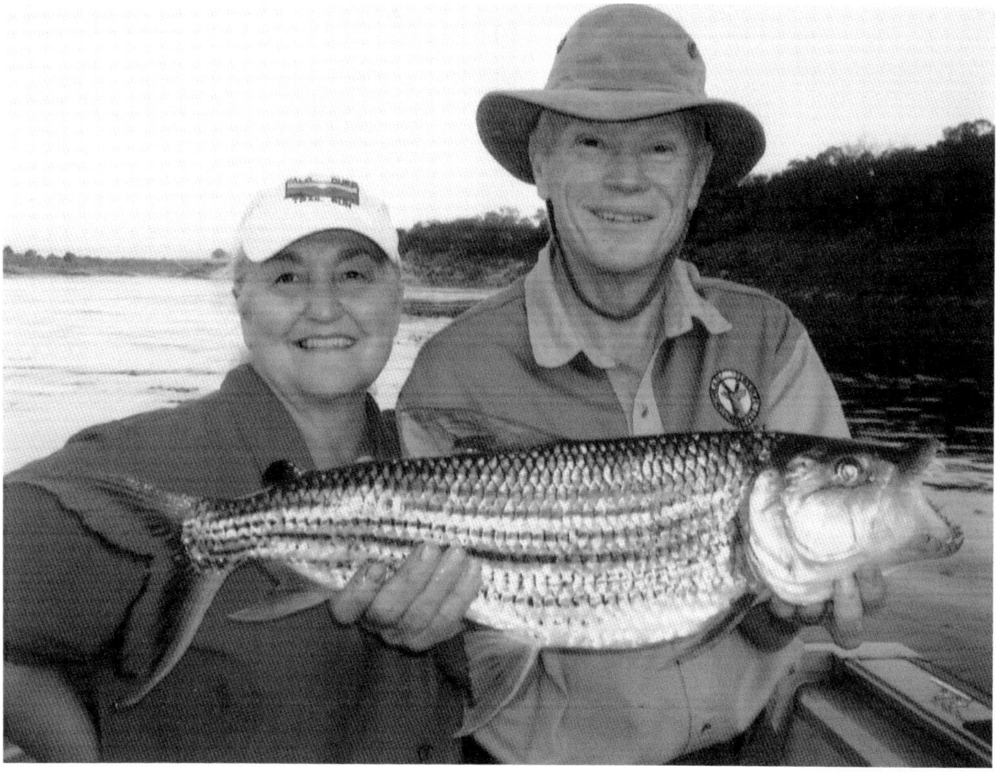

The Sprayberrys

Big-game hunter Jack Sprayberry and his wife, Judi, owned the Game Trail from 1993 to 1998. Jack founded the Rocky Mountain Elk Foundation's Alamogordo chapter, was president of the Friends of the NRA, and provided facilities for gun safety training. They sold the business to travel to Africa, Australia, and New Zealand, researching to set up a safari booking agency, but in 2002, God called them to be missionaries. The Sprayberrys lived in Kenya and then Zambia, and in 2010, they founded Help4Hope Afrika. They teach carpentry and earthbag building; meet medical, clothing, and hunger needs; and provide schooling for youth. (Courtesy Sprayberrys.)

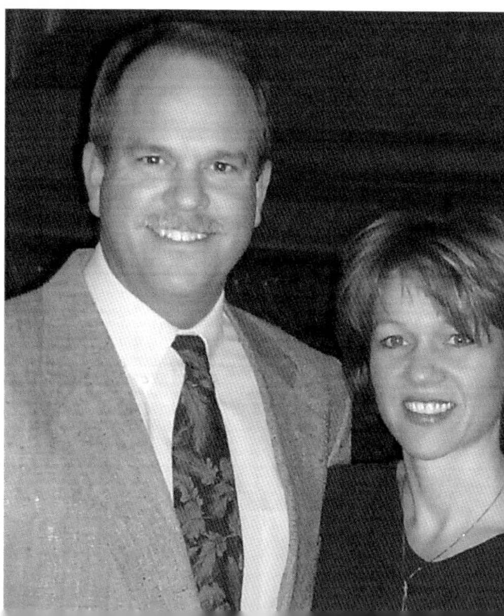

The Richardsons

Stan and Jane Richardson founded Southern New Mexico Outreach to help young women through unintended pregnancies. Operating under Youth with a Mission, they offer medical testing and parenting programs. The couple also operates King's Treasure Thrift Store, which helps fund the organization. (Courtesy Stan Richardson.)

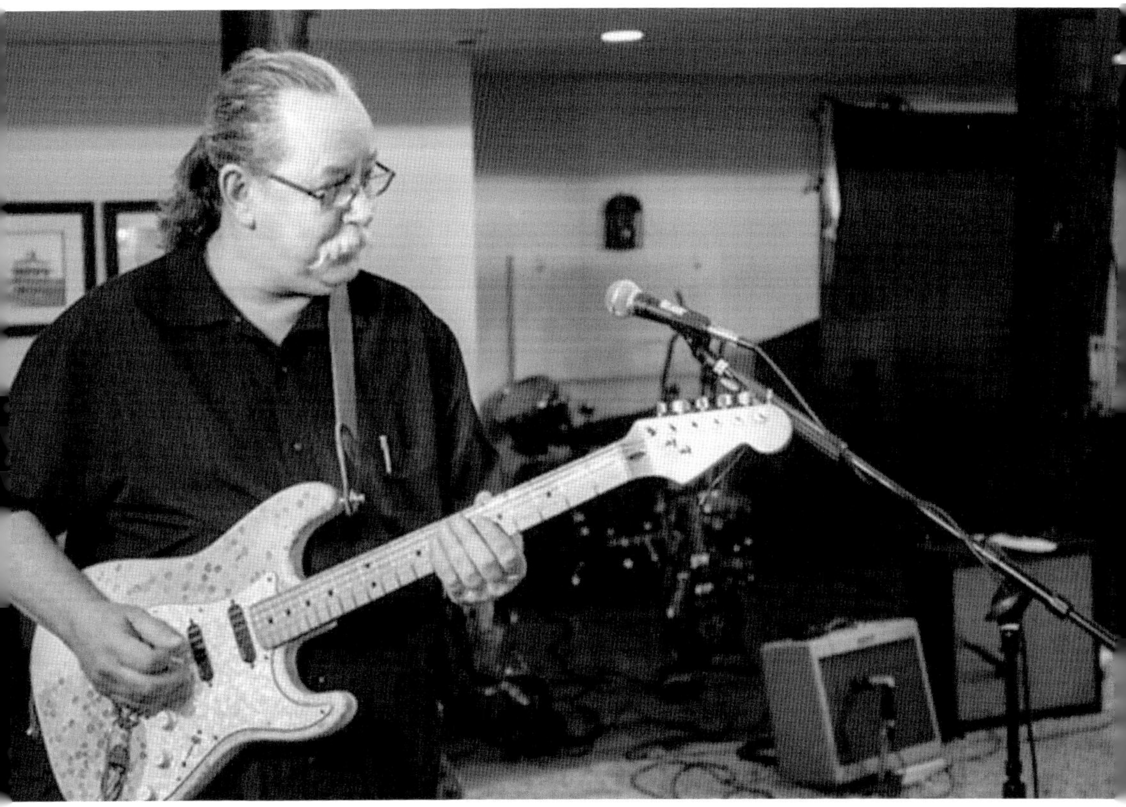

Ellis Neel

Selling rare books in Philadelphia had lost its luster. Regardless of the lucrative position, the noisy city and frenetic pace did not meld well with the soul of an artist. So, after a visit to the Grand Canyon's north rim in 1996, Neel felt the tug of peaceful deserts and big mountains and skies. He gave his employer eight months' notice, and sold, gave away, or left on the sidewalk nearly everything he owned except a few pair of Levis, a handful of T-shirts, two guitars, an amplifier, and three cameras. He hit the road and ran out of money in Alamogordo. Art-school studies had honed the fine-artist's eye, which he put to use behind the camera lens, and he walked into the *Alamogordo Daily News* to ask for a job. Over the next 15 years, Neel photographed the community's life. Parents trusted him to freeze their young athletes' finest moments. He captured historic events at Holloman Air Force Base and once tramped through nearly impassable foliage in the wee hours of the morning to help locate the crew of a downed German air force Tornado. Neel earned more than 40 regional and national awards for photography and writing before becoming an award-winning restaurateur. Eventually, he returned to the East Coast, where he handcrafts guitars and jams out the blues in area clubs. (Used with the permission of Ellis Neel; photograph by David Wolanski.)

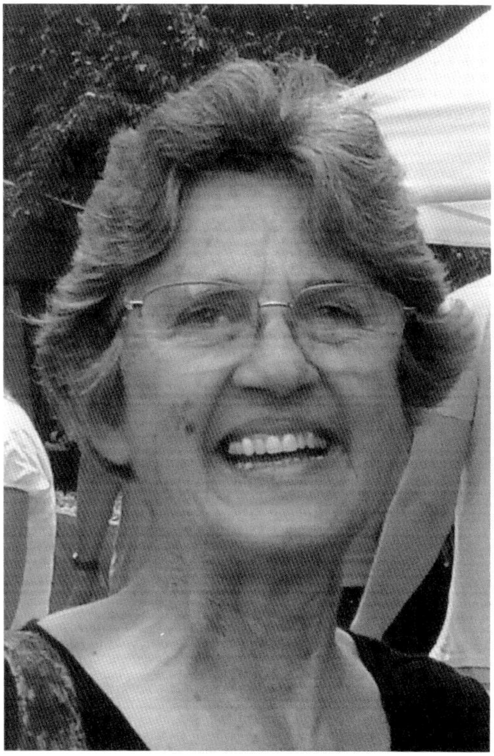

Yvonne Oliver

Oliver keeps Otero County's ranching heritage alive as an Otero CowBelle. The local chapter of the state organization touts the benefits of beef and highlights ranching custom and culture. Her husband, G.B. Oliver II, spent his life ranching after his World War II service. He became a county commissioner and a New Mexico CowBelles Man of the Year. The couple spent 36 years on their White Sands Ranch, running horses and managing a cow/calf operation. (Courtesy Yvonne Oliver.)

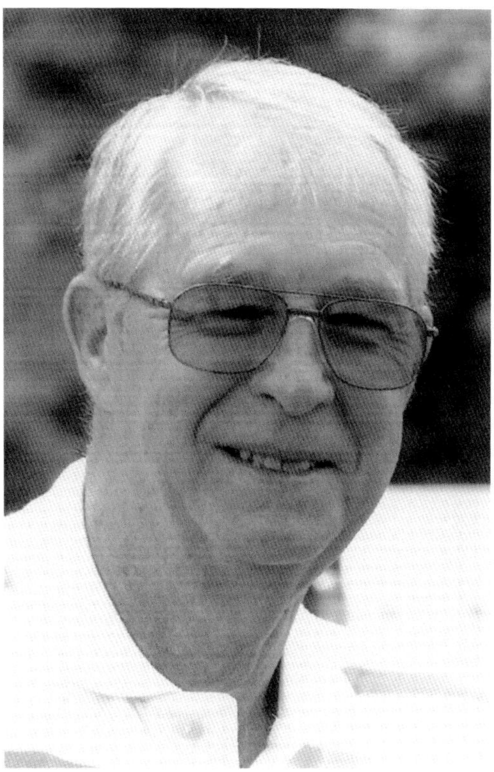

Junior Stoots

Stoots helped found the Alamogordo-based Paragon Foundation, which defends ranchers across the United States in land-rights battles. He was instrumental in bringing cowboy singer Michael Martin Murphy to central New Mexico for a benefit concert on behalf of a rancher under fire from the federal government. (Courtesy Junior Stoots.)

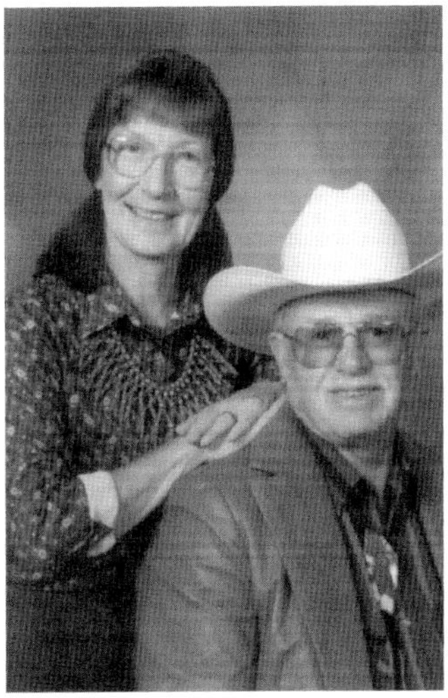

Jean Vallance
In 1998, Vallance, shown here with her husband, Carl, was on a government watch list, suspected of radicalism after she spoke against the United Nations. *New American* magazine featured her story. Vallance was media reporter for People for Otero County and Eagle Forum–New Mexico, and she interviewed nationally known conservatives on KRSY AM. Before her 2011 death, the Otero County Commission declared "Jean Vallance Day." (Courtesy Carl Vallance.)

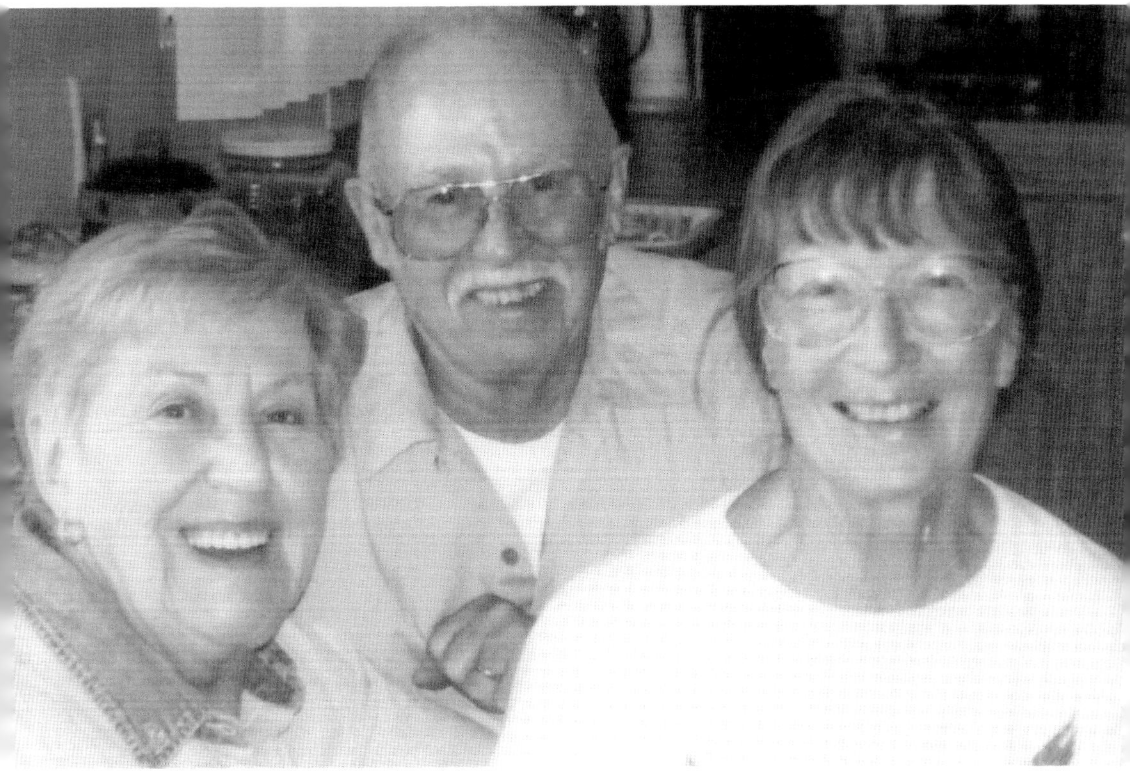

Betty Bennett Stoots
In the mid-1990s, People for Otero County gathered steam after standing against Washington's property-rights attack on the West. An Otero County native, Stoots (left) chaired the organization. In addition, she belonged to the Otero CowBelles, which promotes beef and ranching custom and culture. Stoots was a child when the Trinity Site atomic bomb was detonated, and she told of a school field trip to the Alameda Park Zoo, where she petted radiation-burned livestock. At right is Jean Vallance, on whose KRSY radio program Stoots was a frequent guest. Carl Vallance, Jean's husband, is in the center. (Courtesy Carl Vallance.)

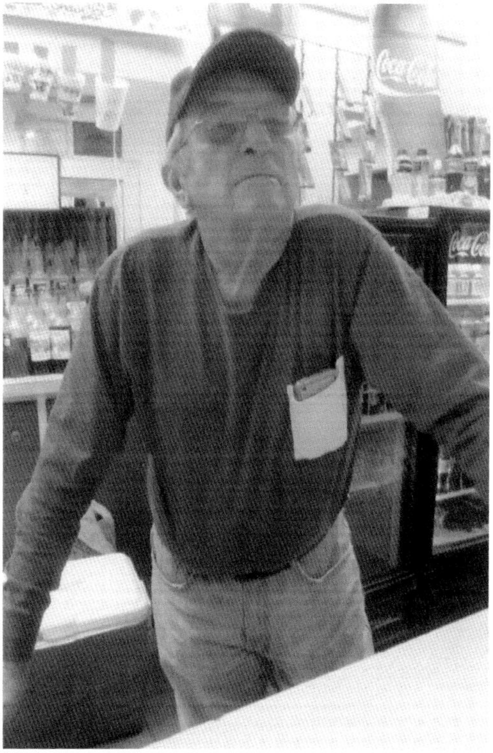

Ron Walton
Through his Tropical Snow business, Walton helps local youth projects, fundraises for cancer research, and educates Americans on their sovereign freedoms. Cancer took Walton's father and a young son, and Walton battles the disease. Outspoken, he tells nearly everyone that, if they do not value their God-given rights, they could lose them. He relates the story of being in Columbus, New Mexico, when Pres. John Kennedy was assassinated and seeing military tanks with the Red Chinese star across the border in Mexico. (Courtesy Michael Shinabery.)

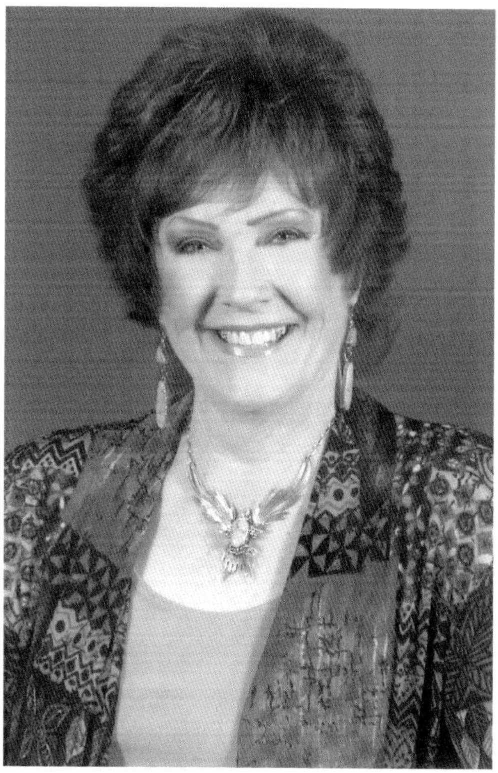

Marcia Stirman
Stirman's 2008 letter to the *Alamogordo Daily News* got worldwide headlines and criticism when she warned readers that Barack Obama would impose a socialist agenda on America. Stirman, who was Miss Southwest Rodeo International in 1971, has been politically active since she was 18. A devout Christian, her passion is biblical studies. She hosts a weekly conservative show on KRSY AM as well as an Internet program. (Courtesy Marcia Stirman.)

CHAPTER SEVEN

Others

Virtually everyone in Alamogordo has a tale to tell. Unfortunately, their stories often do not get told until the *Alamogordo Daily News* publishes an obituary. Both the Tularosa Basin Historical Society and the New Mexico Museum of Space History interview for, and archive, oral histories, as does the Sacramento Mountains Historical Society in Cloudcroft.

The names are many. In education, Charles Reidlinger is hailed as a guiding force at New Mexico State University–Alamogordo, which named the science center in his honor.

Those who admire Rayford Kissiah's professional photographs hanging in local businesses may not know that, before coming to Alamogordo, he was North Carolina's Golden Gloves boxing champion. After serving in the Marines during World War II, Kissiah earned his law degree and joined the FBI. He was liaison between the FBI and Pres. Dwight Eisenhower's office and taught crime-scene photography. After retiring, Kissiah was an assistant professor at New Mexico State University–Alamogordo, teaching criminal justice and photography. He was a cofounder of Alamogordo Music Theatre, where he acted and sang.

June Harwell, now librarian emerita of the Alamogordo Public Library, is responsible for acquiring the extensive collection of Western author Eugene Manlove Rhodes's work.

Mick Heljeson never went to the Moon, but his project was used on the lunar surface. After Apollo 17 lifted off, Heljeson's packages of explosives detonated and returned seismic data.

For much of his adult life, Bill English's name was synonymous with the UFO-related Projects Grudge and Blue Book. English wrote on the phenomena and spoke across the country, enduring heavy criticism. In the early 2000s, he walked away from the subject, turning his ultraconservative energies on hosting an Internet political radio show and writing his blog, *Been Franklin*.

Clif McDonald is well known for his business, political, and ranching endeavors. As the Charlie T. Lee Memorial Relief Route was being built, the city asked McDonald to remove his livestock from grazing land adjacent to the construction. KRSY AM radio host Mike Haymes rode herd on the city when he found out that McDonald went to return his cows to the grasslands after the road's completion and the city said no. The municipality had annexed the land, and ordinances prohibited livestock within the town limits. Charlie T. Lee was the grandson of ranching legend Oliver Lee. His maternal great-grandfather, however, Harry Ackley, was the railroad engineer who drove the first engine to Alamogordo.

At some point, everyone should sit down and put pen to paper, fingers to keyboard, or voice to recorder and document his or her experiences. Their stories would fill volumes, and they deserve to be read. Here are just a few.

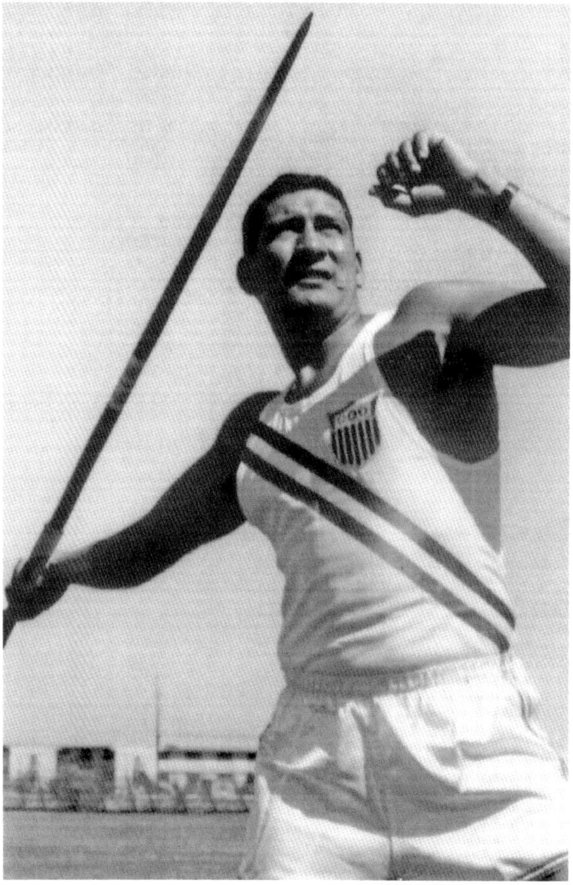

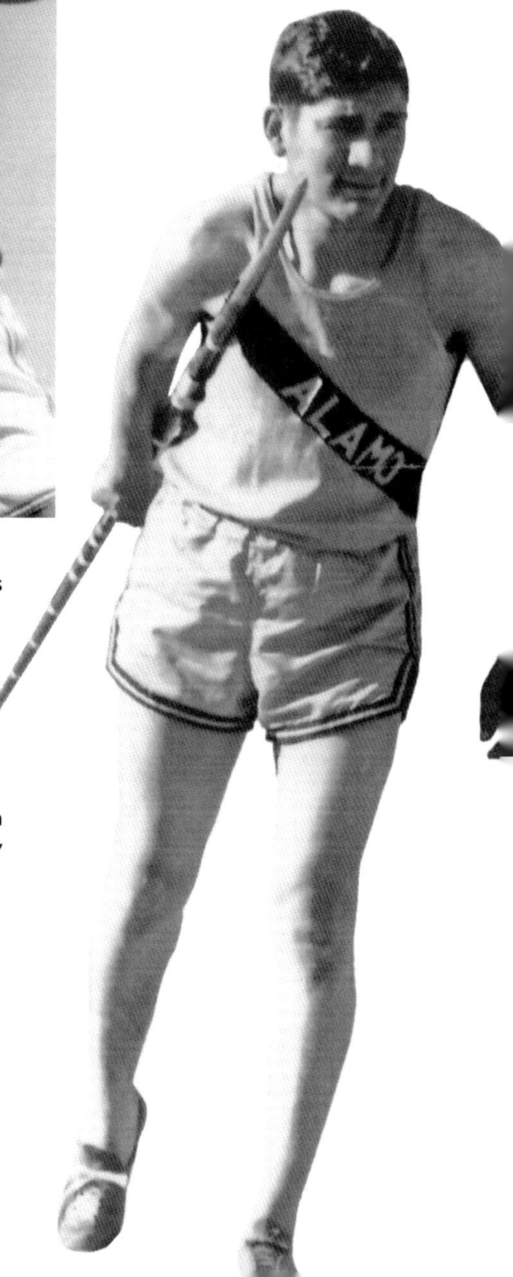

Benny Garcia

Garcia is Alamogordo's only Olympian, as well as the first Olympian from New Mexico. He was a member of Alamogordo High School's 1950 state championship football team, coached by Rolla Buck. The next year, he set the New Mexico javelin record (right), which remained unbroken for decades. Garcia was a four-year letterman at Arizona State. In 1956, as a member of the US Olympic Team (above), he placed eighth in javelin in Melbourne, Australia. He died in 2015. (Both courtesy Garcia family.)

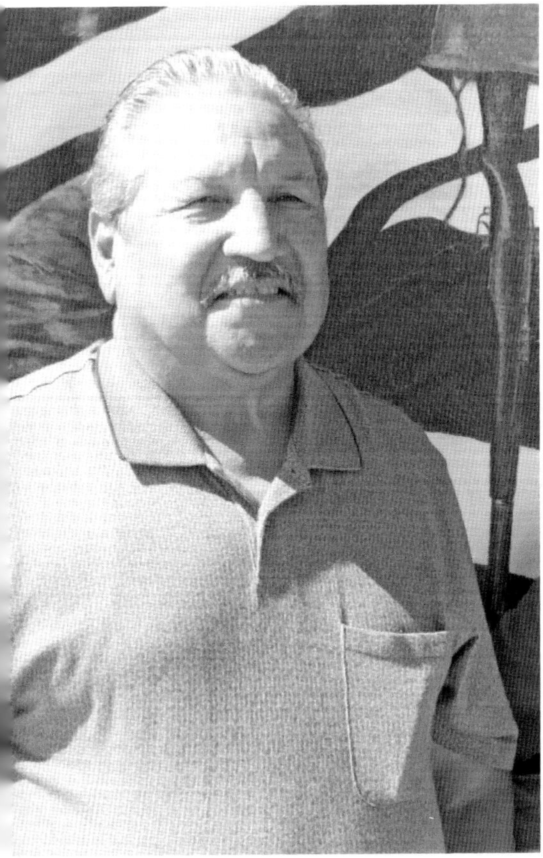

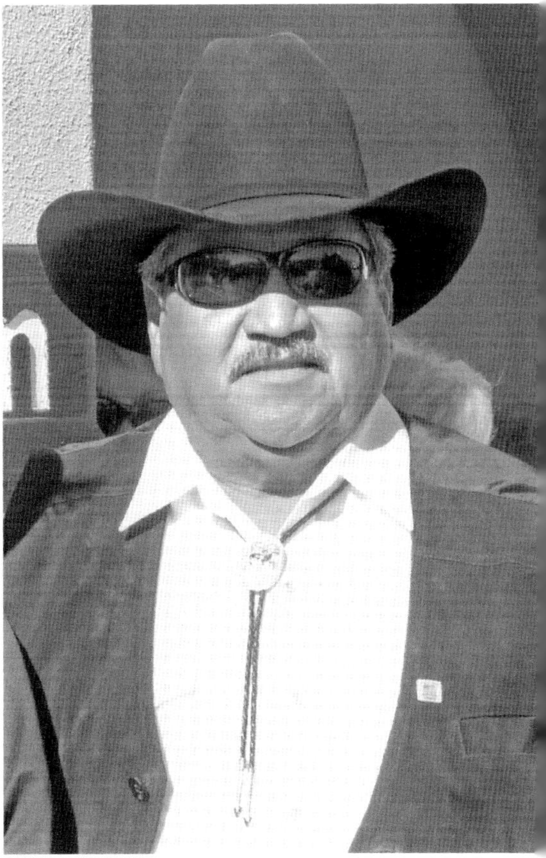

Zeke Castro

Born in his parents' home at 605 New York Avenue—in the same neighborhood where future secretary of the treasury Katherine Ortega's family lived—Zeke Castro (above) spoke little English until he attended Dudley School. That was not unusual for Spanish-speaking youth in the segregated era. While playing one day, Castro saw train cars carrying German V-2 rocket parts through town. He is a member of the Western Writers of America and a historian. Castro's book on Billy the Kid presents evidence that Sheriff Pat Garrett did not kill the Kid, who instead lived to a ripe old age. The photograph at right shows him in period dress on January 6, 2012, during the New Mexico centennial. (Both photographs by Don Larsen.)

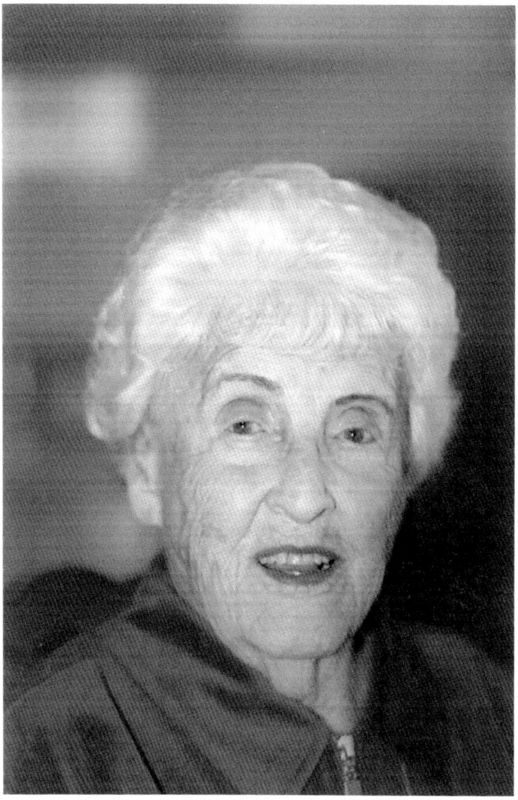

Ruby Hays

Hays's golf game suffered because, whenever she was on the links and a plane flew overhead, she looked up and ignored the fairway. Hays learned to fly in 1947 in a cloth-covered "rag wing." In July 1954, she and her copilot, Ruth Deerman, beat 45 other pilots to win the Eighth Annual All Women's Transcontinental Air Race. Speed did not determine the victor but, instead, how pilots used their time. Prior to takeoff, Hays and Deerman polished Deerman's Cessna with Glass Wax. After a photograph of them on their backs under the prop plane was published, the company shipped Hays and Deerman a case each. Embarking on a world tour was one of the perks of their victory. Another was that Belgium Airlines gave them membership in the Lady Sabena Club. The plane and their trophy now hang in the War Eagles Museum in Santa Teresa, New Mexico. Hays sold her own plane (below), which she had named *Sugar Baby*, in the early 1990s after taking one final flight in West Texas. (Left, photograph by Ellis Neel; below, courtesy Faye Hays.)

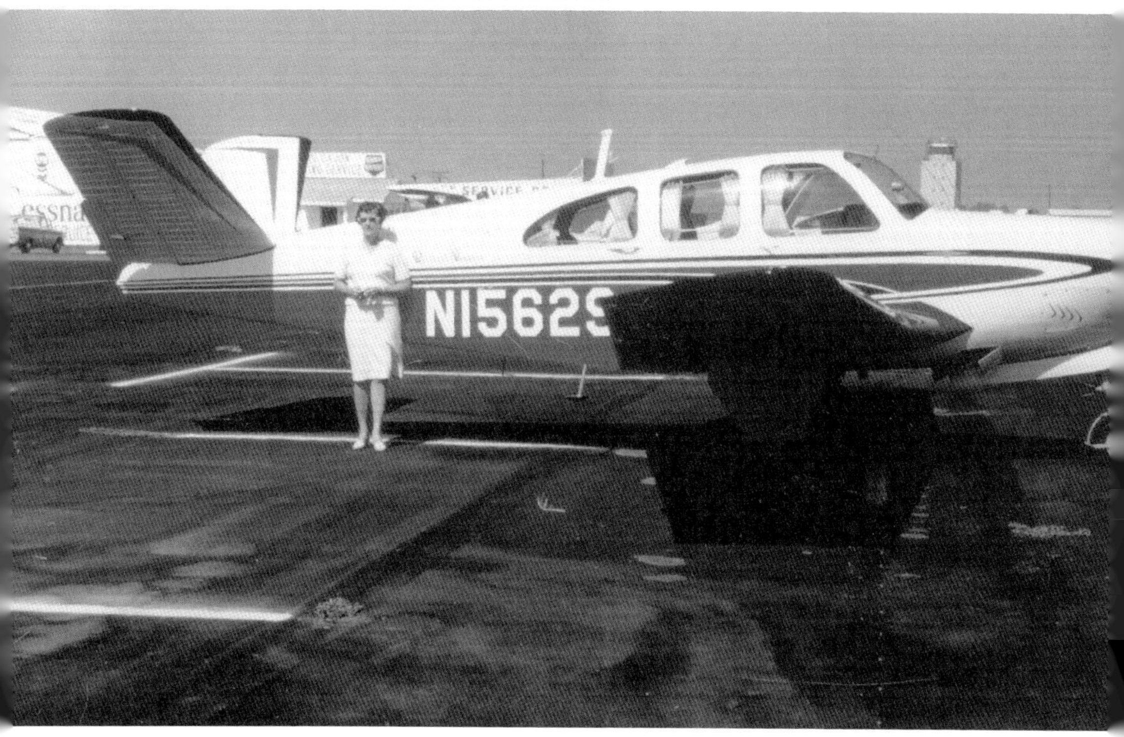

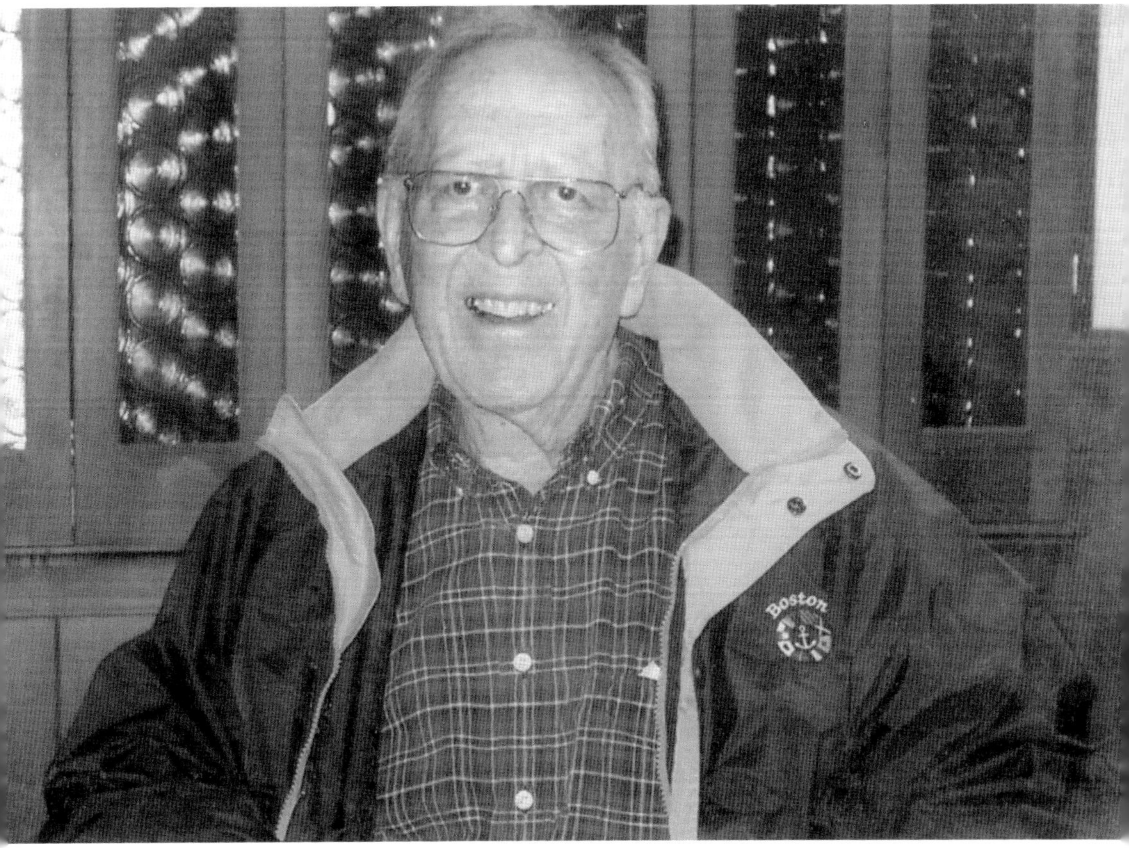

Dr. Richard Sherman

When the Rotary Club of Alamogordo recognized a member's birthday, it was not uncommon for Sherman to point out that he had delivered that person. Sherman moved to Alamogordo in 1956 after residency in El Paso. A man of great Christian faith, he met his future wife, Tina, while riding a bus in Waco, Texas—he saw her give up her seat for an African American woman. As a US Marine during World War II, Sherman twice escaped death when kamikaze pilots attacked his ship, the USS *West Virginia*. The second attack, on Easter 1945, carried a 500-pound bomb that miraculously failed to explode. From his ship, Sherman witnessed the Japanese surrender. He also witnessed the raising of the American flag on Iwo Jima.

When Sherman retired from his daily practice, he became a traveling physician. He filled in for vacationing doctors around the country. In his later years, he was an emergency room physician at Holloman Air Force Base. Sherman was 89 when he died in January 2015. He maintained his credentials until just four years before his passing. (Courtesy Sherman family.)

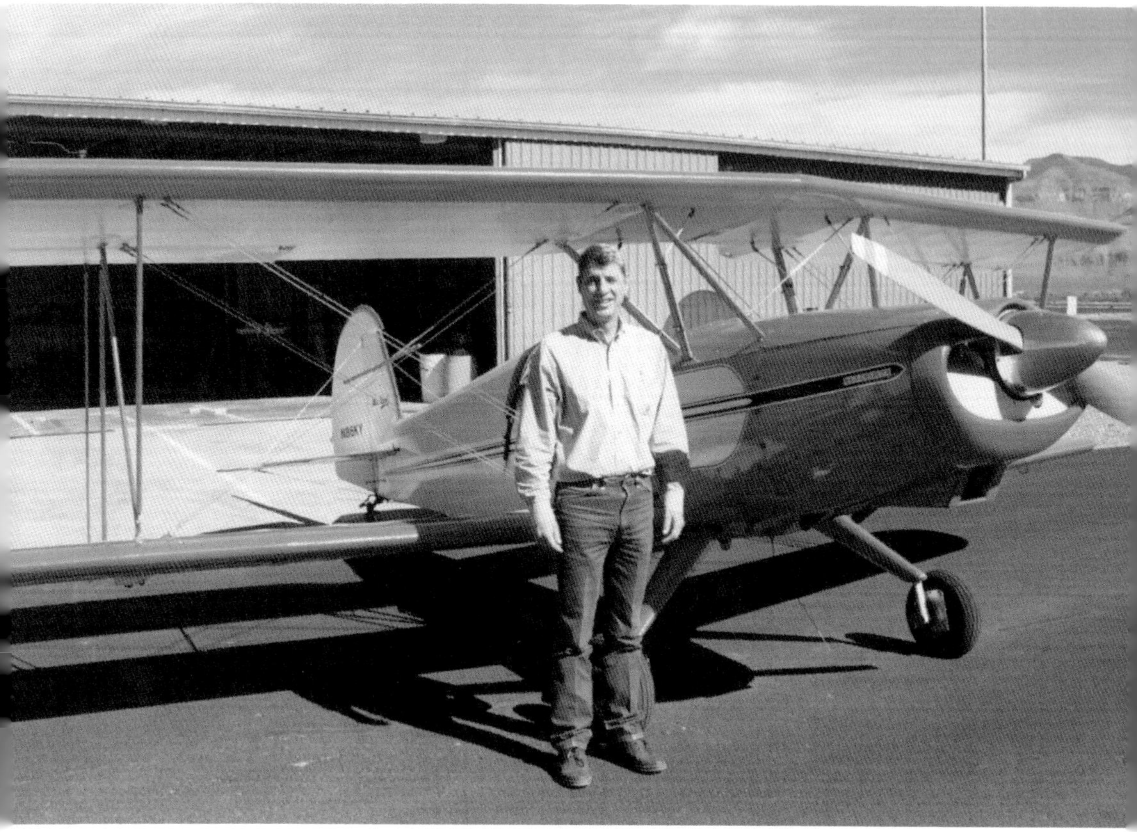

Mike Haymes

Haymes is a grassroots voice amid political correctness. In 1996, he helped create The Paragon Foundation, which fights governmental encroachment against ranchers and landowners. In 2001, Haymes began a popular radio program on KRSY AM, taking political correctness to task. The show lasted several years. When Alamogordo's relief route opened after 25 years of planning, Haymes, a private pilot, flew overhead in his biplane (shown here) and dropped popcorn to mimic snow. He pointed out that someone had said it would be a cold day in July before the road ever opened. (Used with the permission of Mike Haymes.)

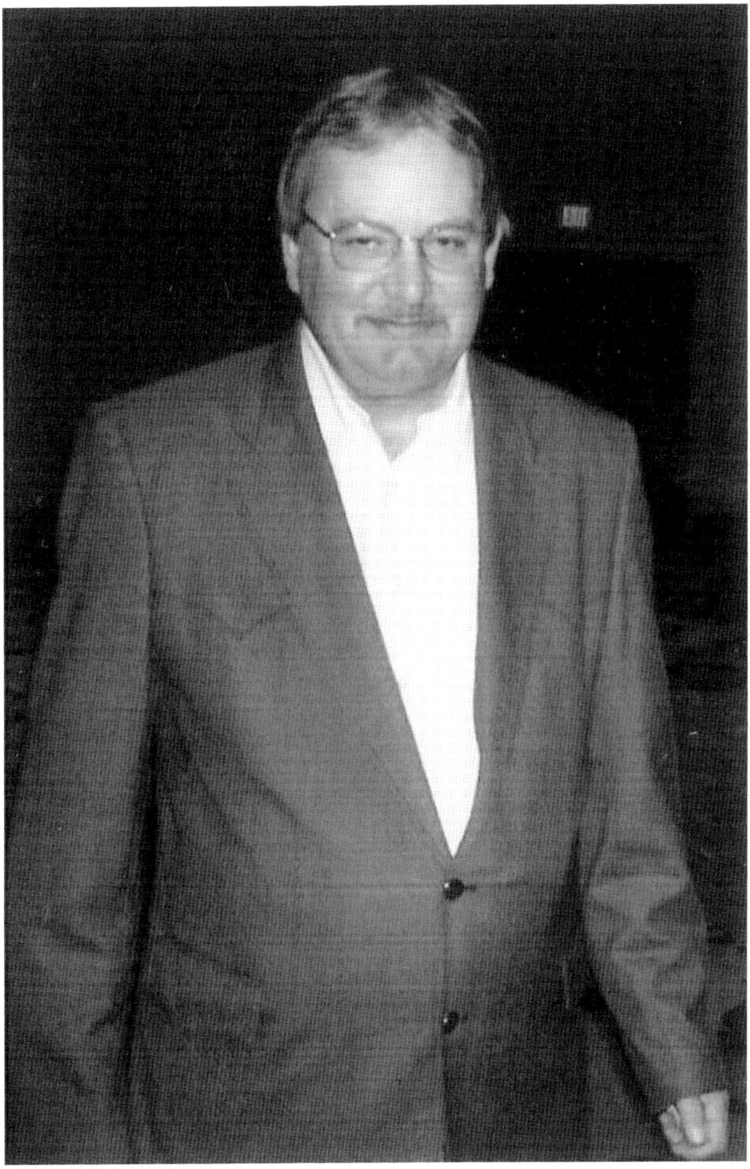

Erik Ness

News was in Erik Ness's blood. Among the stations for which the 1972 Alamogordo High School graduate worked is powerhouse KGRT, Las Cruces. He was a southern New Mexico correspondent for 50,000-watt KKOB and Albuquerque stations KOB and KOAT. While attending New Mexico State University, Ness cofounded campus station KNMS, "Ozone Ranger Radio." In 1981, Ness joined the New Mexico Farm Bureau as communications and media-relations director. He was twice recognized as the nation's most effective agriculture public relations spokesman, and ABC's Paul Harvey quoted his commonsense commentaries. Ness was also an award-winning songwriter and recording artist, producing at Las Cruces' legendary Gold Dust studios. When Ness won the American Collegiate Talent Search, which Michael Martin Murphy judged, the two became friends and collaborators and toured the country together. Ness died prematurely at age 57. The New Mexico Farm and Livestock Bureau set up an agricultural communications scholarship in his honor. (Courtesy Ness family.)

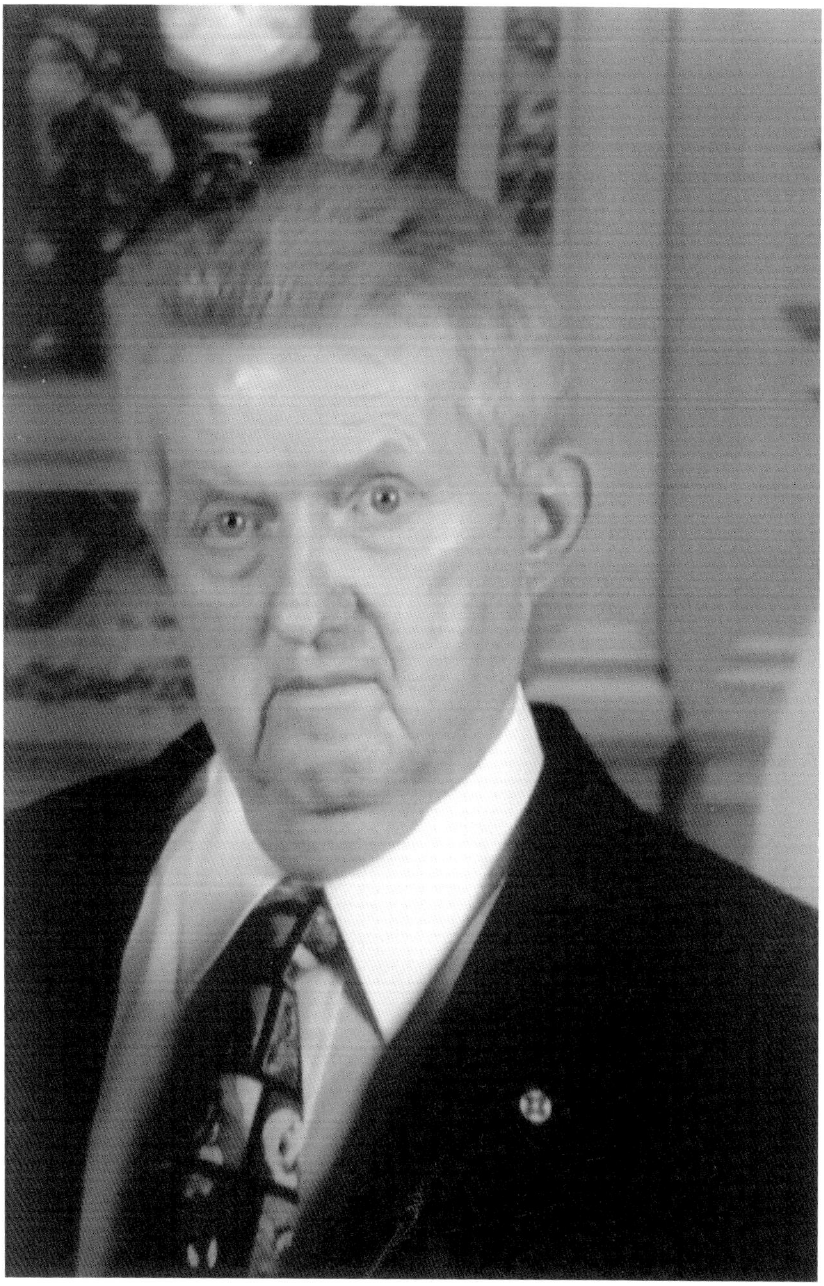

"Doc" Karl Wuersching

On a university trip to a rural Chinese province in June 1985, a Mescalero Apache student of Wuersching's, Molly Gayton, was astounded when she understood some of the language. Wuersching theorized that the region's ancestors, at one time, made their way over the Bering Strait to the Americas. As a professor at New Mexico State University–Alamogordo, Wuersching taught geology, geography, German, real estate, linguistics, and city and regional planning. A hands-on teacher, he took students on trips throughout the Southwest, including rafting along the Colorado River, and overseas. Wuersching was also a real estate broker and a volunteer fireman. (Courtesy Wuersching family.)

Katherine Davalos Ortega
Ortega (on right, with Reagan) served for six years as secretary of the treasury under Presidents Ronald Reagan and George H.W. Bush. Born in Tularosa, her first job was at Otero County State Bank, and she would become the first woman in California to be a bank president. During her term, Ortega raised $40 million for Ellis Island as well as for the Statue of Liberty's restoration. Prior to becoming treasurer, she served on the Presidential Advisory Committee on Small and Minority Business Ownership. When Ortega left the Treasury, Bush named her an alternative representative to the United Nations. In the photograph at right, Ortega (right) is at the White House with Reagan. Below, she takes the oath of office, administered by Donald Regan. The woman to Regan's right is unidentified. (Both courtesy the Tularosa Basin Historical Society.)

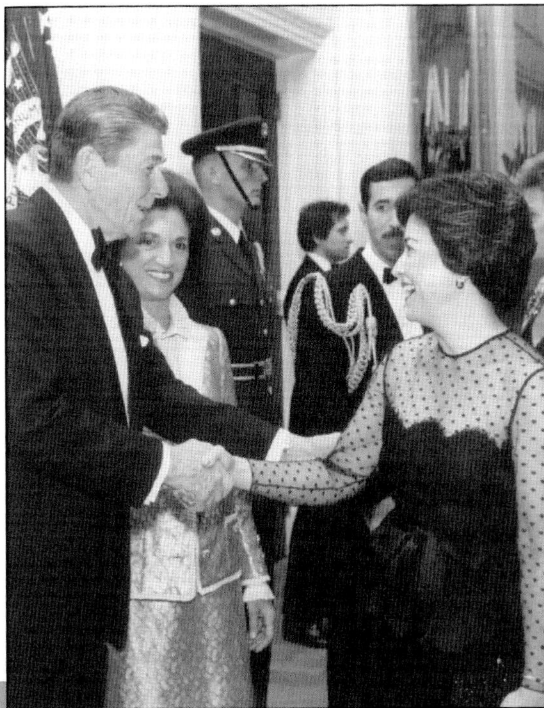

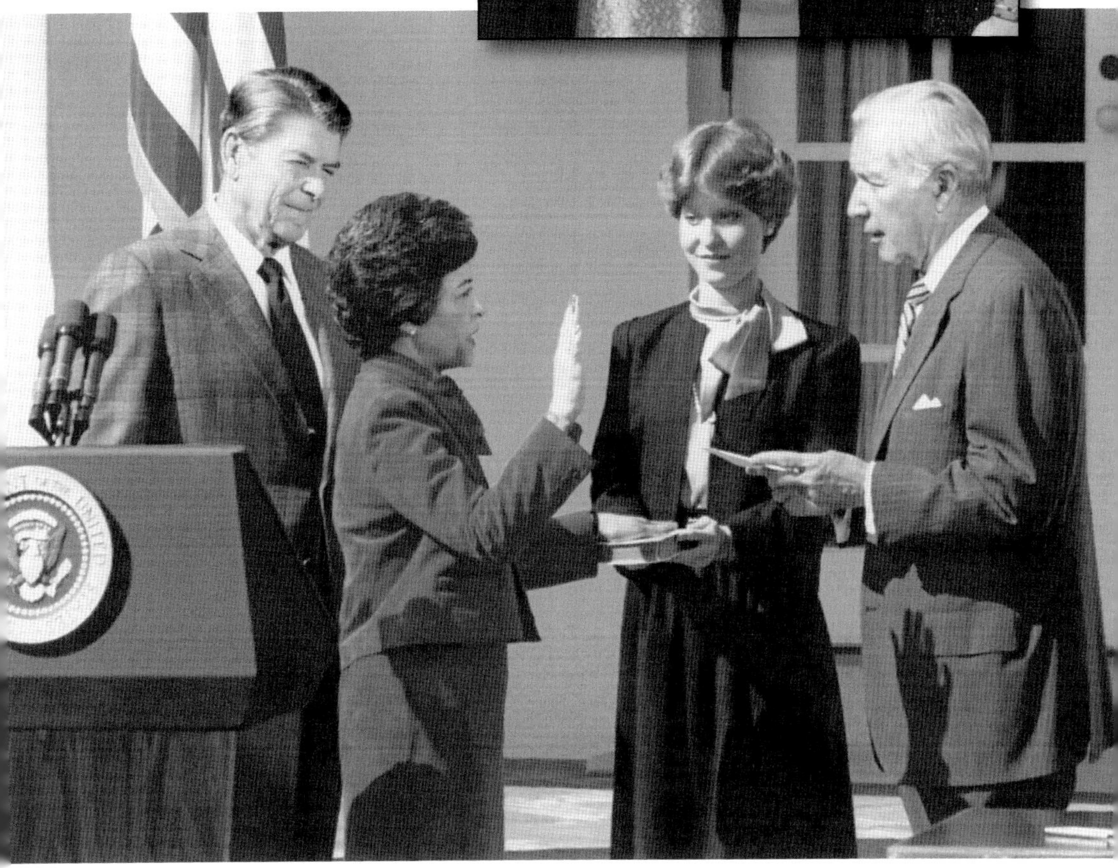

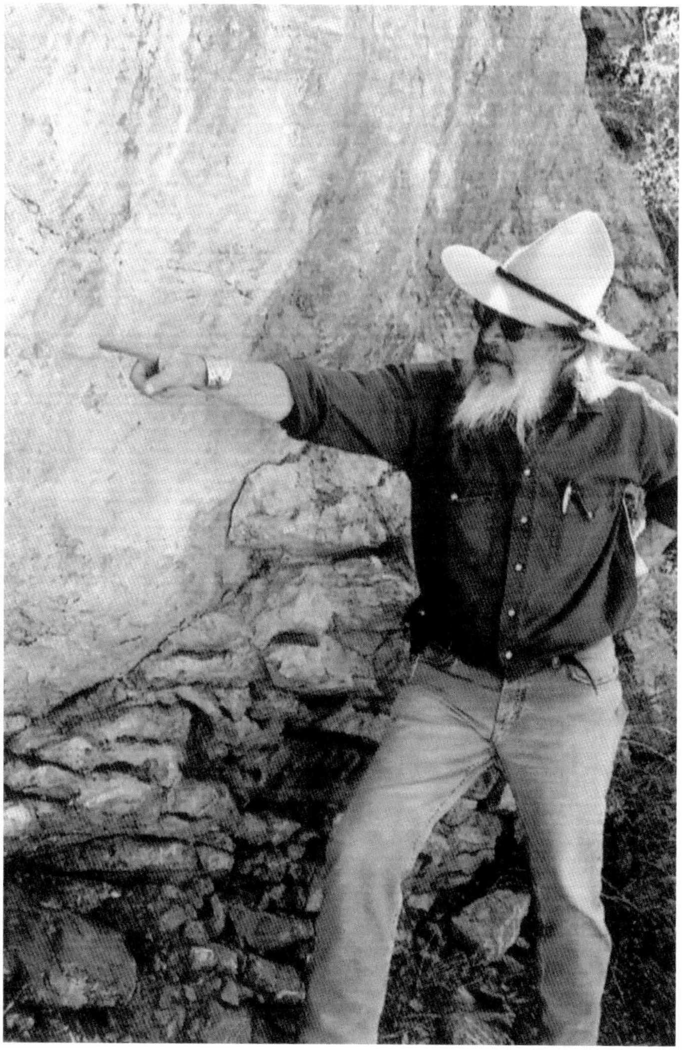

Pete Eidenbach

Eidenbach is an anthropologist, historian, and teacher whose 44-year professional career has focused on the archaeology, history, and traditions of southern New Mexico. He has authored monographs, research reports, and plans in prehistoric and historic archaeology, rural historic architecture, Cold War architecture and military history, and oral history.

In the early 1970s, Eidenbach helped direct excavations at Fresnal Shelter, which contained some of the oldest evidence of domestic maize and beans in the Southwest. In 1972, he and his colleague, Mark Wimberly, founded Human Systems Research to investigate the Tularosa Basin. In the late 1970s, both excavated Frenchy's Cabin in Dog Canyon and discovered several prehistoric solar observatory sites in the Sacramento Mountains. In 1979, Wimberly was killed in a helicopter crash while photographing Wizards Roost.

In the next decade, Eidenbach directed public archaeological excavations of the Oliver M. Lee Dog Canyon Ranch House prior to its restoration. Eidenbach is also a New Mexico State University–Alamogordo professor and an artist who works in a variety of media, from cloth to stone. He carves highly detailed prehistoric motifs in catlinite, or pipestone, and serpentine. (Used with the permission of Pete Eidenbach.)

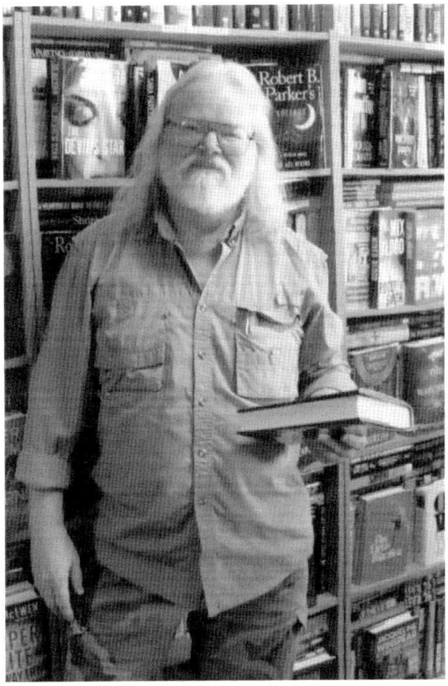

Ed Woten

An author, artist, anthropologist, elementary school teacher, and bookstore owner, Woten has taught Three-Dimensional Mathematics, Caving, and Origami at New Mexico State University–Alamogordo. A member in of the National Speleological Society, Woten has led hundreds of school youth, Boy Scouts, senior citizens, and even students from the New Mexico School for the Blind and Visually Impaired into the region's caves. From his experiences, he pens tales for the Cloudcroft *Mountain Monthly*. (Courtesy Elizabeth Beasley.)

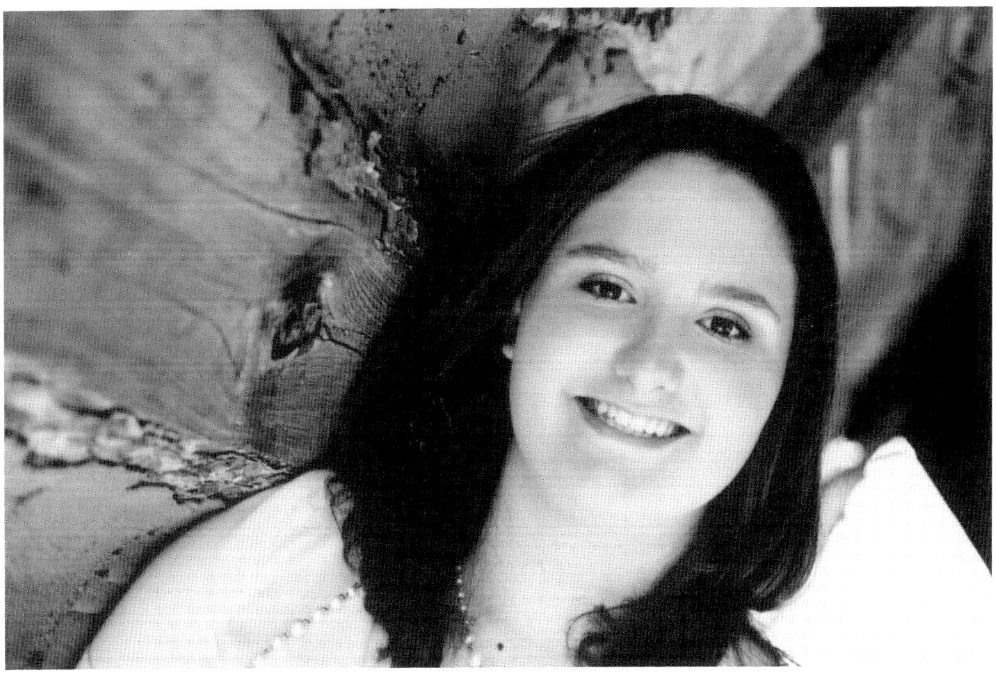

Shara Shinabery

Shinabery was 12 when the New Mexico Museum of Space History needed someone to wear the costume of its mascot, the chimpanzee HAM, and her dad brought the costume home. Shinabery was the only person who could fit into it. Until she grew out of it at age 17, she wore the suit at the New Mexico Legislature and appeared at museum events alongside space shuttle astronaut Mike Mullane and Apollo 17 moonwalker Dr. Harrison "Jack" Schmitt. (Courtesy Dixie Landrum.)

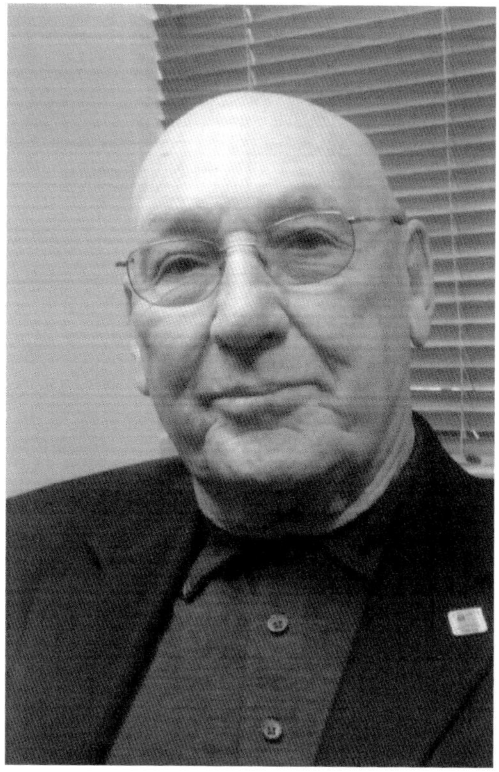

Tommie Herrell
Herrell developed his first subdivision in 1970 near Weed. Subsequently, he opened his own insurance and realty agencies, built the Tres Lagos subdivision and the Spur Landing Town Homes in Cloudcroft, donated the land for the German school, and helped bring First American Bank to Alamogordo. He served on the Cloudcroft School Board and the Otero County Commission. (Courtesy Michael Shinabery.)

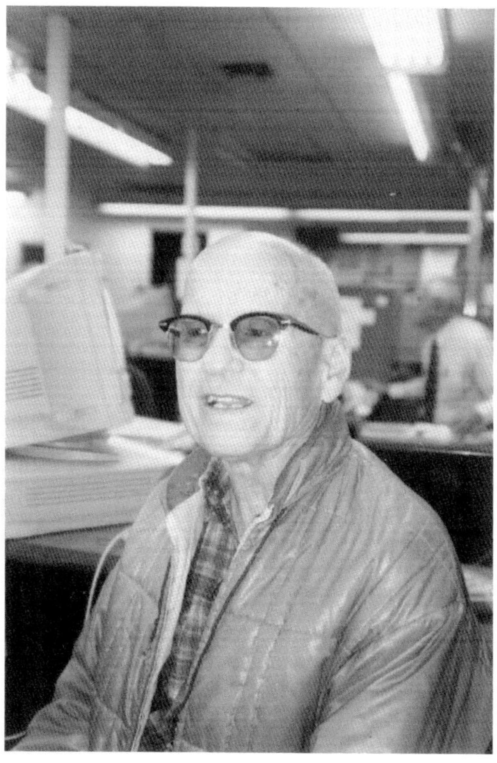

Fred Wilcoxson
He was a private pilot in Roswell in 1947 when the alleged alien crash occurred. Wilcoxson believed the official story until the late 1950s, when he said he saw UFOs flying in an Air Force "V" configuration. Wilcoxson spent the rest of his life arguing in the media that if the American government made secret UFO technology public, wars would end and the economy would boom. (Courtesy Michael Shinabery.)

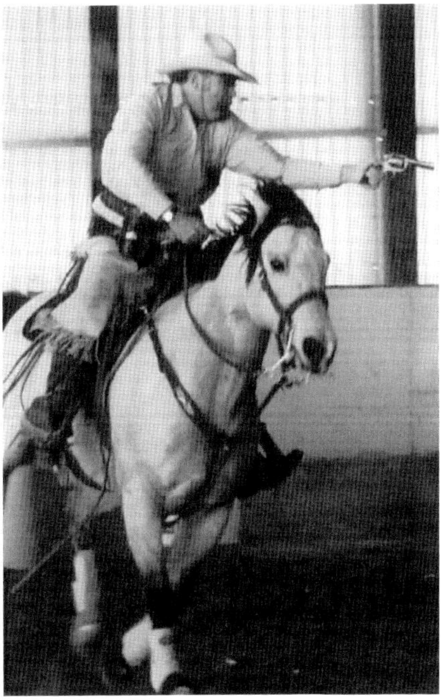

Jim Huff

A move from Seattle to Wyoming introduced Huff to the lifestyle of the West. He fit in, but in 1984, after eight years of harsh winters, Huff migrated to Alamogordo. He was a disc jockey and a farrier, and he and his wife, Louise, own a small horse farm. In New Mexico, his discovery of cowboy mounted shooting combined his love for horses, firearms, and cowboy hats. Huff formed the Borderland Pistoleros, who perform monthly at the New Mexico Farm and Ranch Heritage Museum in Las Cruces. (Both, used with the permission of Jim Huff; left, photograph by Bobby Goode; below, photograph by Amber White.)

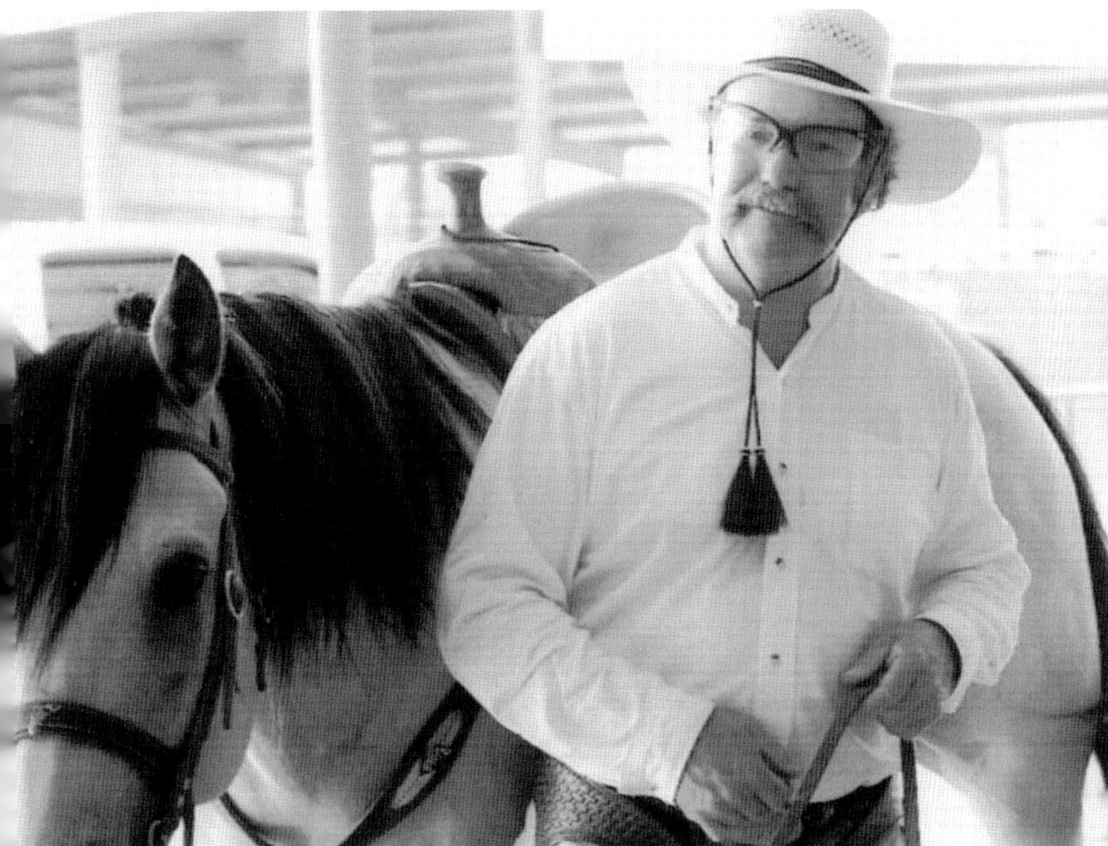

INDEX

INDEX

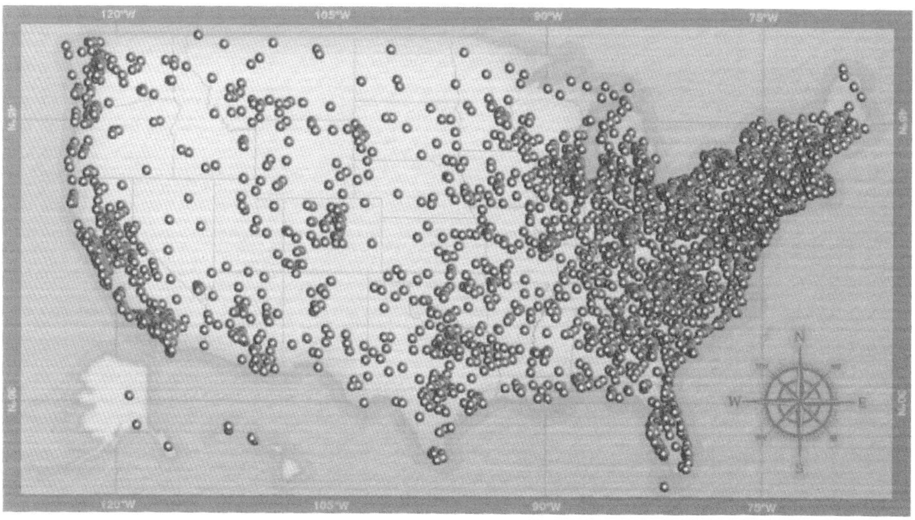